Using Software Samplers: Skill Pack

Nick Batzdorf

Course Technology PTR
A part of Cengage Learning

COURSE TECHNOLOGY
CENGAGE Learning·

Australia • Brazil • Japan • Korea • Mexico • Singapore • Spain • United Kingdom • United States

COURSE TECHNOLOGY
CENGAGE Learning·

Using Software Samplers: Skill Pack
Nick Batzdorf

Publisher and General Manager,
Course Technology PTR: Stacy L. Hiquet

Associate Director of Marketing:
Sarah Panella

Manager of Editorial Services:
Heather Talbot

Senior Marketing Manager:
Mark Hughes

Acquisitions Editor: Orren Merton

Project Editor: Karen A. Gill

Copy Editor: Gene Redding

Interior Layout Tech: MPS Limited

Cover Designer: Mike Tanamachi

Indexer: Sharon Shock

Proofreader: Megan Belanger

For product information and technology assistance, contact us at
Cengage Learning Customer & Sales Support, 1-800-354-9706.
For permission to use material from this text or product,
submit all requests online at **www.cengage.com/permissions.**
Further permissions questions can be emailed to
permissionrequest@cengage.com.

Logic is a trademark of Apple Inc., registered in the U.S. and other countries.

Pro Tools and Structure are registered trademarks of Avid Technologies, Inc. in the United States.

Reason is a trademark of Propellerhead Software.

Kontakt is a trademark of Native Instruments Software Synthesis GmbH.

All other trademarks are the property of their respective owners.

All images © Cengage Learning unless otherwise noted.

Library of Congress Control Number: 2011923930

ISBN-13: 978-1-4354-5853-6

ISBN-10: 1-4354-5853-2

Course Technology, a part of Cengage Learning
20 Channel Center Street
Boston, MA 02210
USA

Cengage Learning is a leading provider of customized learning solutions with office locations around the globe, including Singapore, the United Kingdom, Australia, Mexico, Brazil, and Japan. Locate your local office at:
international.cengage.com/region.

Cengage Learning products are represented in Canada by Nelson Education, Ltd.

For your lifelong learning solutions, visit **courseptr.com.**

Visit our corporate Web site at **cengage.com.**

Printed in the United States of America
1 2 3 4 5 6 7 14 13 12

*This book is dedicated to all the musicians who
make the field of sampling so much fun.*

Acknowledgments

Special acknowledgment to the people at Cengage Learning for the opportunity to write this book, including but not limited to my very bright friend Orren Merton and to Karen Gill, who did a great job of editing the book and managing my stupendous ego without resorting to violence.

About the Author

Nick Batzdorf is a composer, multi-instrumentalist, audio engineer, music technology expert, magazine editor and publisher, and journalist. He has written and orchestrated music for feature films, television, advertising, and other media, and he has played in venues ranging from jazz clubs to pit orchestras. For more than a decade, he was the editor of *Recording* magazine, and then in the mid-2000s he launched *Virtual Instruments* magazine, which he also edits. His articles on music and audio technology have appeared in many other industry publications.

Contents

Chapter 3
Building Programs in Apple EXS24   39

Chapter 4
Building Programs in Native Instruments Kontakt   63

Chapter 5
Building Programs in the Propellerhead Reason (and Record) NN-XT Advanced Sampler   85

Chapter 6
Building Programs in Avid (Formerly Digidesign) Structure   107

Chapter 7
Looping   135

Chapter 8
Release Samples

159

Chapter 9
Using Kontakt Scripts

187

Online Content at www.courseptr.com/downloads

Introduction

It's easy to forget how far sampling has come in the past decade. The commercial libraries we have now are remarkably sophisticated—far more expressive and responsive than anything around during the first couple of decades that sampling existed.

What happened is that in the late 1990s a software sampler called GigaSampler, now defunct as a product but superseded by others, came along and revolutionized the whole field. Rather than having to fit all the samples into memory, Giga (Figure I.1) streamed them off a hard disk. Suddenly it was no longer necessary to worry about how large the sample recordings were, so all previous restrictions on their length, duration, and especially number of dynamic layers and articulations were gone.

The quality of the sounds took such a leap that—for better *and* worse—sampling began to dominate the commercial music scene, and the art of MIDI programming became a whole new musical medium. This spawned a vital industry of sample library developers who continue to raise the bar every year.

Meanwhile, the move from dedicated hardware to computers allowed software engineers to create samplers with all kinds of new capabilities. What's more, in some samplers these capabilities can be extended with scripts, which are custom programs that control their built-in parameters in all kinds of sophisticated ways. Given the complexity, it's not uncommon for an advanced sample library to take years to develop—and that's just for version 1.

If that has you hiding under the bed, please crawl out. You know how the last 5 percent of any project takes 99 percent of the time? Well, it's only the first part we need to be concerned with. Far from being intimidating, the advances in sampling technology have made it easier than ever to create custom sample libraries that sound right at home next to commercial-grade ones.

We can record libraries that sound good, and we can download and import some remarkably sophisticated scripts into our samplers. Perhaps most importantly, we can do a good job of editing and mapping samples to the keyboard so that they play well under the fingers.

Figure I.1 Nemesys GigaSampler revolutionized sampling.

And that's what this book is all about: creating custom libraries that bring unique instruments to our productions, taking advantage of the inherent life that makes sampling such an exciting technique for creating sounds.

What You'll Find in This Book

The software samplers available today make it more practical than ever to create your own sample libraries for a unique sound. This book demystifies and guides you through the whole process, including easy, step-by-step tutorials for all the popular samplers: Native Instruments Kontakt, Apple EXS24, Avid Structure, and Propellerhead Reason.

This book includes the following and more:

- Practical tips for planning your custom libraries and then recording your samples so they sound professional

- Editing and processing your instruments creatively

- Mapping instruments so they feel right when you play them
- Building advanced and expressive programs in the popular samplers, with easy tutorials you work through using samples that you download from the companion Web site

Who This Book Is For

This book is for musicians who want to create their own custom sample libraries or who just want to explore the advanced features of their software samplers.

How This Book Is Organized

Here's a breakdown of what you'll find in these pages by chapter:

- Chapter 1 covers what to record so that you sample just what you need and nothing more. You'll also learn how to record a sample so that your libraries will sound good enough to blend with the commercial ones you're already using.
- Chapter 2 is about slicing and dicing the samples. Read about making creative choices about tuning, noise reduction, and dynamics processing.
- Chapters 3 through 6 offer information on building programs in the popular samplers (Apple EXS24, Native Instruments Kontakt, Propellerhead NN-XT, and Avid Structure). Tutorials start with basic playable programs and then add more and more sample layers and performance features.
- Chapter 7 is all about looping. You'll discover how to repeat sections of your recordings to extend their length—without the listener knowing you're doing so. Tutorials are included for each sampler.
- Chapter 8 is where you'll learn about release samples. You'll edit and trigger samples that are triggered when you let go of the note. Tutorials are included for the individual samplers.
- Chapter 9 covers using Kontakt scripts. You'll read how to install these programs to extend Kontakt's functions.

Companion Web Site Downloads

This book has a companion Web site offering additional content related to this book. You can download files from www.courseptr.com/downloads. Please note that you will be redirected to the Cengage Learning Online Companion Web site. Simply enter this book's title, ISBN, or the author's name in the Companion Search field at the top and click on the Search button. You'll be taken to the book's companion page, where you can download the related files.

On the companion page for this book are the audio files you'll use to go through each chapter's tutorials. In addition, you'll find two bonus chapters. Chapter 10 shows how to create the popular stutter effect, and in the process introduces some important features in your sampler. Chapter 11 explores the samplers' synthesis parameters—filters, envelopes, and modulation matrixes—to create both wordly and unworldly effects.

1 Planning

There are several decisions to make before starting to record a custom library. And as with anything else, what you're *not* going to do (to avoid spending man-years) is often the biggest decision.

Obviously the more you record, the more work you'll have editing your samples. That will affect things like how many volume levels you record, whether you sample chromatically or use pitch shifting to fill in the gaps, how many mics you use, what articulations you record, whether you record release samples, what sample rate and bit depth you're going to use, and so on.

The other factor affecting how much you record is how heavily you want to tax the computer or computers running your custom library. In the real world, your custom samplers are likely to become integrated into the rest of your system alongside many other virtual instruments, and the whole load is cumulative. So with that as the backdrop, let's start with a look at the computers themselves.

Computer Performance

Streaming sample programs can be as large as necessary. Yet three finite resources have an effect on playing them back: processing power, memory access, and disk streaming. The first two are becoming less critical these days, and the third promises to become history when solid-state drives reach the mainstream. For now, however, Sampling Nirvana remains elusive.

Processing Power

On its own, streaming samples off a drive is child's play to a computer's processor. GigaSampler ran on inexpensive Pentium 3-level machines when it first came out years ago, and even back then you could open up the Windows Task Manager and see the processor sticking its tongue out at you and laughing.

If you look at Figure 1.1, you'll see that streaming samples alone is very light on the CPU. This ancient 2.4 GHz Pentium 4 machine is streaming four tracks/80 stereo voices inside GigaStudio 3, and much of the 82% processor it's using is being taken up by other programs running simultaneously. (Namely, Audio Impressions Audioport and the Plogue Bidule VST plug-in; in place of audio and MIDI hardware on this computer, GigaStudio is receiving MIDI and streaming audio over an Ethernet network into another computer that's running a sequencer.)

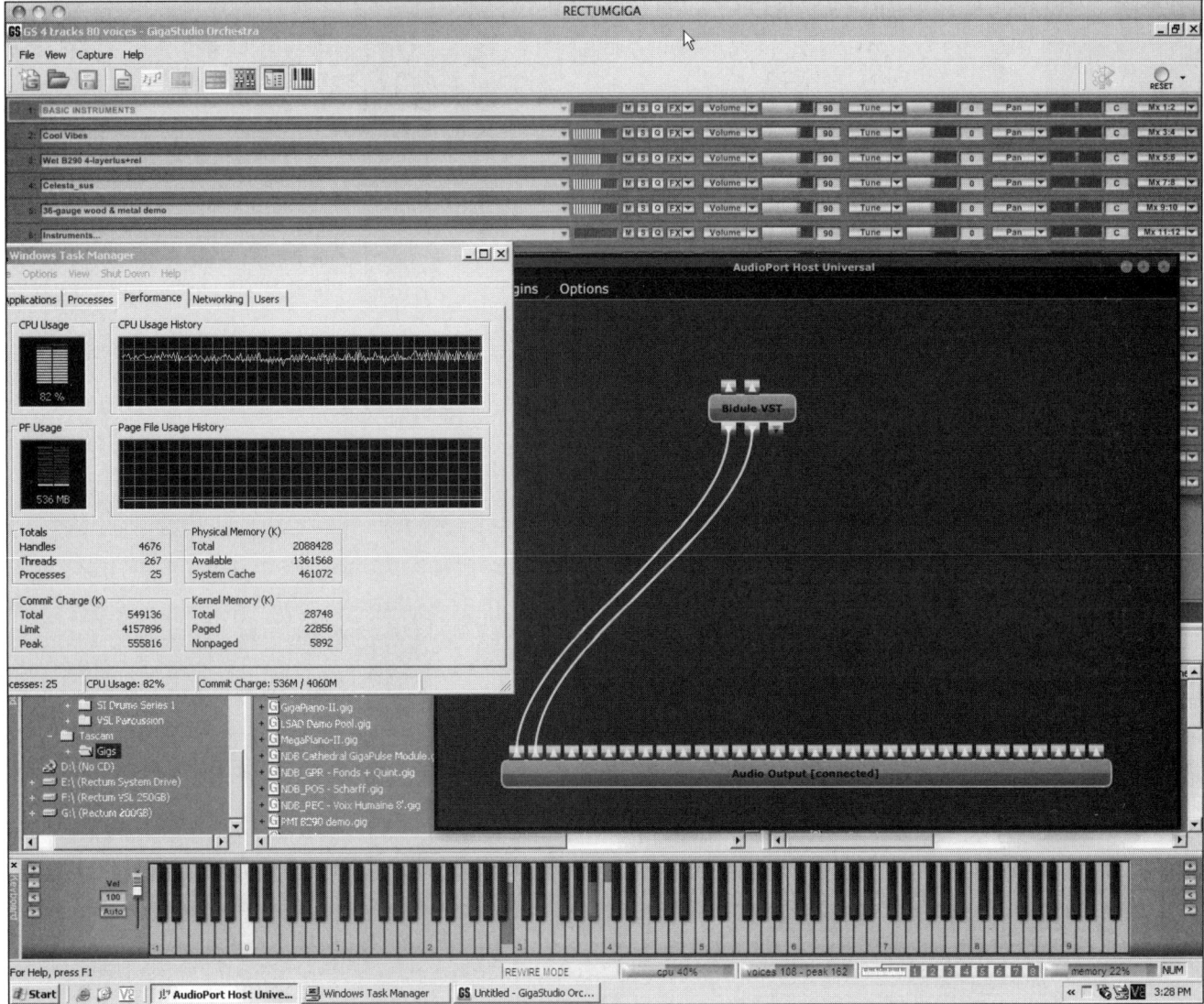

Figure 1.1 Streaming samples without doing a lot of processing is very light on the CPU.

However, sampling has advanced a lot since the early Giga days, to the point that we're usually doing a lot more than just streaming. Modern samplers now include all kinds of DSP (digital signal processing) features that use the huge amounts of power existing in modern computers. These processes include advanced "morphing" filters, built-in reverb, and especially convolution processing, which we'll discuss in some detail later (these processors apply the "sonic footprint" of sampled spaces—or anything else—to your samples).

Complicated scripts can also tax a computer's processing resources. Sometimes it's hard to figure out what's causing this to happen, but usually it's just because their programming language is high-level by design—meaning it's an additional layer that sits "above" the more efficient lower-level instructions.

You can also tax the computer's processing power with aggressive playback settings. Samples are first read off the hard drives they're stored on into a "head start" RAM buffer for playback, because conventional rotating hard drives are nowhere near fast enough. Computer memory is many times faster, with response measured in microseconds rather than milliseconds.

As the size of the RAM buffer goes up, the amount of processing power used goes down—but the latency increases, meaning the time between playing a note and hearing it back gets longer. So we're always trying to reduce the size of the RAM buffer before the playback starts glitching, balanced against CPU use on the opposite side of the scale. This scale runs into the ceiling and the floor, however—it only applies up to a point.

Given today's multiprocessor computers with several cores as powerful as the single processors that preceded them, it may seem odd to talk about running out of power. The problem is that, say, an 8-core machine isn't quite the same thing as eight single-core computers. Between the operating systems and the way the software is written, the load isn't always divided evenly; one instrument might be assigned to a single core and do some damage.

One of the cores in the powerful 8-core machine shown in Figure 1.2 is running a lot more than the other seven, possibly because it's using advanced sampler scripting.

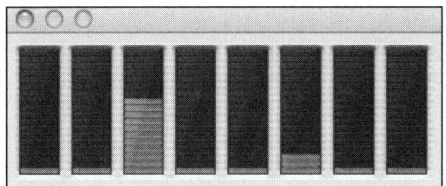

Figure 1.2 Efficiency is always a good idea, because a single instrument can overload a single processing core.

In reality it isn't usually necessary to avoid programming a sampler feature just to avoid taxing the processors in a modern computer, but the cumulative load can make it necessary to raise the RAM buffer and increase the latency to a noticeable level. Efficiency is always a good idea; maybe it would be better to share a big honking reverb plug-in among several instruments in your sequencer's mixer, rather than to program it permanently inside the sampler, for example.

Memory Access

RAM access limitation has been the biggest thorn in the backside of sample users for years, but the issue is finally, um, behind us, at least with most music software. Memory access remains something to consider when creating libraries, however, because there are still limits to how much you can run on a single machine.

Now, the more programs you have loaded and ready to play, and the more samples in all these programs, the greater the amount of memory the software you're running needs to access. That's true whether these programs are all different instruments or just various articulations (meaning playing techniques) of the same instrument. It's necessary to have lots of programs cued up; the alternative would be stopping to load a new one every time you needed to switch from, say, long to short notes. No thanks.

For a few years, the amount of RAM you could access for samples on a single machine was quite limited—not much more than 1GB—even if the machine was physically capable of holding more memory. So musicians typically ran a few computers to accommodate larger sampled ensembles. It wasn't difficult to fill up a whole machine with a single large instrument like a piano, which of course has lots of samples, and things had become quite unwieldy by the time the major orchestral sample libraries came on the scene in the early 2000s.

This was due to both hardware and software, but it had a lot to do with the limitation of 32-bit operating systems (OSs). The theoretical maximum a 32-bit OS can access is 4GB of RAM per program (due to the number of memory addresses that can be defined using 32 bits), and in the real world you're lucky to be able to load 3GB before things become unstable.

Still, that's 3GB per application, and the first big breakthrough was when you could run multiple applications, each with its own 4GB allotment. At first the solution was to load up a sequencer with its 3GB and then launch either standalone samplers or another virtual instrument host program on the same machine (such as the now defunct Steinberg V-Stack or current Plogue Bidule). Sometimes you could resort to workarounds like giving the second instance of a sampler or virtual instrument host a different name (such as "Copy of xxxxx").

The next step was when the samplers themselves created their own "memory servers" outside the host program, tricking the OS into thinking that each server was a separate program with its own memory allotment. VSL's dedicated player for its own libraries was the first to do that, soon to be followed by Apple's EXS24 sampler built into its Logic Pro sequencer. Native Instruments Kontakt introduced a memory server, along with EastWest's dedicated PLAY sampler for its own libraries.

Figure 1.3 shows Kontakt's memory servers. In the shaded area, you can see KxMemServer0 accessing 3.43GB of samples loaded inside Apple Logic Pro (with 1.41GB loaded), spilling over to KxMemServer1 with 1.74GB loaded.

But the real answer is 64-bit computing, which allows access to essentially unlimited amounts of RAM. There's a small catch, however. To run 64-bit samplers, everything has to be 64 bit—the computer's processor(s), the OS, the driver for your audio interface, the host program and/or sequencer you're running, and all the other instrument and processing plug-ins.

As of this writing, the world is making the transition to 64 bits. The operating systems are there, but not everything else is. For example, Logic Pro uses a somewhat clumsy "bit bridge" to run 32-bit instruments and processors in its 64-bit version, while the Vienna Ensemble Pro host takes a different approach, providing both 32- and 64-bit server programs. (You can run as many of each as you need.) Avid Pro Tools hasn't turned 64 yet, but Steinberg Cubase has, as has Native Instruments Kontakt 4.1. We're in a state of flux.

Of course, small sample programs can fit into RAM without streaming, in which case the performance issues disappear. Most samplers have an option to turn streaming on and off.

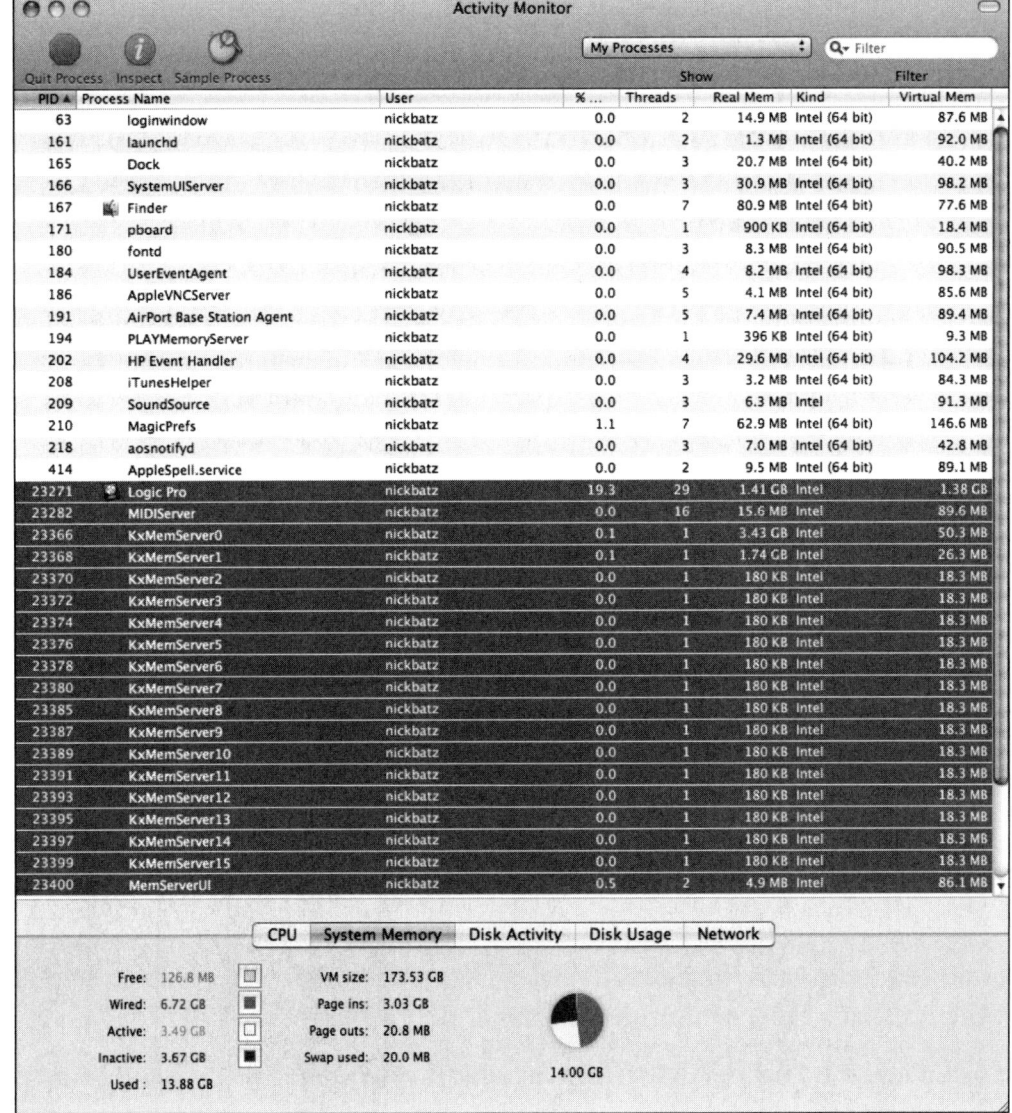

Figure 1.3   Native Instruments Kontakt 3.5 introduced memory servers to break the theoretical 4GB per program limit.

Drives

When streaming samples, the hard drive's read head has to grab samples very quickly from all over the place. Its ability to do that is called *seek time*. Standard hard drives with rotating platters have steadily been gaining capacity and becoming less expensive over the years, but the seek times have been locked in the 7–10 millisecond range. Some high-performance drives spin at 10,000 RPM; standard ones spin at 7200 RPM, but the basic spec is always in the same ballpark.

That means the number of simultaneous voices a single drive can play is finite. Exceptions are starting to appear, but note that the amount of data that can go across the drive bus—the transfer rate—is not normally important in our application; instead it's the drive's finite ability to grab smaller amounts of data quickly that sets the limit.

For that reason, RAID (Redundant Array of Independent Drives) setups, which increase the bandwidth, are not usually much help with sampling. (On the other hand, video playback does require bandwidth, so RAID may be useful for working with reference video in scoring applications.)

What can help with the sample load is JBOD: Just a Bunch of Drives. If you distribute the seeking a sampler has to do among different hard drives, you reduce the amount of seeking each drive has to do. It can be helpful to put different instruments on different drives.

The real answer is here, but it's still relatively new: solid-state drives (SSD), which use memory for storage and aren't electromechanical devices at all. SSDs are still relatively expensive as of this writing, and there are some bugs in the system, but they're dropping rapidly. On some setups, however, people are getting performance that totally slays conventional drives, and it seems likely that the days of spinning platters are numbered.

The performance increase we're talking about is manifested in the number of simultaneous voices a single drive can play back, in smaller head-start buffer settings (i.e., lower latency), and equally importantly in the shorter amount of time it takes to load programs. Until now, there's been a practical limit to the amount of RAM it makes sense to install in a single computer, simply because it takes so long to load larger templates. Nobody wants to sit around waiting 25 minutes for an orchestral template to load—especially after a computer crash!

Multiple Machines

So far we've been discussing the limits of a single machine, and the practical way around them is to use more than one of them. That's true even in this day and age of really powerful machines.

Somewhere in this discussion there's another issue: old machines that are still perfectly viable only they aren't capable of running as many sample programs at once as current computers. At least one highly successful, modern commercial library—Audiobro LA Scoring Strings—was developed on modest Pentium 4 computers precisely to ensure efficiency.

Whether you're using old or new computers, integrating them into a rig is as simple as putting inexpensive audio and MIDI interfaces on them. Nowadays it's more elegant just to run audio and MIDI into your main DAW on another machine over a gigabit Ethernet cable. VSL's Vienna Ensemble Pro and Audio Impressions' AudioPort Pro are two programs that take the place of hardware interfaces on slave computers.

Recording Choices

The first questions when planning a custom library are these:

- What are you going to record?
- How are you going to record it?

In fact, the two are inseparable, and many of the decisions you'll make are intertwined. A few of the considerations you'll encounter follow, in somewhat random order.

Stereo versus Mono

If you're making a live recording of a solo instrument, there's no question: you want to record it in stereo, most likely spread out pretty wide to fill in the soundscape. But we're not recording performances, we're capturing "snapshots" that we'll use to create playable instruments—or at least instruments that require a minimum of tedious programming in a sequencer to sound right.

If you're sure you won't need stereo, mono does use half the computer resources, and mono samples tend to be more versatile. More often than not you absolutely will want to record in stereo; in fact, it's sensible to record in stereo if you even *think* it might sound better somewhere down the line. But it does add some complexity even before the larger question of how many mics you're going to use.

For example, you may want to use a solo instrument as part of a group, and a stereo image that sounds good when the instrument is on its own may be too wide in another context, or it may just take up too much space in a mix. That can certainly be changed—it's not difficult to narrow the spread in most sequencers' mixers without even inserting a plug-in—but if you collapse it all the way to mono—or for that matter if you use a mono channel strip—you can get a phasey sound. That's why it's important to record in a mono-compatible way; refer to Figure 1.4 for the simplest stereo miking technique (X–Y), which works well in small rooms.

Figure 1.4 X-Y, the simplest and most foolproof stereo miking technique.

The idea is to use two mics with a cardioid pickup pattern, tails spread out between 90° and 130°, with their heads as close to the same position as possible (avoiding phasing problems).

There's another way to avoid phasing between the channels when you create mono: mute one of them. That works best if the recording isn't too ambient (because it can sound a little odd to remove half the ambience). The caveat is that the level can go up and down if the performer moves back and forth during the recording. If you use both recorded channels, the image simply shifts—which can be another issue, but it's less noticeable than level changes.

Turning the discussion around, you can also create artificial stereo from a mono recording. It may not be quite as good as real recorded stereo, but it's still very effective. The simplest way of doing this is to use a reverb unit—specifically the early reflections rather than the reverb tail. Early reflections are the first bounces off the walls, ceiling, and floor, and they tell the ear about the space an instrument was recorded in.

Please refer to Figures 1.5 and 1.6, showing a concert hall reverb program inside Audio Ease's Altiverb convolution processor. In the first screenshot, the early reflections are on, and in the

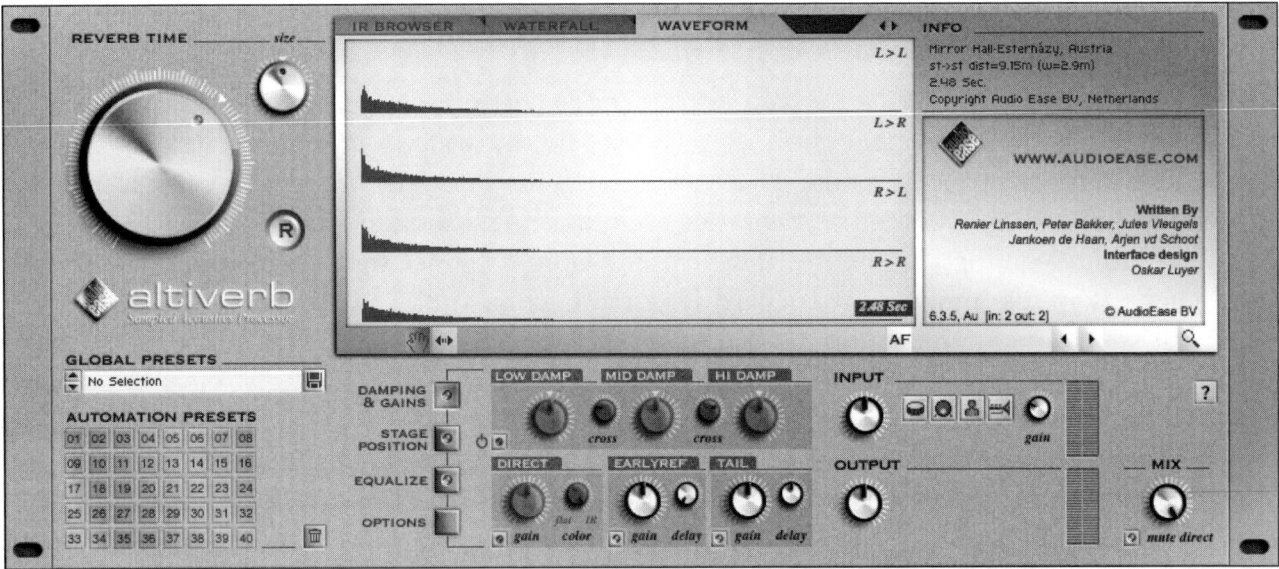

Figure 1.5 Altiverb early reflections plus tail.

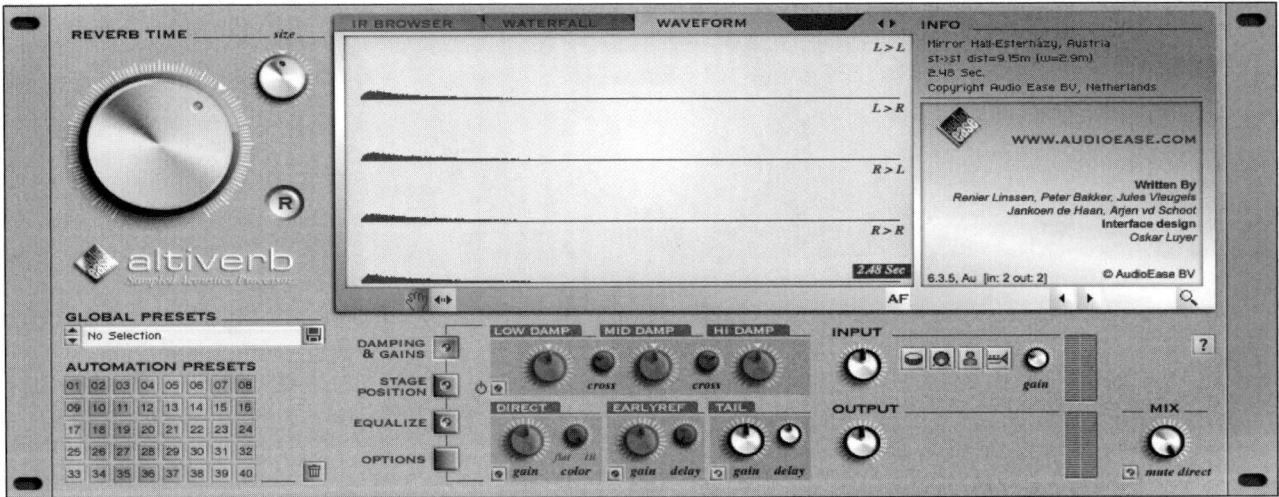

Figure 1.6 Altiverb tail without early reflections.

second they've been turned off. You can use early reflections without the tail to create very convincing stereo out of a mono recording.

A more basic way of making artificial stereo is just to create two walls using a stereo delay plug-in, panned hard left and right, with one side set around 15 milliseconds and the other maybe 40. If mono compatibility is important, you can detune the two sides from one another a couple of cents with a pitch shifter to avoid phase weirdness when the channels are collapsed to the middle. I mention this technique here because it uses minimal computer resources, and it might make sense to put it inside the sampler as part of your programming. This effect is "more than mono but not quite real stereo," and maybe it can let you get away with recording in mono.

Figure 1.7 shows artificial stereo created with a stereo delay to simulate bounces off two walls, here in Avid/Digidesign Pro Tools.

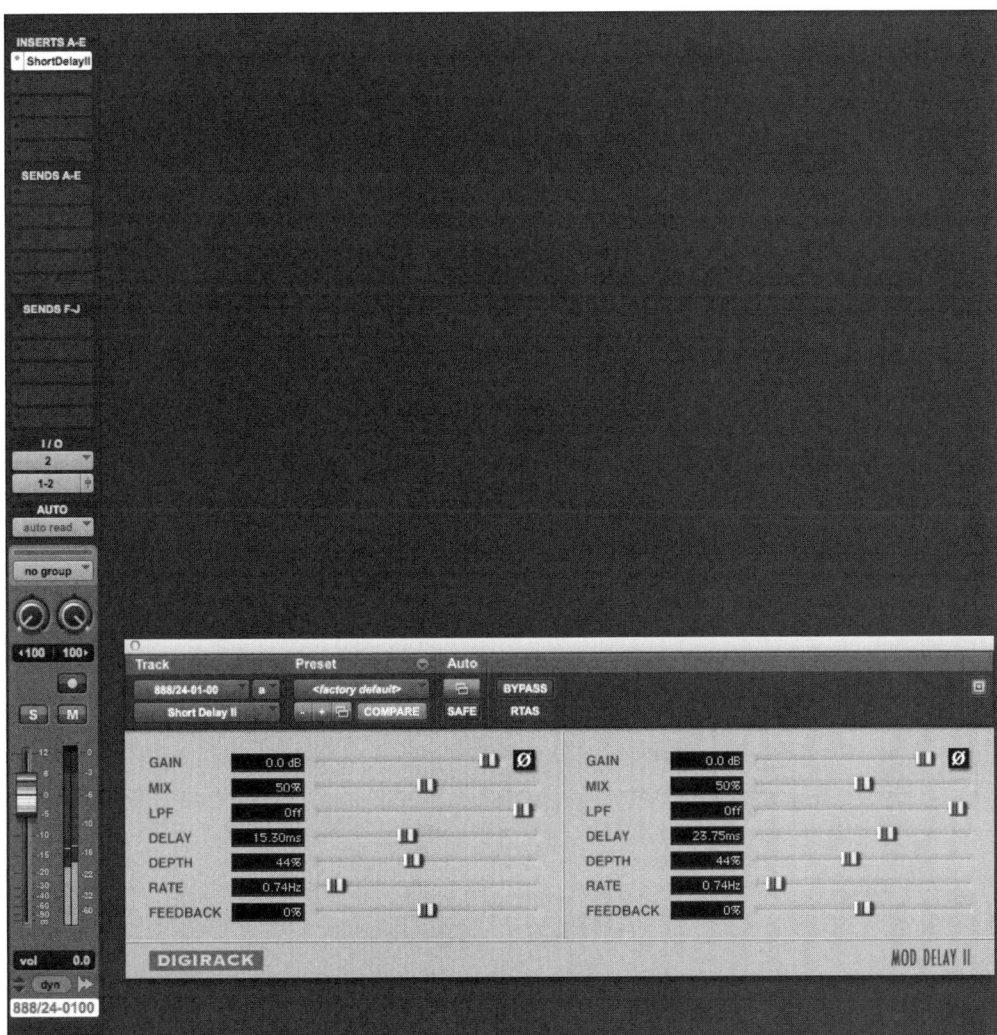

Figure 1.7 Artificial stereo created with two delays.

One more point about recording in stereo as it applies to samples: you may end up with more room sound than when you record in mono. The reason is that stereo usually requires a little more distance from the source. Not only does that tend to make the quality of the room you record in more critical, recorded ambience can restrict the samples' versatility.

The flip side of that is that recorded ambience can add a whole lot of spark to the recordings. Stereo is wonderful; it can make mono sound dull and lifeless by comparison. You just want to be sure there's a good reason for recording stereo samples.

Finally, it's unlikely but worth considering whether you want to record an instrument in its actual stage position. This is mostly applicable to acoustic instruments. For example, you could record a harp at about 10 o'clock relative to the conductor's position. If you're only going to use the harp that way and can record it in a good-sounding hall—and if you're not concerned about being locked in to that position—then why not take advantage of the natural ambience?

Multiple Mic Positions

It doesn't cost extra to record with multiple mics in different positions—even if you're using two mics but not really recording in stereo. The best engineers aren't embarrassed to do that, and not necessarily as a safety measure (although that is a benefit) but because of the flexibility it affords, letting you balance the mics to come up with a composite sound you like.

The question is whether you want to keep the individual mic position samples separate or mix them down to mono or stereo before editing. No question, keeping them separate makes editing a lot more cumbersome, to say nothing of the extra computer resources you're taking up. This is especially true when you're miking from a distance, due to the more noticeable amount of time it takes sound to travel to the mics.

The EastWest Quantum Leap Symphony orchestra was one of the first commercial libraries to do this on a huge scale, with close, Decca tree over the conductor, and hall positions. EWQLSO also has recorded reverb tails, so when you release a note you get real ring-off. If ever there was an editing nightmare, that must have been it. On a more practical level, a number of commercial drum libraries keep the mics separate to simulate the way real drums are recorded (overheads, snare and tom mics, etc.); the bleed between the various mics is part of what we expect from a drum sound. Ocean Way Drums is a good example.

In general you'd probably want to avoid keeping the multiple mic positions separate when editing, but there are times when it makes total sense. An example would be both close and room mics on a guitar cabinet, or for that matter direct and amped versions of a guitar. It's easy to edit stereo—two tracks—but beyond that it can start to become unwieldy in a hurry.

One thing you'll notice right away is that mics don't behave like the human ear; if you use more than one, you have to adjust the positioning to avoid phase cancellation issues when the tracks are combined. Really bad phasing sounds like the recording was made inside a tin can, but more often than not the problem is more subtle.

As a starting point, the 3:1 rule is good for multiple mics: separate additional mics by at least three times the distance the first one is from the source (see Figure 1.8). So if a mic is 1 foot away from the source, the other must be 3 feet away from the other mic. That rule is violated all the time—for example, it doesn't matter if the mics aren't pointing in the same direction— but it won't steer you wrong.

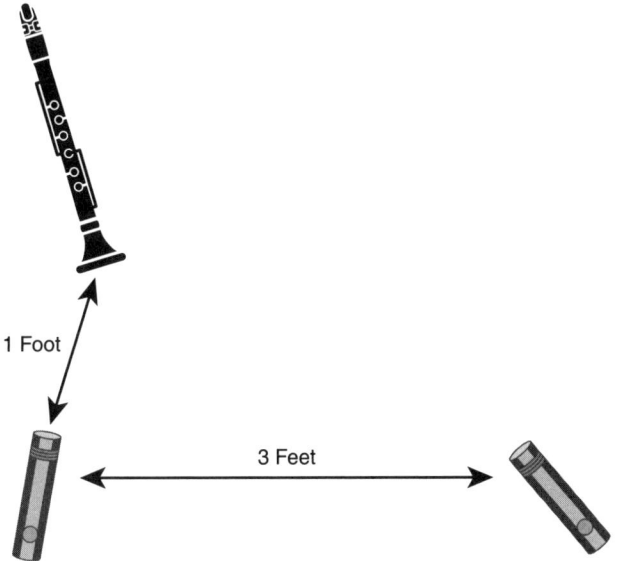

1 Foot

3 Feet

Figure 1.8 The 3:1 rule: One mic is 1x from the source, while a second mic should be 3x away from the other mic.

It's also possible to slide tracks inside the audio editor to phase-align them, but it's better to get it right while you're recording.

Rooms

It's pretty apparent that moving mics back from a source will lower the source and bring up the room. And since rooms that weren't designed for recording have an unfortunate tendency to sound perfectly awful, the conventional wisdom is that project studio recordings should normally be close-miked. Furthermore, dry samples are more flexible, since you can always add reverb but you can't really take it away—nor can you remove the signature sound of a bad room.

But the room is an integral part of the sound. If you haven't heard how weird a recording made in an anechoic chamber sounds, you certainly have heard the difference between a totally dry synthesizer and one run through a reverb; few things sound good in a totally dead space. Sure, you can easily surround something with thick foam and remove all the upper mid and high frequency reflections, but then you'll suck all the life out of the recording. So even in bad rooms it's good to work hard to capture some air from the space.

There are commercial products designed for recording in untreated rooms. ASC Tube Traps, which create a portable recording field, are probably the premier product of this type (see Figure 1.9). But what you can't see is that underneath the fabric, Tube Traps have a combination of absorption and reflection—one side has a hard reflective surface behind the cloth, and you mix and match the two to come up with a good sound.

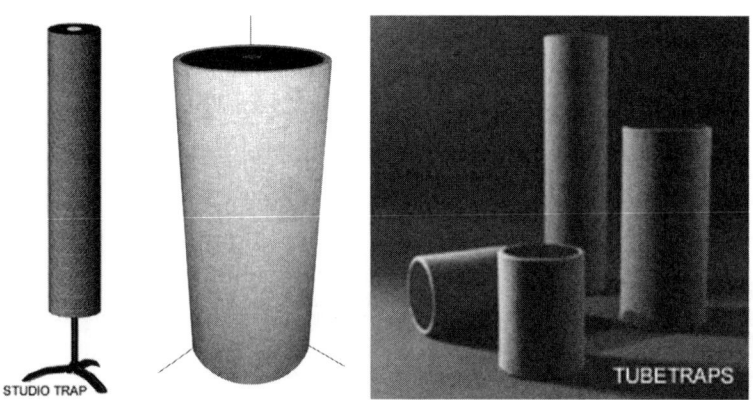

Figure 1.9 ASC Tube Traps, one of the most ubiquitous and effective acoustic treatment products on the market.

It's not difficult to apply that same basic concept without using a commercial product. If you need to use foam to get rid of horrible reflections in a room, try leaving the opposite side of the room reflective. Maybe leave curtains partly open so there's some reflective window between them. Place a mattress on one wall but not the other.

On the other hand, there's no shortage of excellent recordings from the '70s that were done in very dry studios. Drums and vocals are still normally recorded inside isolation booths. But they're usually recorded with some air.

Sample Rates and Bit Depths

The standard sampling rates for digital audio are 44.1kHz (the CD rate) and 48kHz (video, and probably the default rate), meaning that the audio is sampled 44,100 or 48,000 times per second. Those rates were chosen because humans hear up to about 20kHz; the sampling rate has to be twice that in order to capture both the tops and bottoms of the waveforms, and all higher frequencies are cut off abruptly with a "brick wall" filter to avoid a noisy mess called *aliasing*.

There have been industry attempts to increase the resolution to 96kHz and even 192kHz in order to raise distortions in the digital filtering system out of the audible range, although the improvement is subtle. While high sample rates might make sense for live recording, absolutely nobody wants to double or quadruple the amount of data and get half or a quarter of the playback performance in a sampler. Samples are almost always recorded at standard sampling rates (the one exception I know about being Vienna Symphonic Library), and nobody releases libraries at high sample rates.

The difference between 44.1kHz and 48kHz is about a semitone, and given a choice it sounds better to transpose down than up. That means 48kHz is a slightly better choice than 44.1kHz, but it doesn't make much difference which you choose; all software samplers are aware of the session sample rate in your sequencer and handle the conversion seamlessly.

Samplers

At some point you're going to choose which sampler to use. It's not really necessary to make that decision before recording or even editing, but the features of the sampler could make a difference.

A very basic example is that neither the NN-XT nor the NN-19 samplers inside Propellerhead Reason do disk streaming, and they don't play release samples. While some of the commercial Reason libraries are quite large—and actually quite good—your library would want to be smaller than it would otherwise be in order to fit into RAM.

By simply importing scripts into your programs, you can immediately add some pretty remarkable features. If you'd like to use scripts in your programs, the choice of samplers dwindles to two—actually one as of this writing. Native Instruments Kontakt, the most popular sampler and the winner of the decades-long sampler format wars, is current the only sampler that has scripting. EastWest's PLAY Pro, which will probably have been released by the time you read this book, will also have a scripting feature.

For an example of what Kontakt scripting can do, R.D. Villwock gave the world a wonderful free script called SIPS (http://nilsliberg.se/ksp/scripts/sips/sips.htm). SIPS does an excellent job of simulating legato transitions between notes. It makes notes sound like they were played in the same breath or bow; if you hold down one note and quickly hit the next one, it adjusts the decay of the source and the attack of the destination notes in real time and sometimes adds subtle pitch glides into the destination. The alternative would be the actual recorded legato samples featured in high-end commercial libraries (first introduced in the Vienna Symphonic Library), and that's probably too much work for a custom library.

But there are reasons to choose formats other than Kontakt, the most practical one being that you already own a sampler that uses a different one. If you're using Logic Pro, for example, the EXS-24 is built in. If you're using Propellerhead Reason or Record, you already have used their samplers. Both Steinberg HALion and Avid (formerly Digidesign) Structure are capable samplers, and we'll have tutorials on using these instruments.

Looped or Unlooped

Before sample streaming came along, all the recordings in a sampled instrument had to be loaded into memory. That meant the recordings had to be as small as possible to fit into the available RAM; if you wanted a note to sustain longer than the recording, you had to loop it, meaning you had to program the sampler to repeat a section of the recording over and over while the note was being held.

Looping is still a viable technique for certain applications, and you can load smaller sampled instruments in RAM. But with disk streaming and very inexpensive drives, it's no longer necessary to make short recordings.

What that means is that you can and should usually record everything for a long enough time that you can avoid looping it. Let sounds ring all the way out, hold notes as long as your breath can play them, and so on.

Efficiency is always a good idea, but obviously you'd prefer to discard what you don't need than to wish you had recorded it.

Alternate Takes

One of the giveaways that you're listening to samples rather than live instruments is the infamous repeated note effect. The worst (unless you're after the effect) is the machine gun sound when you play short notes, as anyone who's tried to program a snare drum roll on a drum machine knows.

For that reason, it's often a good idea to record more than one version of every note. Programming alternating notes in the sampler isn't especially complicated.

The "Sucking" Sound

Musicians naturally swell—get a little louder—when playing round, expressive long notes. The problem is that the next note starts at a lower level when you're using those notes in sampled instruments, and it sounds like the line is getting sucked into the track.

This is what sample library aficionados refer to as "sucking" (for this reason, not because it sucks). The workaround for this problem is to override the recorded dynamics and perform the required ones with a MIDI controller while you're playing the parts.

Friendly Mic Null

Ying: by definition, directional mics have polar pick-up patterns in which they're much more sensitive to sound coming from certain directions, namely the front and to varying degrees the rear. Yang: that means they're equally insensitive to sounds coming from the sides.

You can use that rejection pattern to minimize noise. If there are sounds coming from a window at the front of the room, try to record with the mics pointing to the sides.

What to Record—An Incomplete Checklist

The basic concept of sampling a tonal instrument is simple: record scales of long and short notes to a click. After that, it becomes increasingly difficult to spell out. Some of the questions are

- Do you need to sample the instrument chromatically? It doesn't hurt to do that as long as fatigue isn't a factor (such as huge brass instruments played loudly), but it's not always necessary; some instruments take pitch shifting better than others.
- What tempos?
- How many dynamic levels?
- How are you going to record alternate takes (if you've deemed them necessary)? Should you play, say, a series of 16th notes to give yourself a choice?
- What articulations? Beyond the basic long and short notes, are there any unique articulations you might want to use—or are there any missing from commercial libraries? Please refer to Figure 1.10 for some ideas.

Musical Purpose

And now for a little philosophy.

Sampling technology works as well as it does for a number of reasons, but at the top of that list is that it uses recordings to generate sounds. That gives it an inherent life (despite the fact that the technology consists of piecing together static "snapshots").

Similarly, the most important factor separating the great sample libraries is not technical, it's the performances; every note has a musical purpose behind it. Please consider that when you're determining what to record, and especially in your role as producer—whether you're directing yourself or other people.

Test Recording

With the best laid plans for your custom library in place, you're ready to record. However, bear in mind that commercial sample developers almost always make test recordings before going too far, and if practical that may be a good idea at the custom library level, too.

The reason is that recordings that work well on their own may or may not sound right as playable instruments. So the idea is to record some basic notes and articulations, build one or more quick and dirty programs, and see how well your concept works. Cut the recordings up into a few individual notes, map them to the keyboard, and see how they work.

Figure 1.10 EastWest's Ministry of Rock has a moderate number of articulations, while VSL's solo violin has a vast number.

2 Processing and Primary Editing

After making any necessary adjustments in response to your test recordings if applicable, you've transferred your samples into the program you're going to use for editing, and you're looking at one or more side-by-side tracks with recordings of notes. The first steps are to clean them up if necessary, cut them up into individual notes, and turn them into playable instruments. You may or may not need to tune them as well.

As with all sound production, you need to be able to hear what's going on in order to make the right decisions. It's worth including some quick suggestions on the subject, because an inadequate monitoring setup can cause a lot of frustration.

Monitoring

Functional nearfield monitors (NFMs) as found in most project studios don't have to be expensive. NFMs are fairly small speakers set up maybe four feet away, forming an equilateral triangle with your head. They're usually built to withstand uncontrolled loud sounds that might damage domestic speakers—the kinds of sounds sampling often produces—and hopefully they don't introduce an uneven frequency response that tells a different story from what's really going on. Headphones can also be a useful reference, although they don't have the same sound as speakers and subjectively aren't a very satisfying substitute.

Now, the problem with small speakers is that they're small. That—combined with the issues inherent to the small rooms we tend to work in—means their low frequency response is not very strong. Most NFMs cut off around 60Hz, and things like vocal pops, piano hammer thuds, and foot taps in microphones start just below that, maybe at 55Hz.

In Figures 2.1 and 2.2, a test oscillator plug-in is generating a reasonably loud 55Hz sine wave. The spectrum meter plug-in (in Apple Logic Pro) and iPhone audio analyzer app (iAnalyzer) show it very clearly. These are things you *really* don't want to have in your samples, so you need to be able to hear them.

Ideally you'll have a subwoofer—even an inexpensive one from Costco works fine—or even more ideally a pair of bigger speakers to use as a reference. You can also check for rumbly stuff by placing your hand on the woofer to feel for cone excursions, plus you can use spectrum display

Figure 2.1   Unwanted low frequencies in Logic Pro's spectrum meter.

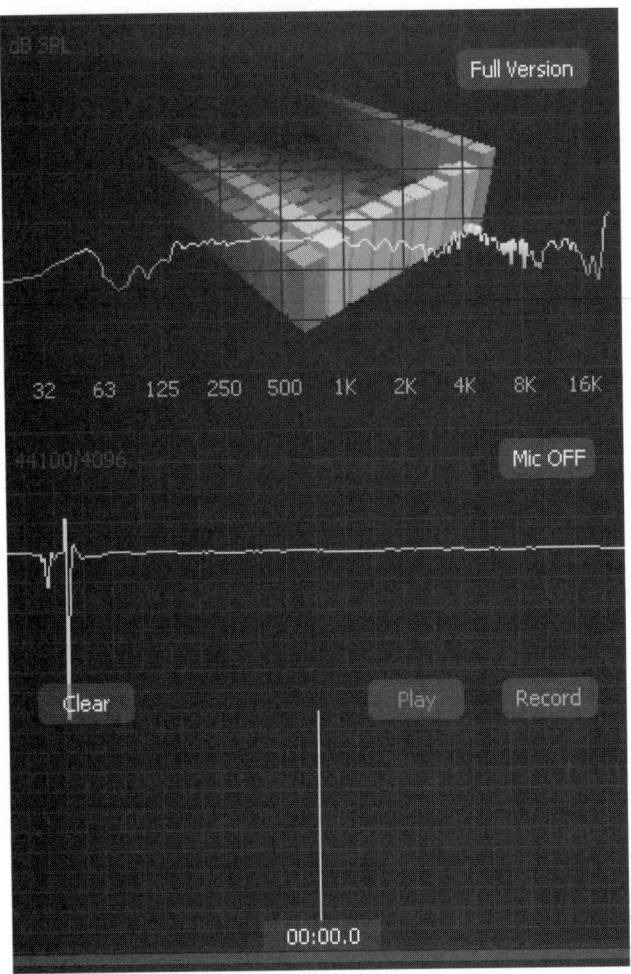

Figure 2.2   Unwanted low frequencies in iAnalyzer running on an iPhone.

plug-ins in your editing software. If you see funny stuff on the graph that you don't hear, something funny is going on.

Next, the room. There are some quick, easy, and inexpensive things you can do that will make even the worst room serviceable.

Now, conventional idea is that because you're near the monitors, you hear them before the room has had a chance to "interfere with" the sound. However, a bad room will indeed interfere with the sound. And in fact you can't and wouldn't want to remove the room, because it actually helps you hear properly. It's true that NFMs tend to work better than speakers that are farther away in less-than-ideal rooms, but that's mainly because you hear a lot of details close up, and the imaging is very precise when you're in the perfect position between them.

It's not necessary to call in the architects. Rather than trying to deaden the entire room, a simple approach advocated by audio guru Dave Moulton (www.moultonlabs.com) works much better: soak up excess reverb at the front of the room with broadband absorption, but keep the sides hard and flat (for example, leave the walls bare). Reflections from the sides actually improve the sound, contrary to the popular "reflection-free zone" theory you may have heard; it's only reflections coming from the same angle as the speakers that cause interference when they combine with the sound coming from them, hence the dead front of the room.

There are all kinds of commercial acoustic products available, but you can also use unofficial materials very effectively. The main thing is not to try to absorb sound with materials that are too thin, such as light curtains. That just removes the high frequencies, and you don't want to be fooled into making the samples too bright to compensate for your having messed up the frequency response of your room.

Like politics, acoustics is the art of the possible rather than the ideal. If it's not possible to, say, make the sides hard and flat, it's not the end of the world; these are just general principles. The main point is that simple treatments to a room can make it usable even if it isn't perfectly "tuned."

Noise Reduction?

Hopefully you were able to record your samples without picking up any extra noise. And that's most likely not the case, so you'll have to do a little clean-up.

Unlike normal recordings, samples are stacked on top of each other, and notes are repeated. That means steady-state ambient noise builds up in layers; a five-note chord has five layers of noise in addition to five notes. And extraneous noises that you wouldn't notice normally—or that are a hallmark of real recordings—will always sound at the same amount of time after the noisy note is triggered.

As is often the case, however, what you don't do can be more important than what you decide to do. You're close to your recordings and hear them over and over under close examination, so there's a tendency to use too much noise reduction and suck the life out of your samples (all noise reduction schemes take out some of the baby along with the bathwater).

The same idea applies to noises. Some are good, some are annoying; the line between beauty marks and blemishes is subjective. But in general it's better to under-process samples than to sterilize them.

There are all kinds of noise reduction plug-ins, and many DAWs come with them. (The plug-in included with Logic Pro is shown in Figure 2.3.) For steady-state noise such as, say, a fan, there are processors that learn the noise footprint and build a custom sliding filter to reduce it. Other processors are focused on removing hum and buzz, tracking the 50Hz or 60Hz harmonics up the series and filtering that narrow band. Still other algorithms are designed to get rid of crackles and clicks, but it's unlikely you'll need to do that to samples. The main thing is to use all of this sparingly.

Figure 2.3 Some sequencers, such as Logic Pro, come with noise reduction processing built in.

If you have pops or similar problems in the rumble range (below about 80Hz), there are two ways to get rid of them. The easiest is to highlight the portion of the waveform with the problem, get a file-based (as opposed to real-time) equalizer, and reduce the low frequencies. If you have lots and lots of pops, you can try using a multiband compressor that kicks and lowers the levels just of the offending frequencies. But it's better if you can remove pops one at a time.

Test Programs

It's important to understand that there aren't always clear separations between the various steps involved in creating sampled instruments. At one stage or another, you'll take the individual samples you're editing and build some simple sampler programs to see how they work. That may be before you're done using the editing program.

That applies to processing as much as anything. You're undoubtedly aware that modern digital audio programs all come with a variety of plug-in processes that can improve samples. The more common operations include changing the levels to balance notes, EQ-ing them to bring out/suppress certain frequencies and make them sound better, using a compressor to even out the sound or punch it up, and noise reduction (but be conservative); less-common processes might include anything from sub-bass enhancement to any number of synthetic effects.

Plus there's any number of creative possibilities, for example, using time compression/expansion and pitch shifting. Perhaps you want to slow down the vibrato within part of a single note. Or you could create a different-sounding second voice for layering by copying all the samples, pitch-shifting them down a step, then transposing them up a step for playback. The sky is not a limit.

Then there's the whole subject of looping samples, which we'll address separately in a platform-independent way; looping is often done inside an audio editor. Let's jump ahead of ourselves and offer an aside: in the context of instruments like our recorder example (as opposed to, say, sampled beats), it's better if you can get away without looping the samples, except that the vibrato long notes are shorter than non-vibrato samples, for the simple reason that they take more breath. So we may want to loop them—in fact we may want to suspend disbelief and loop both sets of long notes in order to hold them longer than humanly possible.

Point being, it's probably more common than not to hear things in samples that require more detailed editing only when you play them inside the sampler. And it's usually not necessary to make complicated programs with every sample you have mapped to the keyboard—very simple programs with fewer samples stretched across a wider transposition range than the final ones can be very helpful.

Editing in Apple Logic Pro

The basic process of editing a recording and preparing it to load into a sampler and create a playable instrument is very similar in all editing programs. Some do make the process easier than others and include some more advanced features, but Logic's built-in audio editing is perfectly fine for the uncomplicated instruments we're creating. Let's go through the process.

Tutorial: Cutting Up the Samples in Logic

Please refer to the file "To practice editing.wav" on the companion Web site at www.courseptr.com/downloads. We're eventually going to build one octave of an alto recorder, with four articulations—and even that is only a partial instrument—but this one file is all that's necessary to get the hang of the sample editing process.

Create a new Logic session and drag the file onto the Arrange window. Logic will automatically create an audio track for it if you didn't drag it into one (Figure 2.4).

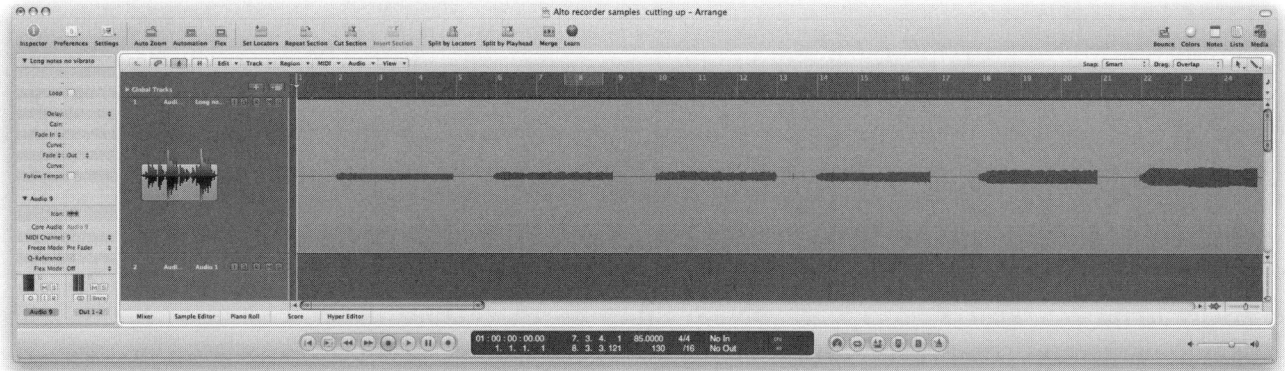

Figure 2.4   Before being separated into individual notes.

The first step is to separate the recording into individual notes. It's not necessary to be precise at this stage, and you can do this without listening just by looking at the waveform. The audio region boundaries are nondestructive, meaning that they only represent beginning and ending pointers to tell Logic where in the recorded waveform to play; the original continuous file(s) isn't/aren't touched.

The simplest way to separate the notes is to highlight the pauses between them with the Marquee tool and press the Delete key (Figure 2.5).

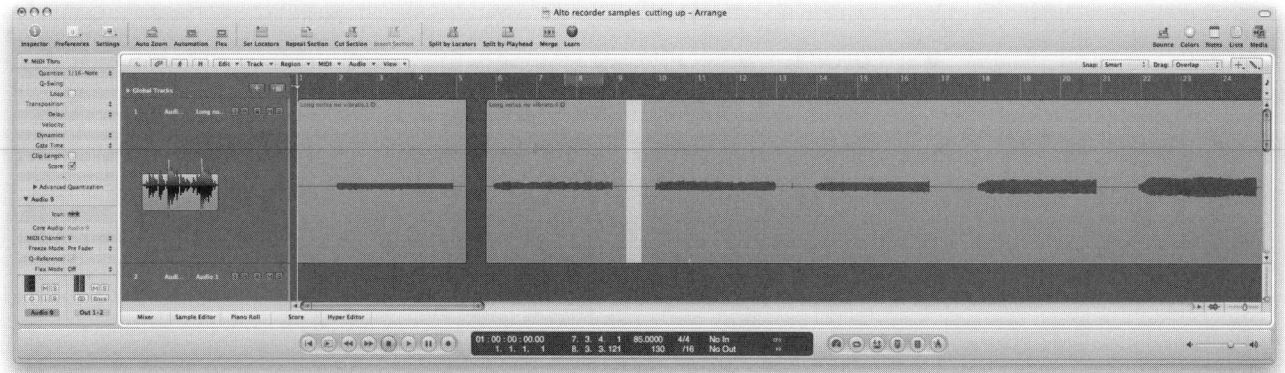

Figure 2.5   Separating notes one at a time.

Alternatively, you might be able to save some time using the Strip Silence command (Figure 2.6). This simply "gates" the audio by placing region boundaries where the audio crosses the threshold setting.

Logic shows you the silence it's going to strip before you tell it to go ahead. If the threshold setting is too high, you will remove quieter sections of the audio (Figure 2.7).

This is more like it (Figure 2.8).

More often than not, you'll still have to fine-tune the results after this, but it'll probably get you close.

The next step is to name the regions (Figure 2.9).

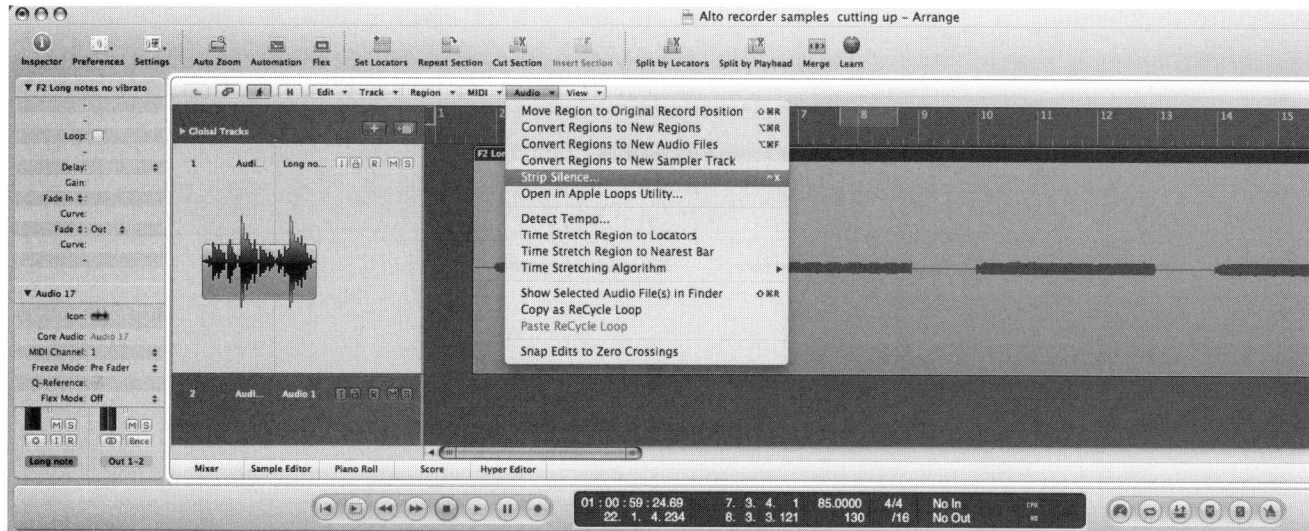

Figure 2.6   Strip silence.

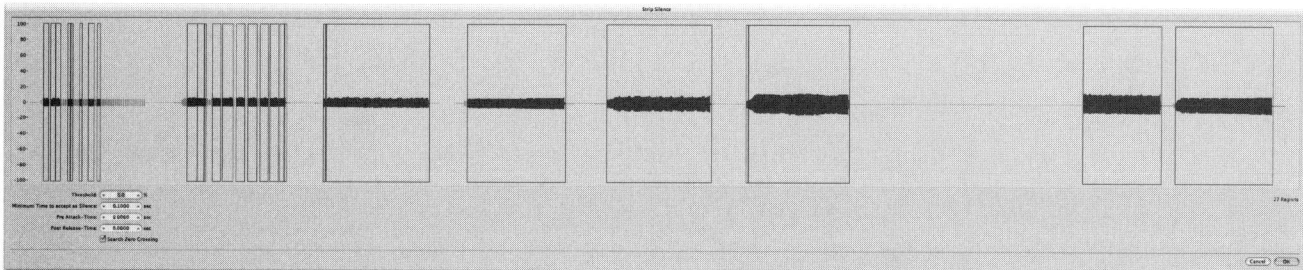

Figure 2.7   The threshold is too high.

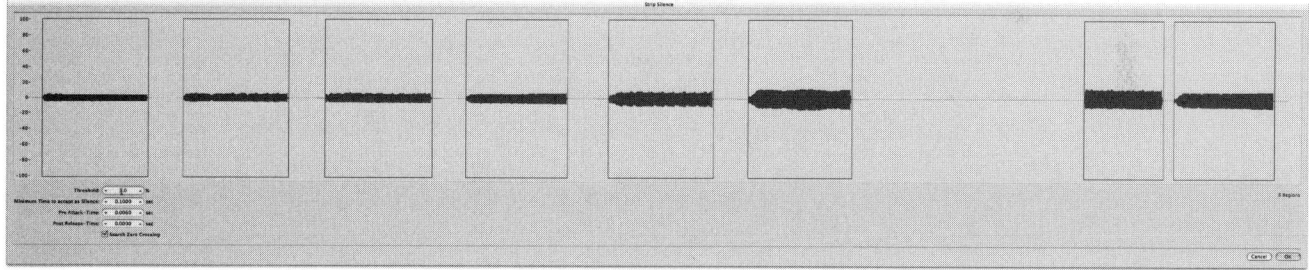

Figure 2.8   The threshold is set properly.

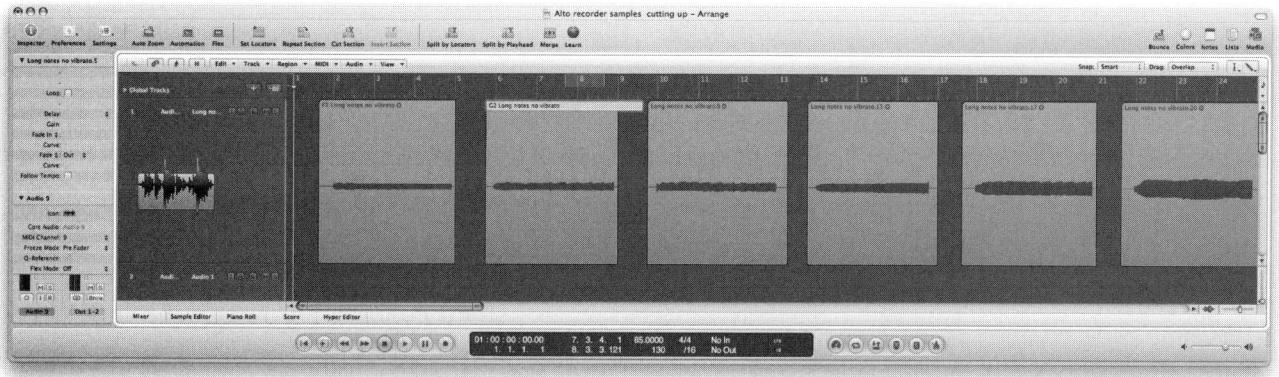

Figure 2.9   Naming each note.

It's important to use adequately descriptive names; we're only dealing with a limited number of recordings in our examples, but when you're dealing with lots of samples it's much too easy to lose track of what's what.

Copying and pasting common text between the sampled notes (including leading space) will save time and cut down on typos, so for example you might only have to type "F3 [command+v]" instead of "F3 pp alto no vibrato long 1" and then "F#3 pp alto no vibrato long 1" and so on.

Now it's time to fine-tune the sample region start and end points. Just double-click on a region to open it in the Logic sample editor (Figure 2.10).

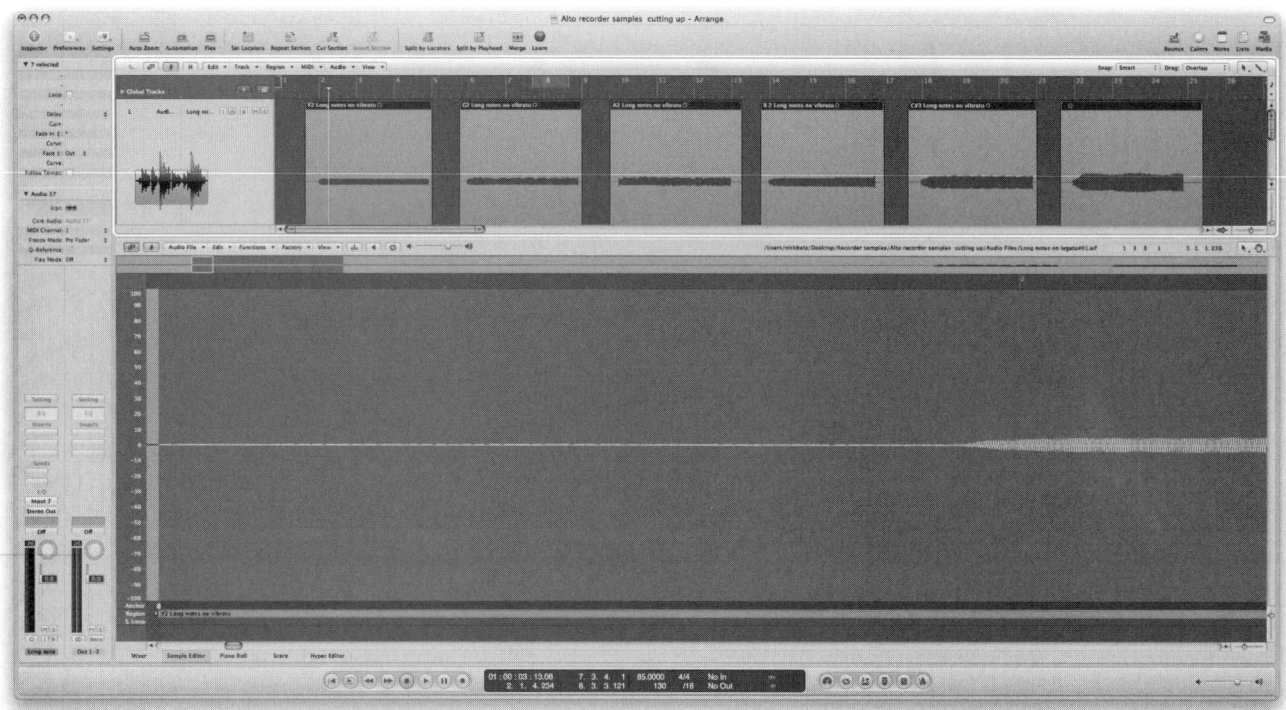

Figure 2.10   A region in the sample editor.

Zoom way in. You can see where the modulation begins, and then click to place the cursor there (Figure 2.11). You can audition it with the little "prelisten" speaker icon above the waveform display (not seen in this screen shot, but you won't miss it).

And now you can drag the region boundaries to the beginnings and ends of all the samples.

Remember the part about how some sample editors are easier to deal with than others? Logic is a fantastic sequencer, and there are some key commands you can assign to help with the sample editing process. But Figure 2.12 shows that when zoomed in far enough to see the first modulation in a sample, you'll still probably have to scroll down to get to the region boundary (this is true even if you open an entire Sample Editor window instead of just using the one in the Arrange Window like we're doing).

Figure 2.11 Zoomed in at the beginning of a note.

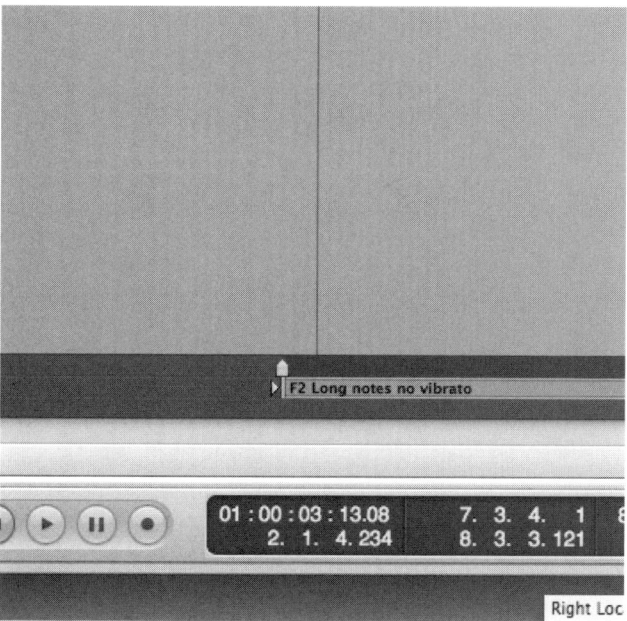

Figure 2.12 Scroll down to view the region boundary.

Then you can drag the region boundary to the Sample Editor cursor. (The region boundary is the bar labeled "F2 Long notes no vibrato" in this screenshot shown in Figure 2.13.)

Figure 2.13   Find the exact beginning of the note.

Do the same to the tail, and the result should look something like Figure 2.14.

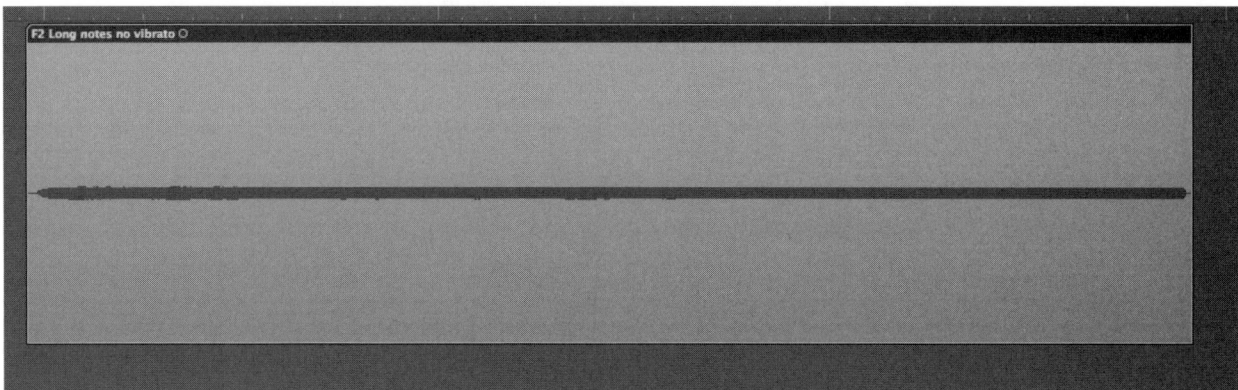

Figure 2.14   The note trimmed neatly.

Ideally you'll trim the ends of samples just to the point where the room sound dies off. In this example, the recording was made in a dry room with very short reverb, so there isn't much of a tail. Still, it's not a bad idea to be conservative and err on the side of leaving the tail too long. If the head is too long, the instrument will have extra and unpredictable latency (because its attack will be delayed after you play it, making it hard to play in time). The only risks with an overly long tail, on the other hand, are that you leave extraneous noises in or that you use more polyphony than necessary while the tail continues playing silence.

With that warning in mind, you might hear things like bad attacks at the beginnings or extra noises at the ends of notes. The first line of defense in any editor is the Fade tool.

Fades into and out of Logic regions are nondestructive until you export the regions as actual files, and you can drag them and edit their curves. Here the Fade tool is being selected, and if you look at the F2 short region, you can see the visual representation of the fades; to edit the fade out length, you simply grab the left vertical line of the white "N" at the end of the region with the Fade tool (Figure 2.15).

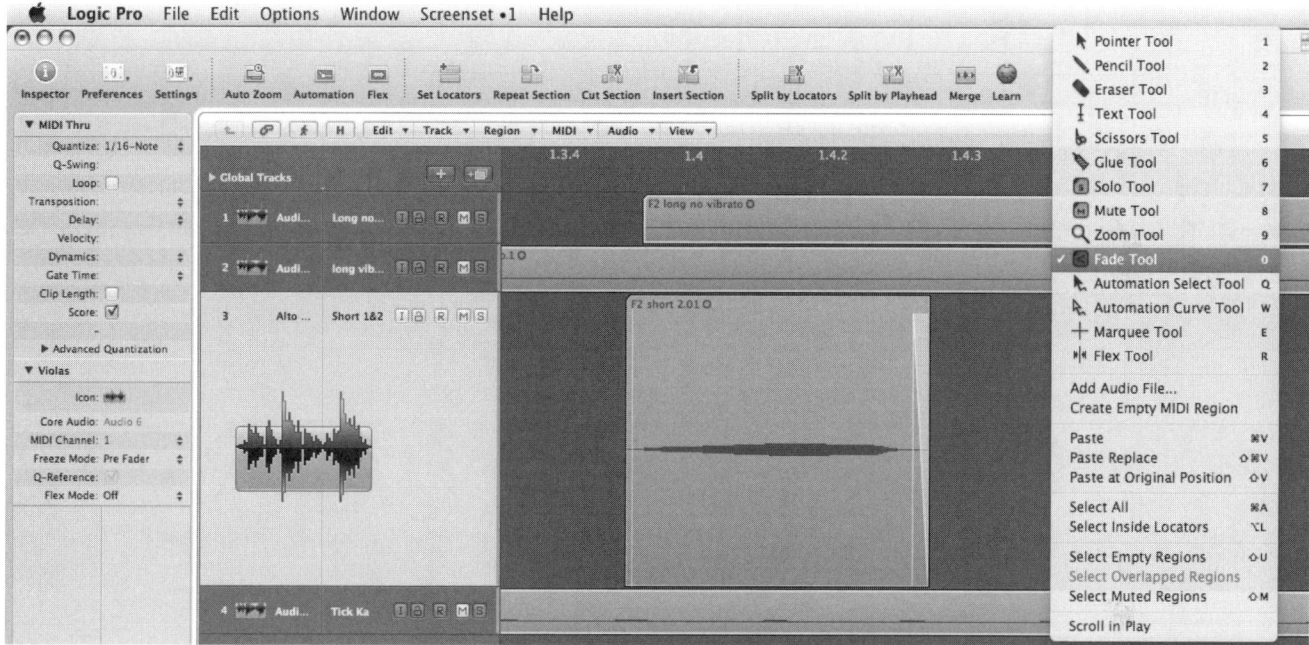

Figure 2.15 Fading out the sample to remove bad decay.

You might still need to do some more detailed waveform editing before building sampler programs, and we'll discuss that separately. But for now let's assume we're finished and export the regions as individual audio files so they can be loaded into the sampler.

Highlight the regions to be exported and select Convert Regions to New Audio Files from the local Audio submenu (Figure 2.16).

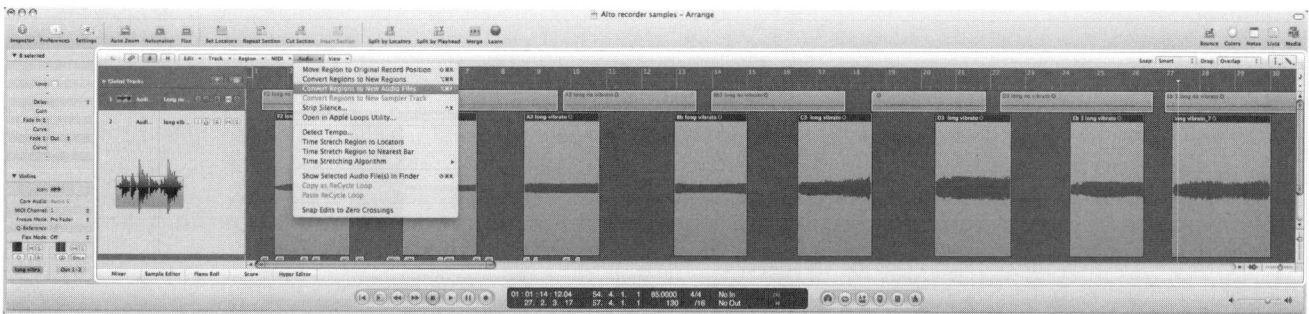

Figure 2.16 Convert Regions to New Audio Files.

A standard Mac OS X file dialog will appear. Use the default name (for example, "8 regions to be exported") to preserve the names you gave the individual notes. It's a good idea to create a new folder with a descriptive name for every group of notes, such as "long vib." Good house-keeping is always important when working with samples.

Editing in Avid Pro Tools

Pro Tools is a great audio editor (among many things). In fact, that was originally its main function; the reason it's remained the standard platform for audio production is that its designers just got the interface right at the beginning. You'll still want to move your samples into the sampler to loop them, but it makes everything else—from recording through editing—very easy.

Here are the basics of separating a recording into individual samples in Pro Tools.

Tutorial: Cutting Up the Samples in Pro Tools

Please refer to the file "To Practice Editing.wav" on the companion Web site at www. courseptr.com/downloads. This is a practice file with only four samples, but the process is the same if you have lots more.

Create a new Pro Tools Session with the parameters as shown in Figure 2.17.

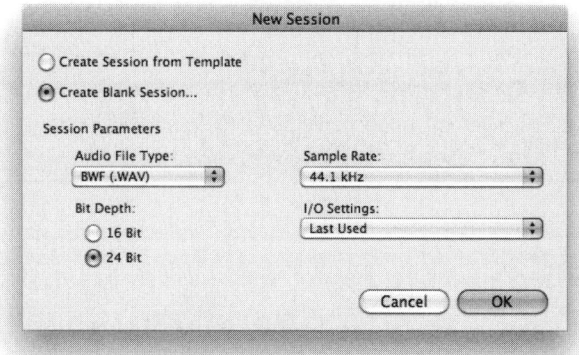

Figure 2.17 Create a new Session.

If the Edit window isn't showing, make it do so (Figure 2.18).

Drag the file "To Practice Editing.wav" into the window. Pro Tools will create a track for it, and it will appear in the Regions bin in the right pane. Your session should look like Figure 2.19.

The simplest way to cut the recording up into individual samples is just to highlight the area between the notes and then press the Delete key to remove the parts you don't want. At this stage, we just want to get close; later we'll zoom in (Figure 2.20).

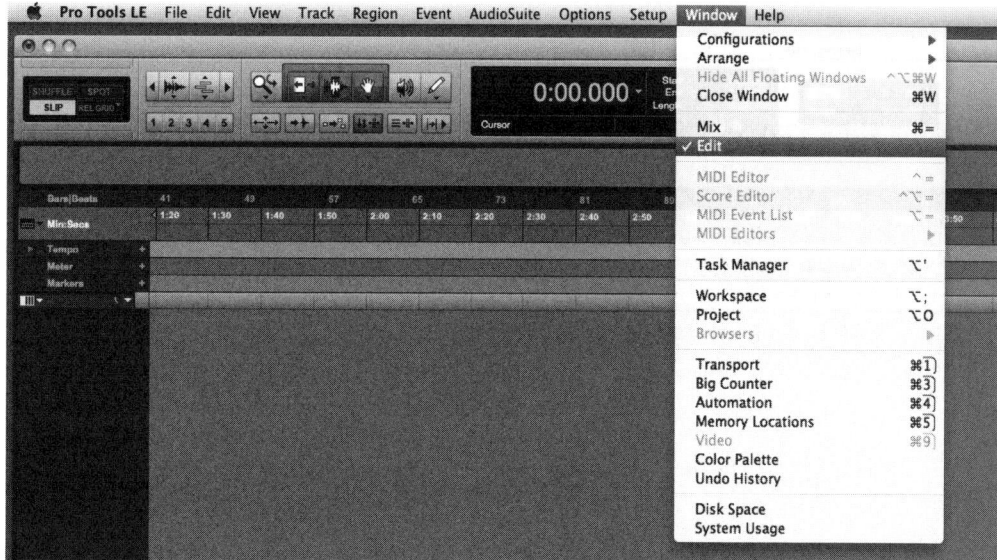

Figure 2.18 Show Edit window.

Figure 2.19 Drag the recording in.

If we had lots of samples, it might be quicker to use the Strip Silence feature. This simply "gates" the audio by placing region boundaries where the audio crosses the threshold setting.

Highlight the whole track by triple-clicking in it outside any region, and then invoke the Strip Silence command from the Edit menu (Figure 2.21).

Pro Tools' Strip Silence feature is a little more finicky than the one in Logic, but that's not a big deal; you have to go in and tweak the results of this operation in any program anyway.

The most important of the four parameters is the threshold. Here it's set too high, so it doesn't recognize the individual samples properly (Figure 2.22).

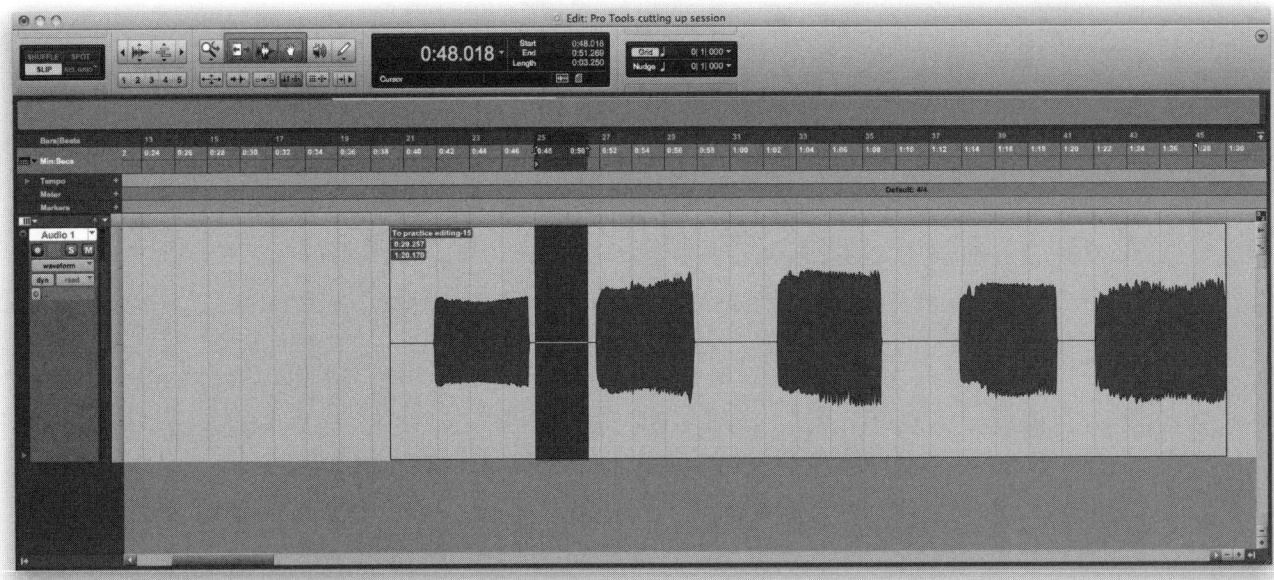

Figure 2.20 Highlight the space between notes.

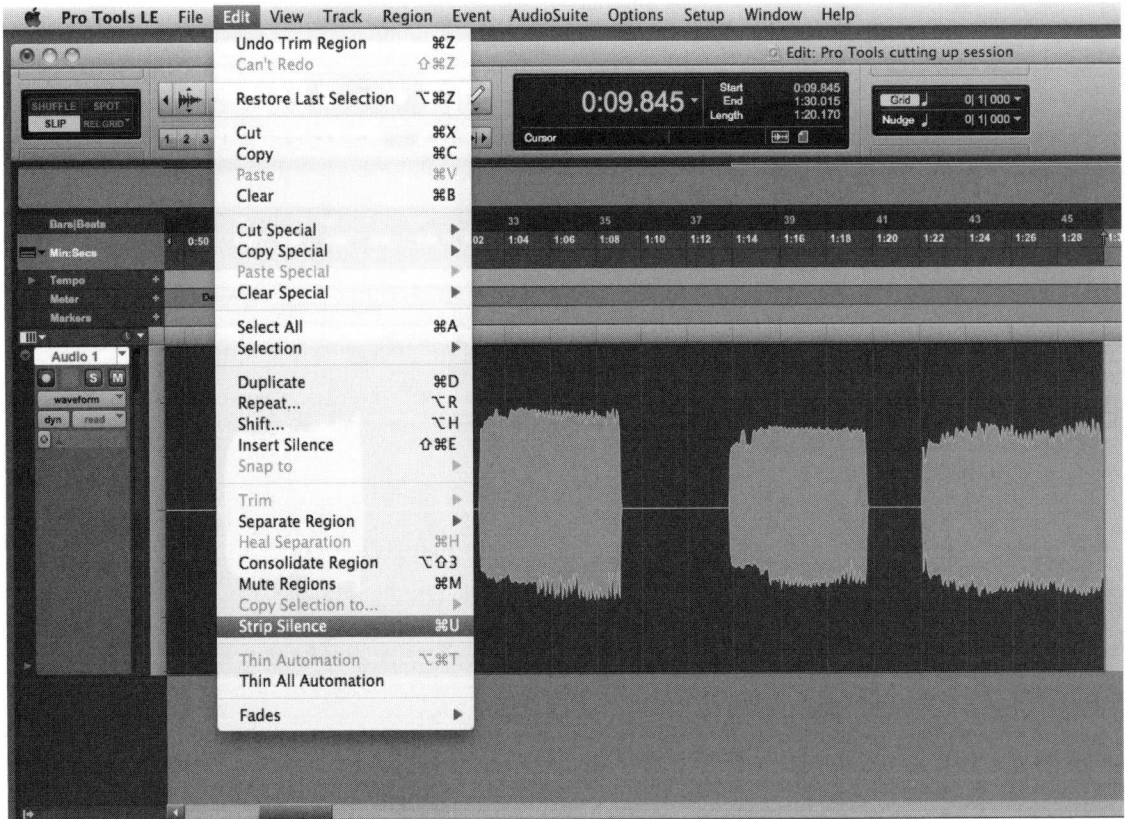

Figure 2.21 Separating notes with Strip Silence.

Figure 2.22   The threshold is set too high.

The following settings are about the best you can do (Figure 2.23).

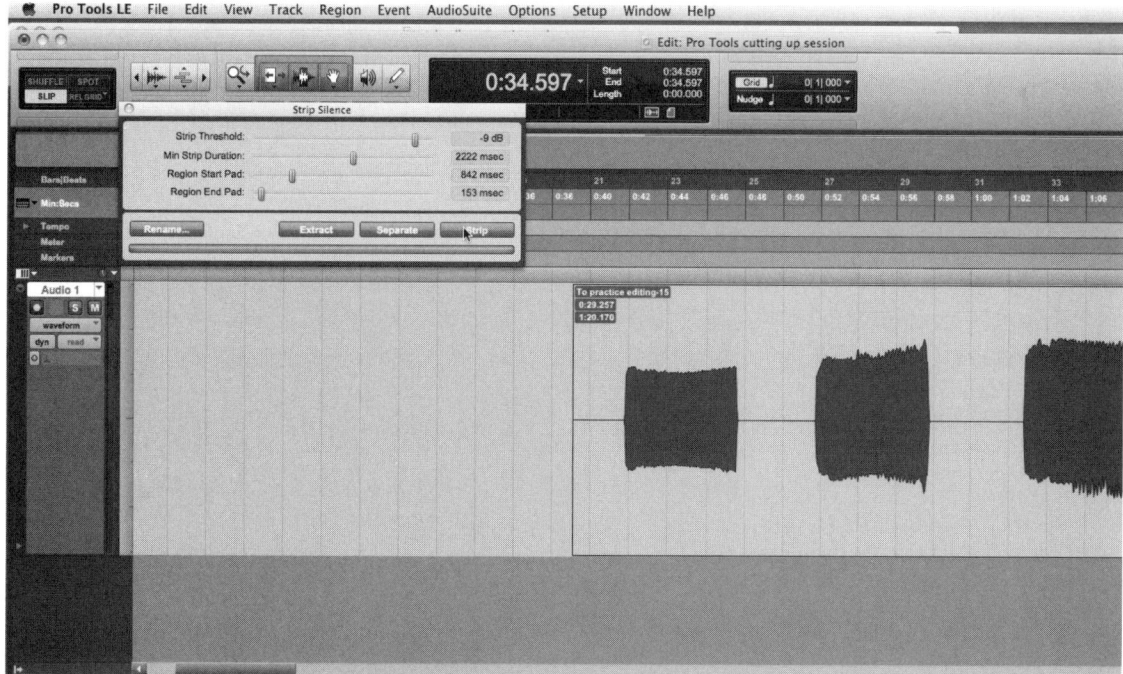

Figure 2.23   Threshold set correctly.

Push the Strip button, which means you just want to create new region boundaries on either side of each sample and remove the silence between. Figure 2.24 shows the result.

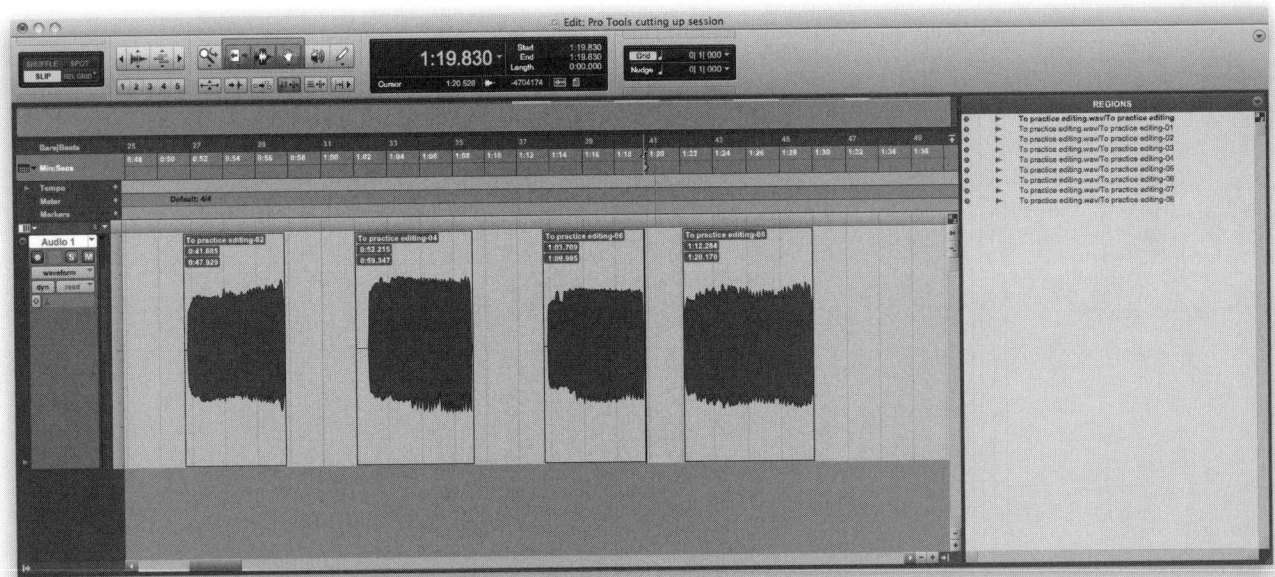

Figure 2.24 Notes separated roughly.

Now zoom in on the beginning of the first sample and move the region boundary over to the start of the waveform, as shown in Figure 2.25. (You're actually using the Trimmer tool, which looks like a staple, but it's only possible to capture screen dumps of the regular arrow.)

Figure 2.25 Zoom in and trim the head of the note.

Notice how that looks perfect? It's not.

You have to zoom way in to see the first modulation (Figure 2.26).

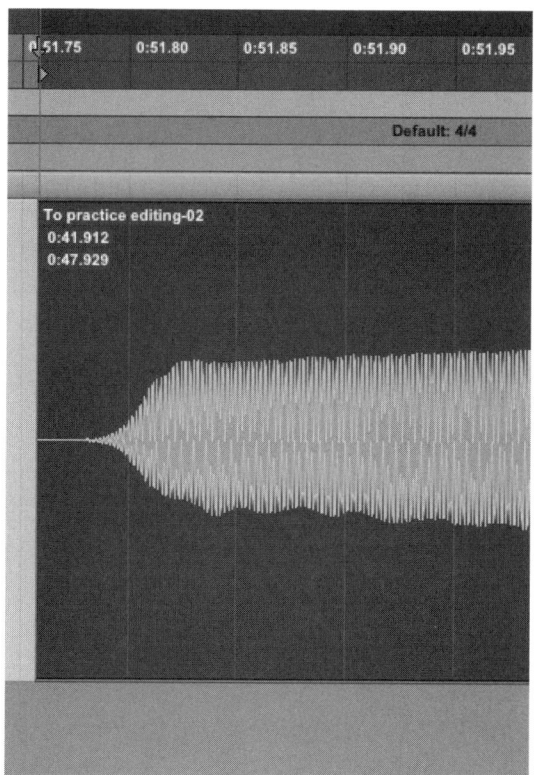

Figure 2.26 Zoom far in to see detail.

Now press the right arrow to navigate to the end of the selection (the region is selected) and trim the tail (Figure 2.27).

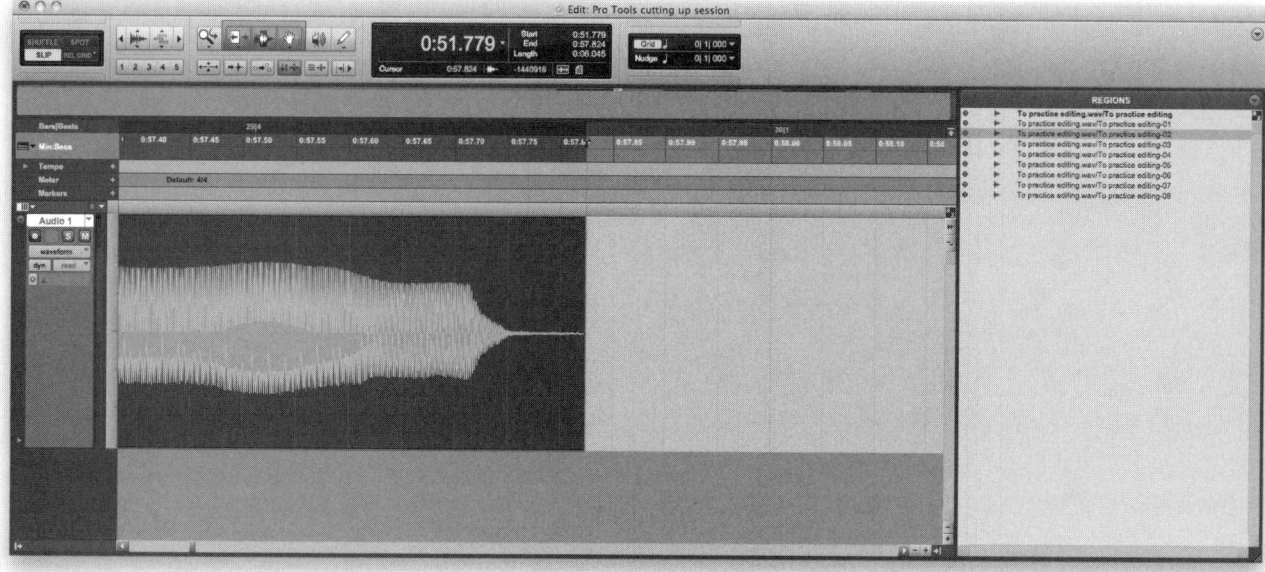

Figure 2.27 Trim the note's tail.

Press Shift+Tab and you'll move to the beginning of the next sample to trim. Notice the small click at the beginning; things like that are fine in recordings, but you don't want to hear that every time you play the sample. We're getting rid of it (Figure 2.28).

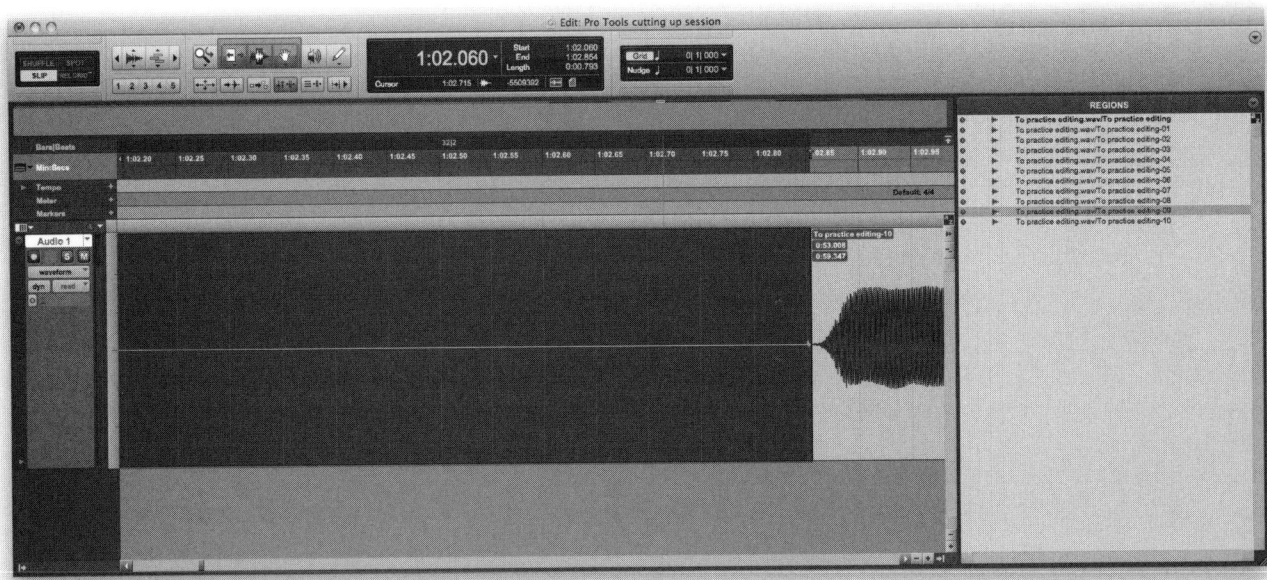

Figure 2.28 Tab to the next note and separate the region.

And the tail (Figure 2.29).

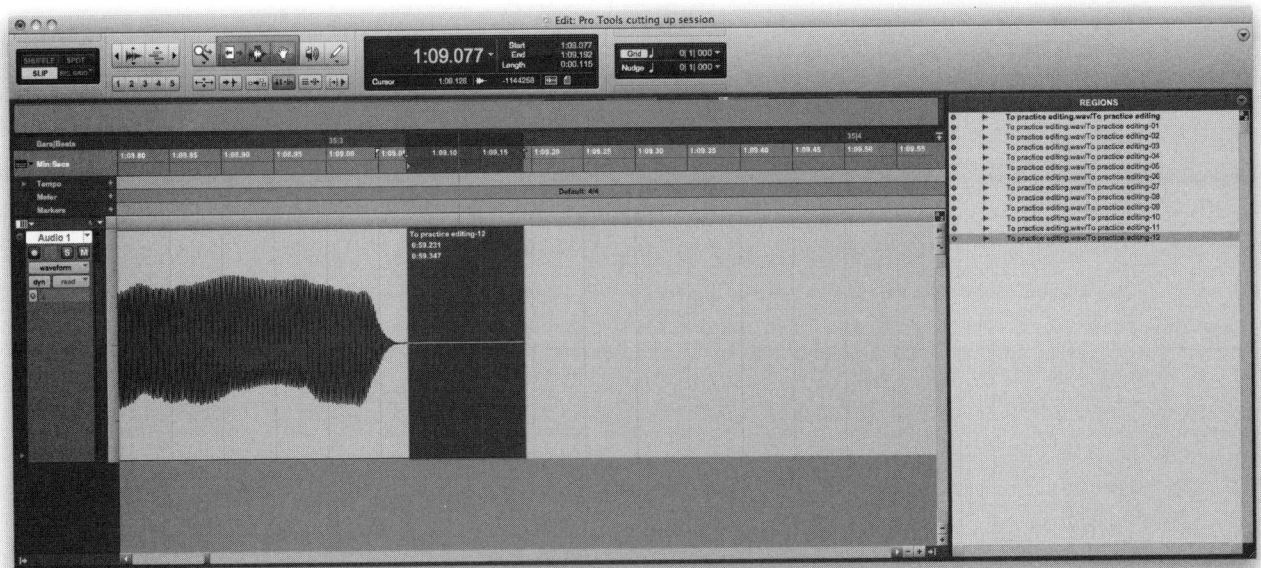

Figure 2.29 The tail.

Now look at the fourth sample in this practice file. See the little bump at the end (Figure 2.30)?

We're going to fade that out. Here again, the arrow cursor is showing in the screen capture instead of the Fade tool, but you can see the yellow lines showing the fade (Figure 2.31).

There are several fade shapes available, but for an edit this short, it really makes no difference; the default is fine.

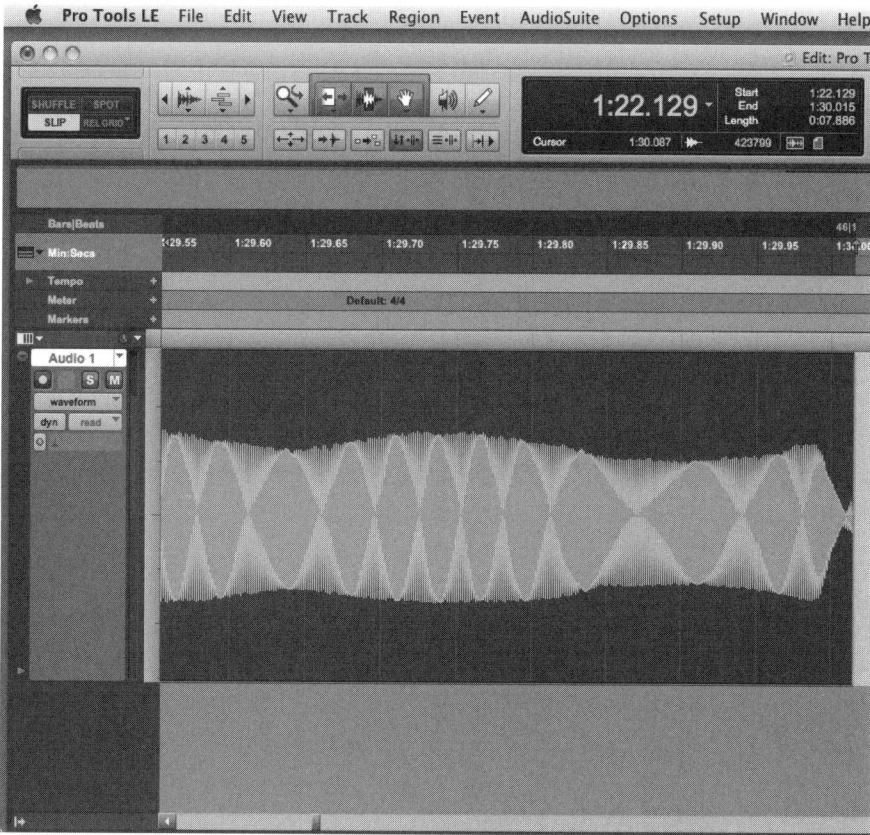

Figure 2.30 This note has a bump at the end.

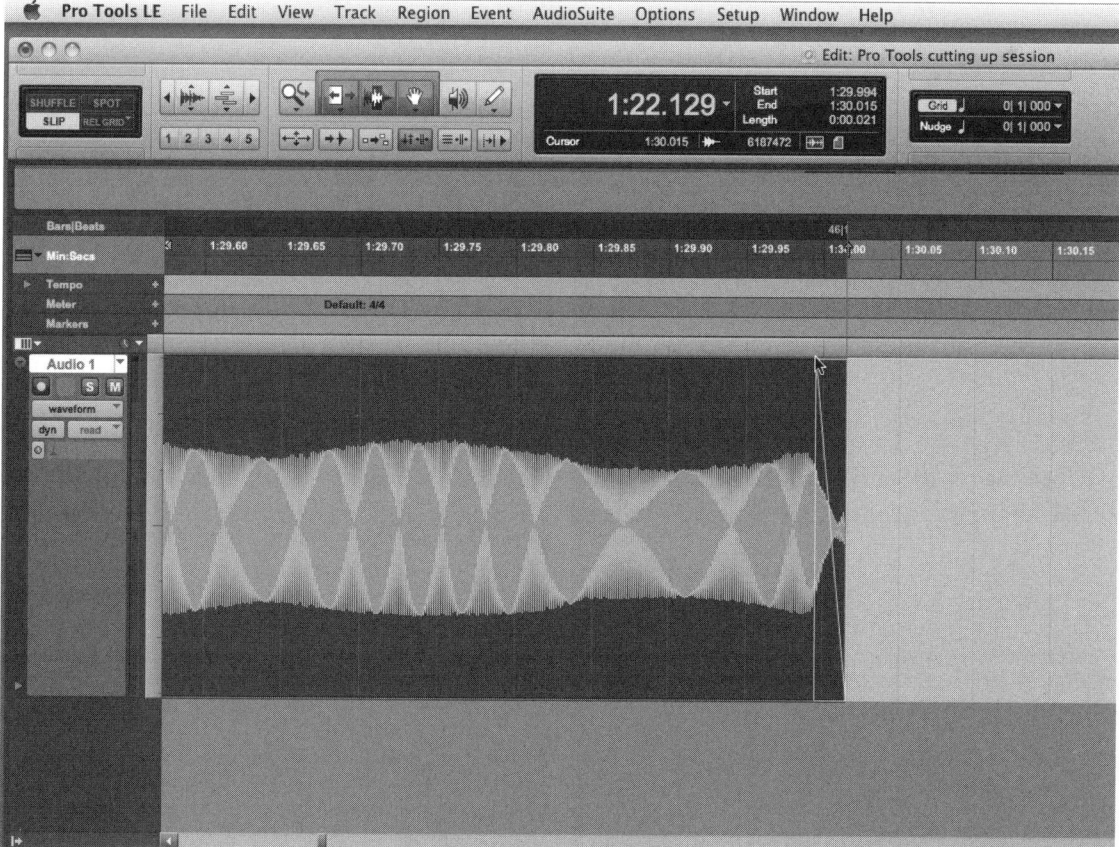

Figure 2.31 Fading out the ending to remove the bump.

Now double-click on each sample (that is, each region) with the Grabber tool to bring up the dialog in which you type the name. As always, copy and paste whenever possible to avoid typos. And to repeat: good housekeeping is really important when you're dealing with lots of samples. We're only dealing with 48 samples in the single octave alto recorder example, and even then it's easy to get confused (Figures 2.32 and 2.33).

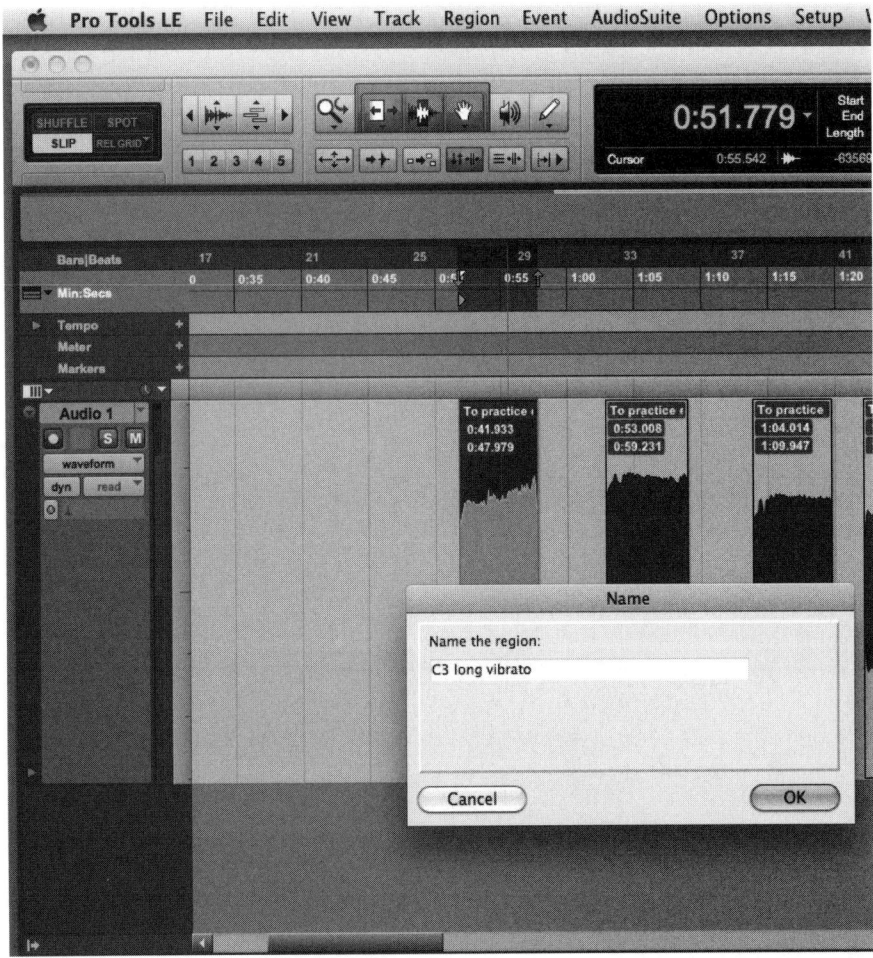

Figure 2.32 Naming the note.

Select all the regions (samples), and in the regions list select Export Regions as Files (Figure 2.34).

Figure 2.33   Named.

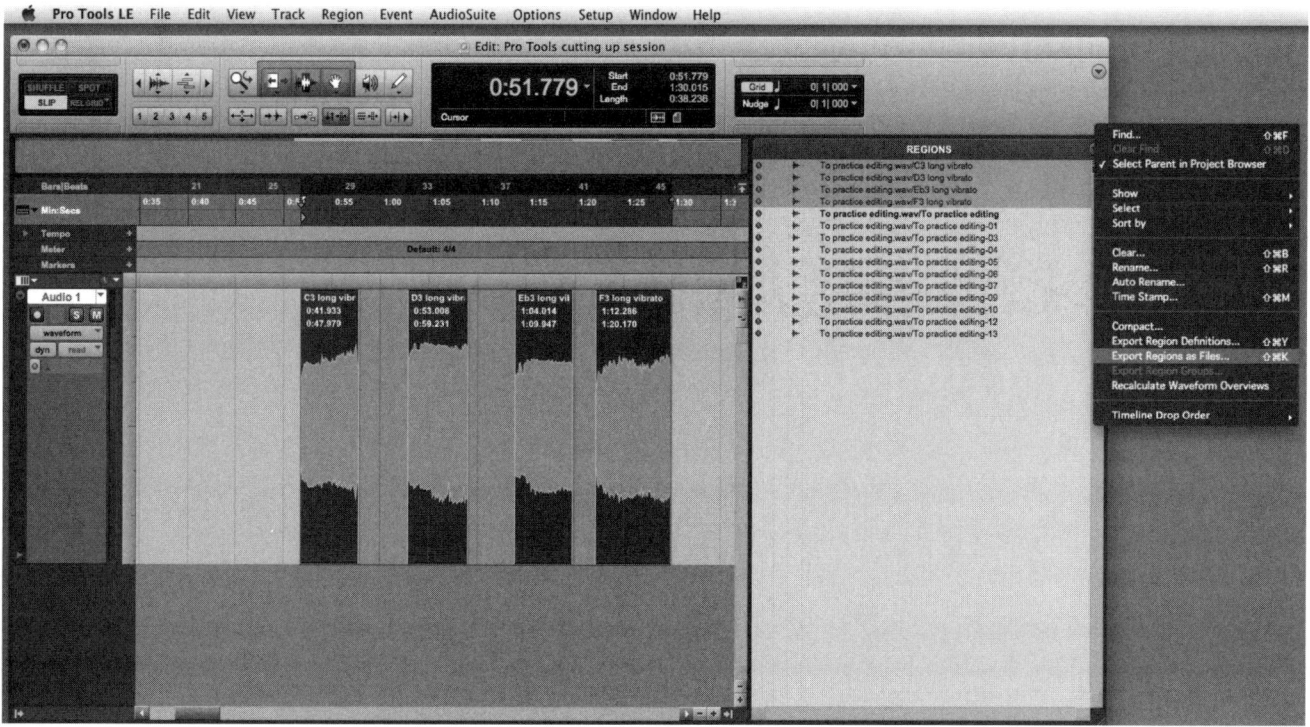

Figure 2.34   Export Regions as Files.

The default options (Figure 2.35) are usually okay, but be sure to choose the appropriate destination director (in other words, file location) by clicking on the button in the middle of the window. Pro Tools remembers the location you used the last time, and you don't want to pollute another folder with 50 million samples that don't belong in it!

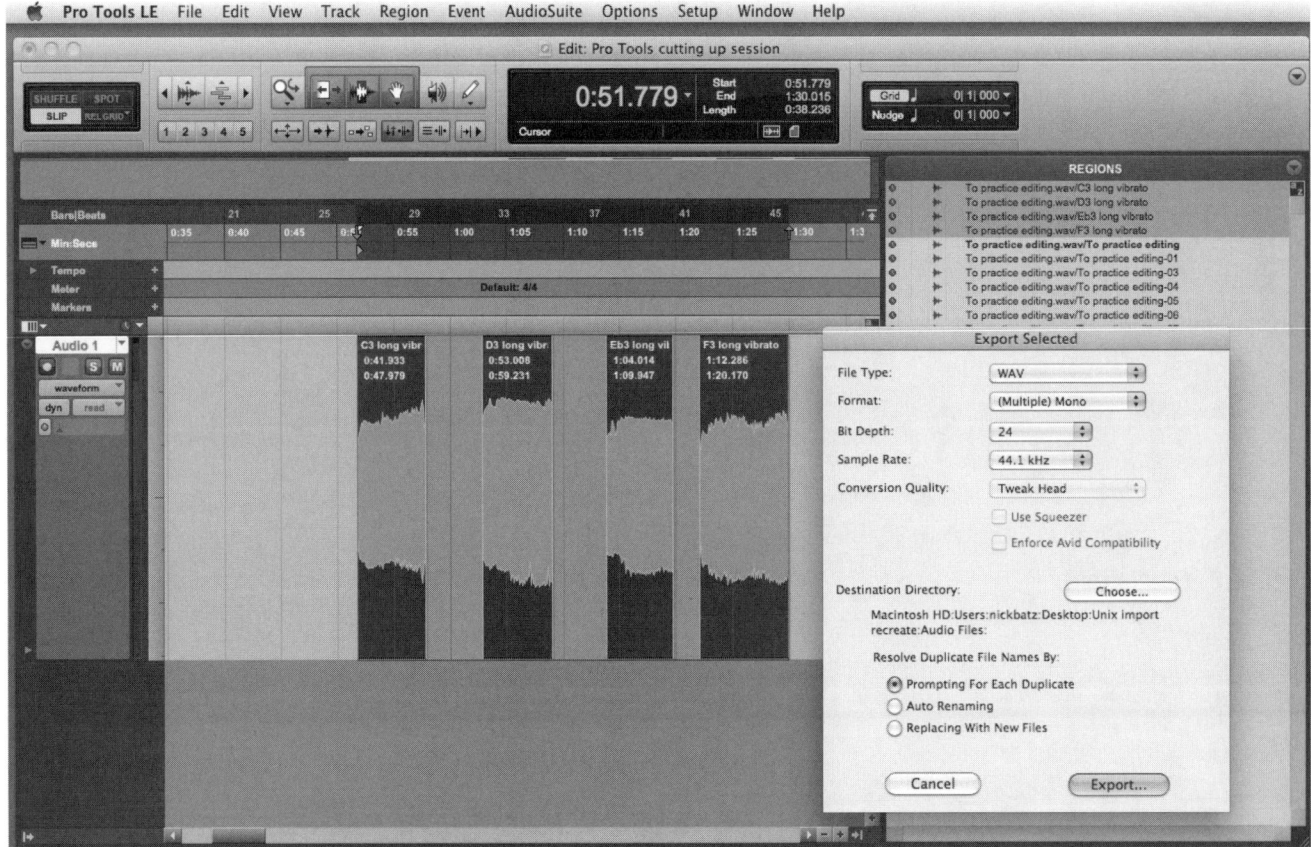

Figure 2.35 Options for exporting the notes.

3 Building Programs in Apple EXS24

The EXS24 sampler built into Apple Logic Pro is competent, convenient due to its integration into Logic, quite easy to use, and by modern standards fairly basic. Interestingly—and subjectively—its front panel is more confusing than its under-the-hood editor, which is very straightforward.

Note that the EXS24 works exclusively inside Logic, which runs only on Mac OS X; unlike other samplers, it is not a standard AU, VST, RTAS, or standalone instrument.

Tutorial: Quick Chromatic Sample Mapping from a Logic Track

This is a quick "pre-tutorial" before we get to the nitty-gritty program.

If you happen to have sampled every note of the chromatic scale—or if you're building any EXS24 program that is to play successive samples as you go up the chromatic scale on the keyboard (whether they're rhythmic slices of a groove or instrument samples)—Logic can map them in one step from trimmed regions in an audio track.

Now, this will not work properly with the example alto recorder samples, since they were sampled every whole step (for the most part). But we'll pretend they're chromatic just to demonstrate the feature.

Select the regions to be mapped into the sampler on the Logic audio track and select Convert Regions to New Sampler Track from the local Audio submenu (Figure 3.1).

Set the starting note range, F2 in our pretend case (Figure 3.2).

BAM. Logic creates an Instrument track with the notes mapped to an EXS24 instrument, ready to play (Figure 3.3).

As an aside, this feature is also intended for working with beat slices, which is why Logic places MIDI notes in the newly created Instrument track; each successive note is intended to trigger its corresponding region (now in the sampler) in its original time position. Let's say we'd been

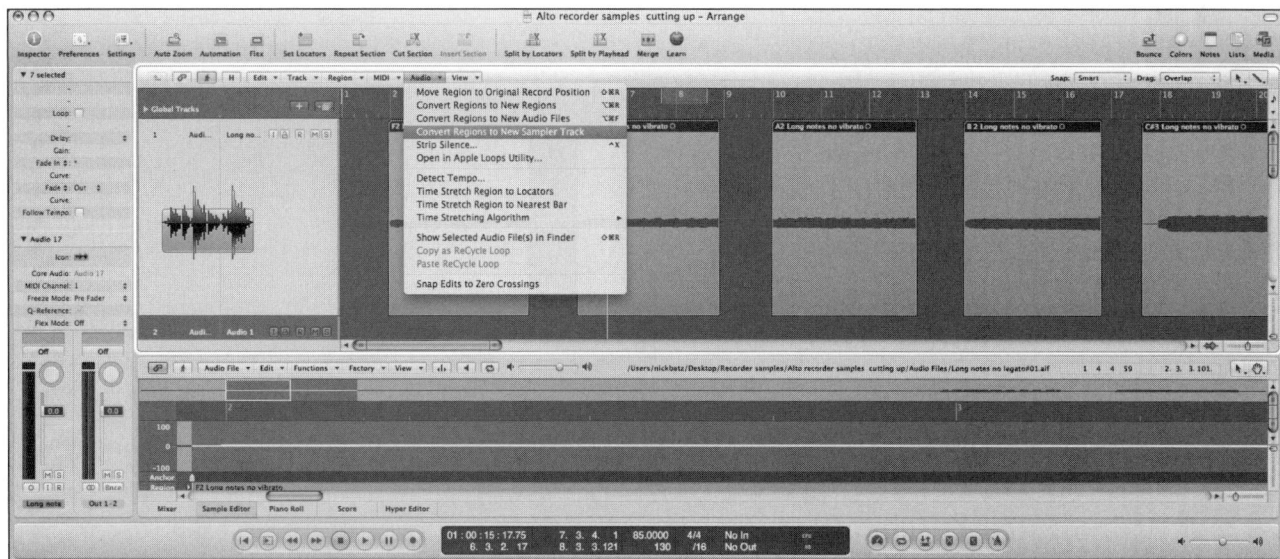

Figure 3.1 Convert Regions to New Sampler Track.

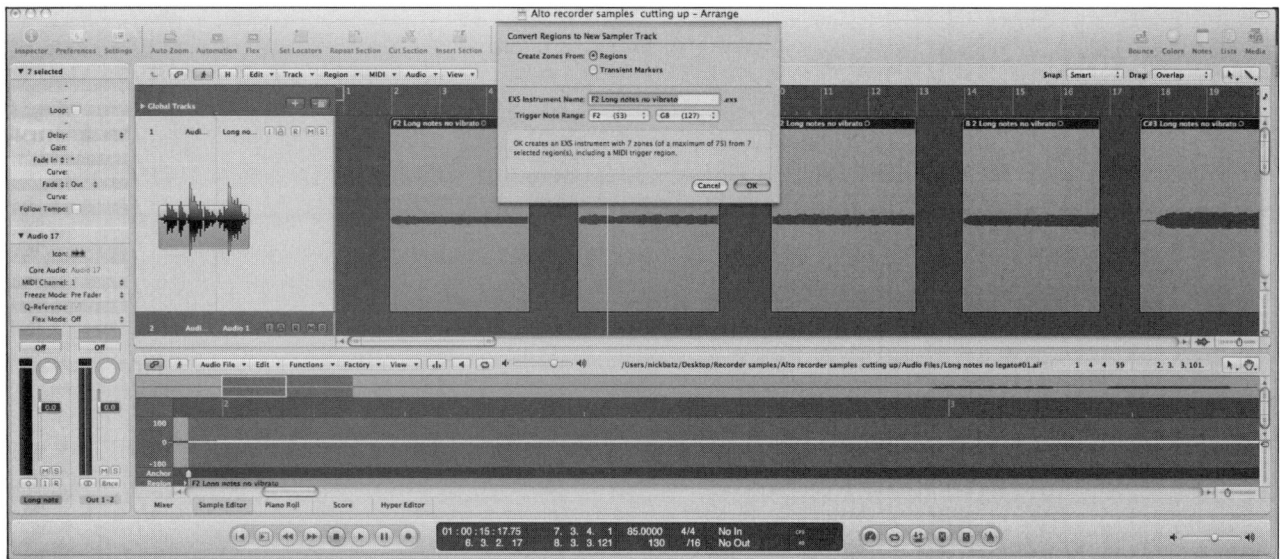

Figure 3.2 Starting and ending ranges.

working with a two-bar drum beat instead of the sampled instrument. In that case, we would have used the option to map transient markers instead of regions, and the MIDI notes Logic created would have played them in time. For this application, you use Transient Editing mode in the sample editor (Figure 3.4).

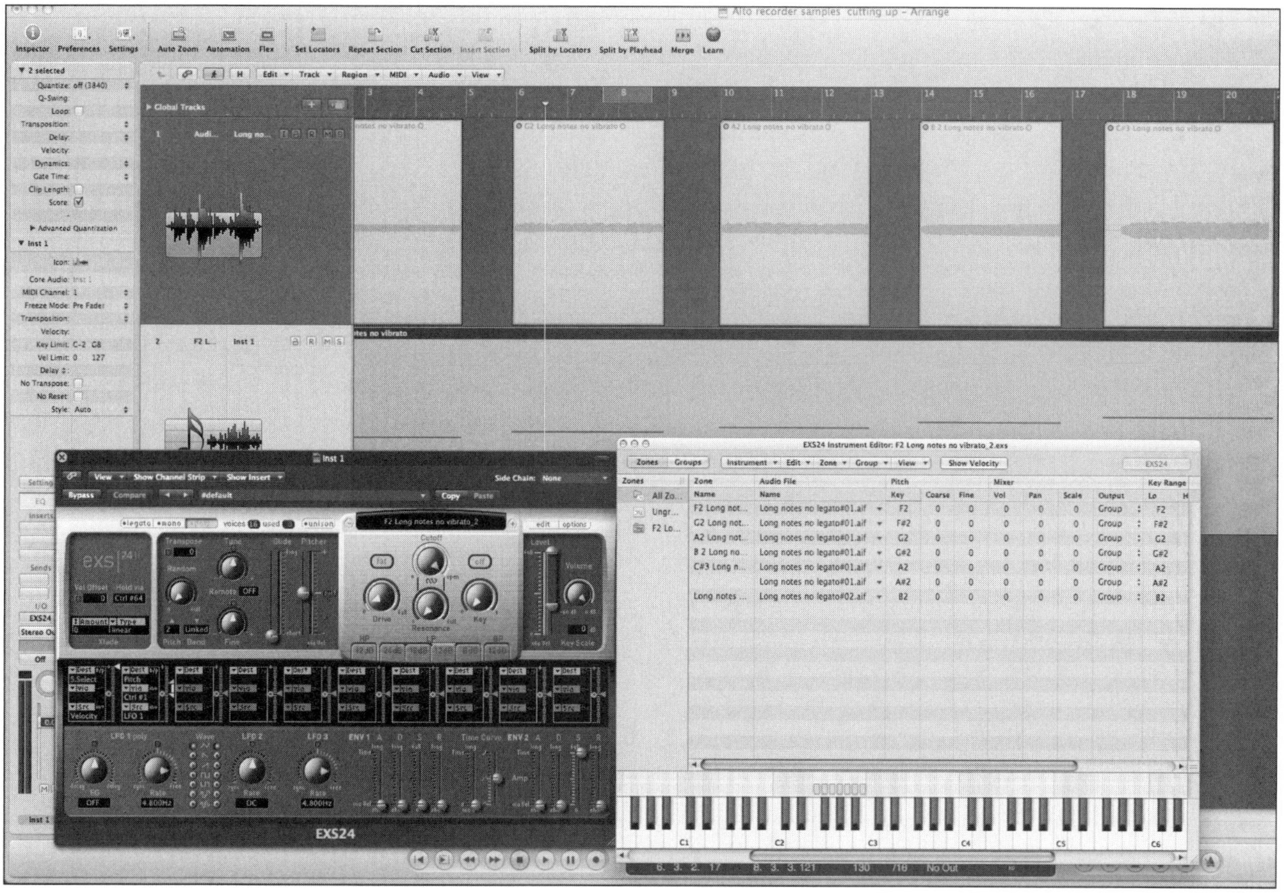

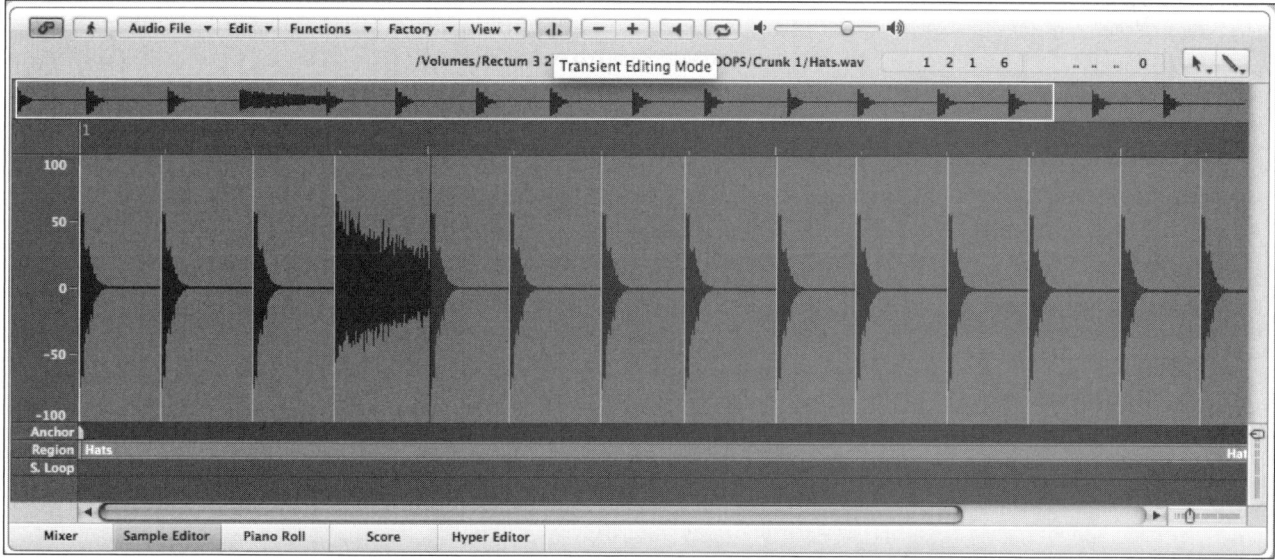

Figure 3.3   Track and sampler ready.

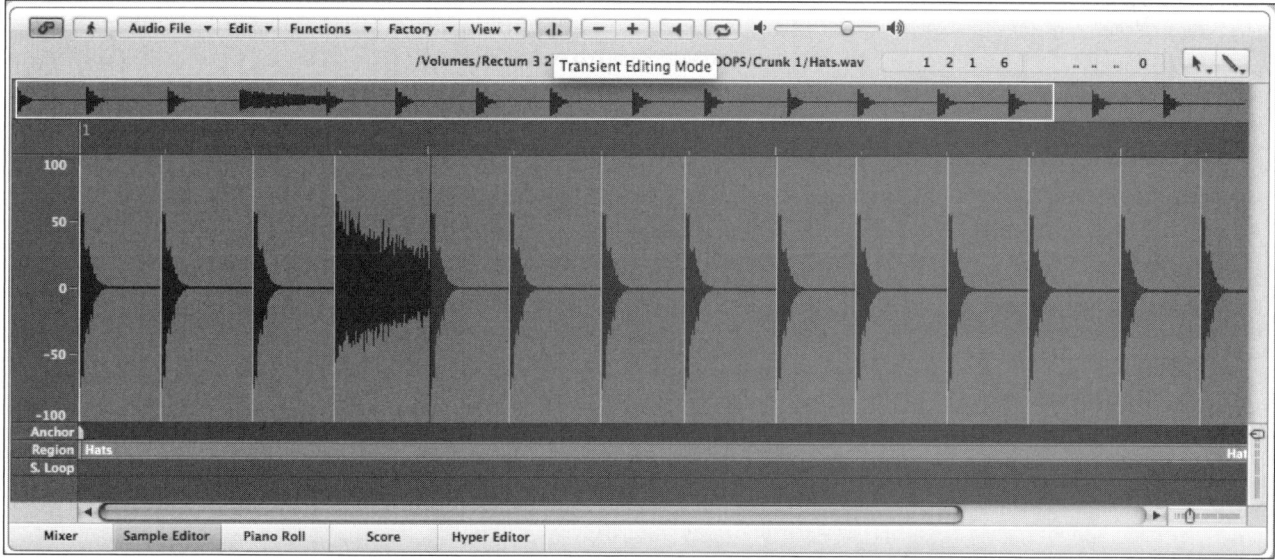

Figure 3.4   Transient Editing mode.

Tutorials: Building a Multivelocity Instrument with Automatic Sample Alternation

In this sequence of tutorials, we'll work with one octave of an alto recorder instrument. We have the four most common recorder articulations: very short ("tick" and "ka"), short ("toot"), long notes with vibrato, and long notes without vibrato. These long note articulations will work for shorter notes, too; the important difference is the vibrato and lack thereof.

The recorder's dynamic range is quite limited, so we only sampled one dynamic layer. However, the way recorder players create a louder feel is by articulating more heavily; the very short "ticka tick" notes tend to have a lighter feel than the regular "toot" ones, so we'll use velocity to switch between the two. We're also going to set up two variations of each short note to alternate automatically. This will help avoid the repeated note effect that gives away the secret that we're using samples right away.

Then to illustrate an example of a useful performance setup, we'll bring in two other multi-sampled programs—long notes with and without vibrato—that will trigger instead of the short notes when the mod wheel is on. The vibrato layer will sound when the mod wheel is over half way, and the non-vib when it's below.

We'll break this down into shorter tutorials. Note that there are often multiple ways of accomplishing the same thing, but due to the limited human lifespan we won't go through all of them. For example, you can map samples by dragging them onto the EXS24 editor's keyboard or by typing in note names in the list above, or select samples graphically or in the list, and so on.

Stage 1: A Basic Playable Instrument

In this example, we'll create a basic instrument. Please open the "short 1 & 2" folder on the book's companion Web site at www.courseptr.com/downloads; we're going to use the short 1 samples—the first of the two short note variations—to create our first program.

Create a stereo Instrument track in Logic (Figure 3.5).

Assign a stereo EXS24 to the track (Figure 3.6).

Figure 3.5 Create Instrument Track.

Figure 3.6 Create an EXS24.

Click on the Edit button in the sampler that pops up (Figure 3.7).

Figure 3.7 Edit mode.

Create a new instrument in the Instrument Editor that pops up (Figure 3.8).

Figure 3.8   New Instrument.

To be safe, save the instrument now.

The usual place to save EXS24 instruments (as opposed to the samples they reference) is in the Sampler Instruments subfolder at ~/Library/Application Support/Logic/Sampler Instruments.

There are two Library folders in OS X (actually three, but one is buried). The ~/ at the beginning of the directory language means that we're referring to the one inside your individual User account, which you access by pressing Command+N from the Finder.

If you want to put your instruments somewhere else, just place an alias of the enclosing folder(s) inside this folder (Figure 3.9).

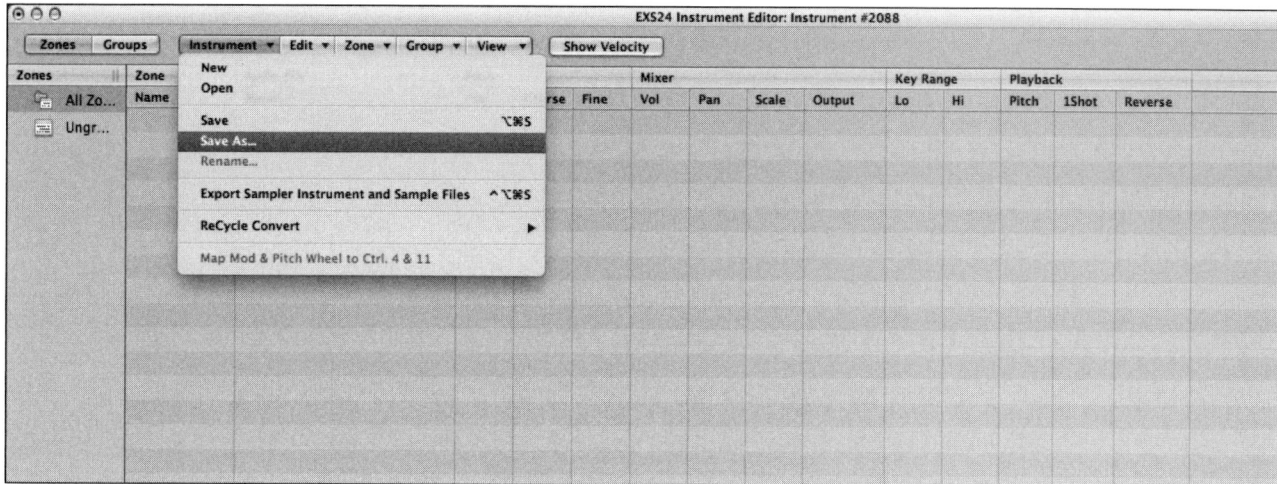

Figure 3.9 Save.

Now we're ready to map the cut-up samples to the keyboard (Figure 3.10).

Figure 3.10 Sample list.

There are a couple of ways to do this, but the simplest is simply to position them individually by dragging them from a folder window on the Desktop. While the EXS24 can analyze and identify sample pitches, it is less fussy just to place them in manually and get it right the first time.

This is where good housekeeping saves lots of frustration (Figure 3.11).

Here the samples are organized in a way that makes it really easy to see what each one is. In case it's not obvious, each articulation is in its own folder in the "Recorder samples" folder. You'll come up with your own system.

Tip Here we've made it even easier for ourselves to see what's going on with colored labels in the OS X Finder (under the File menu) for each type of articulation. It's easy to forget what goes where at this point, and the two seconds this takes makes the mapping process much easier.

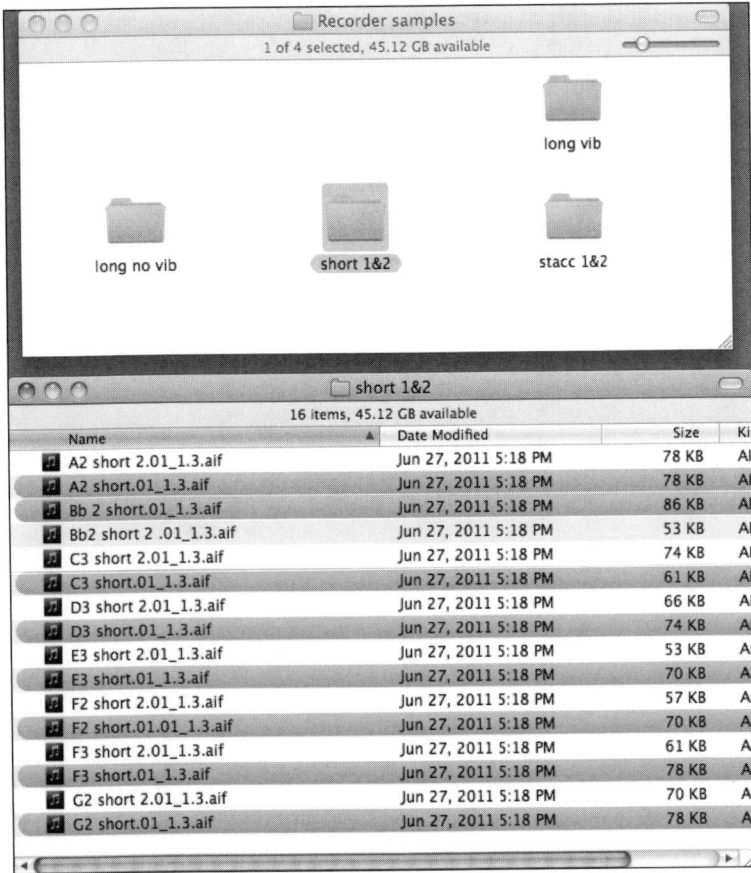

Figure 3.11 Organization makes it easier.

Simply drag and drop the samples onto the root pitches at which they're going to sound. Here the first one, F2, is being mapped (Figure 3.12).

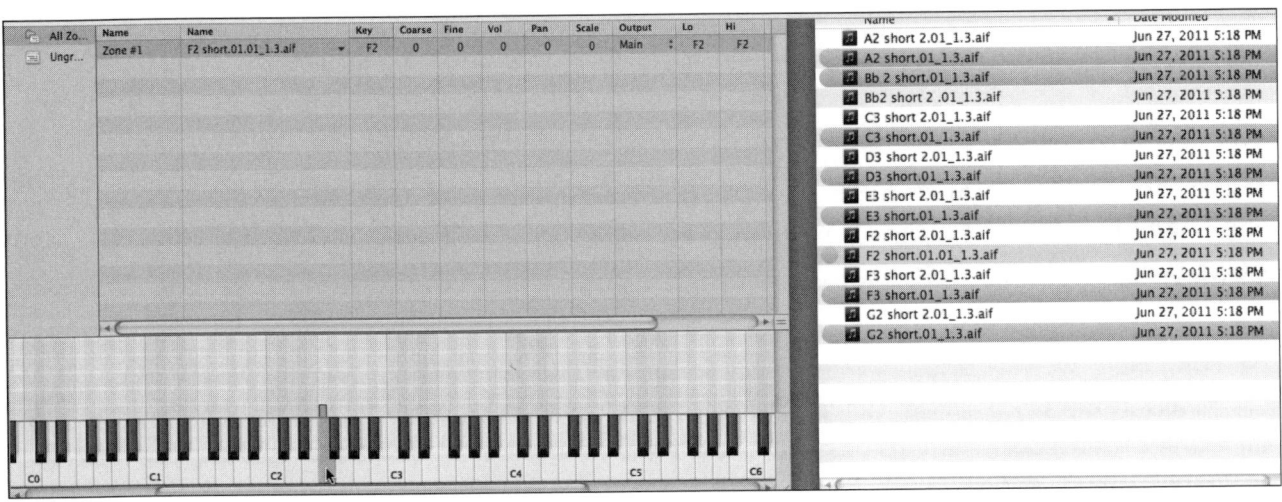

Figure 3.12 Drag and drop the samples in.

Continue with the rest of the Short 1 samples. It should look like this (Figure 3.13).

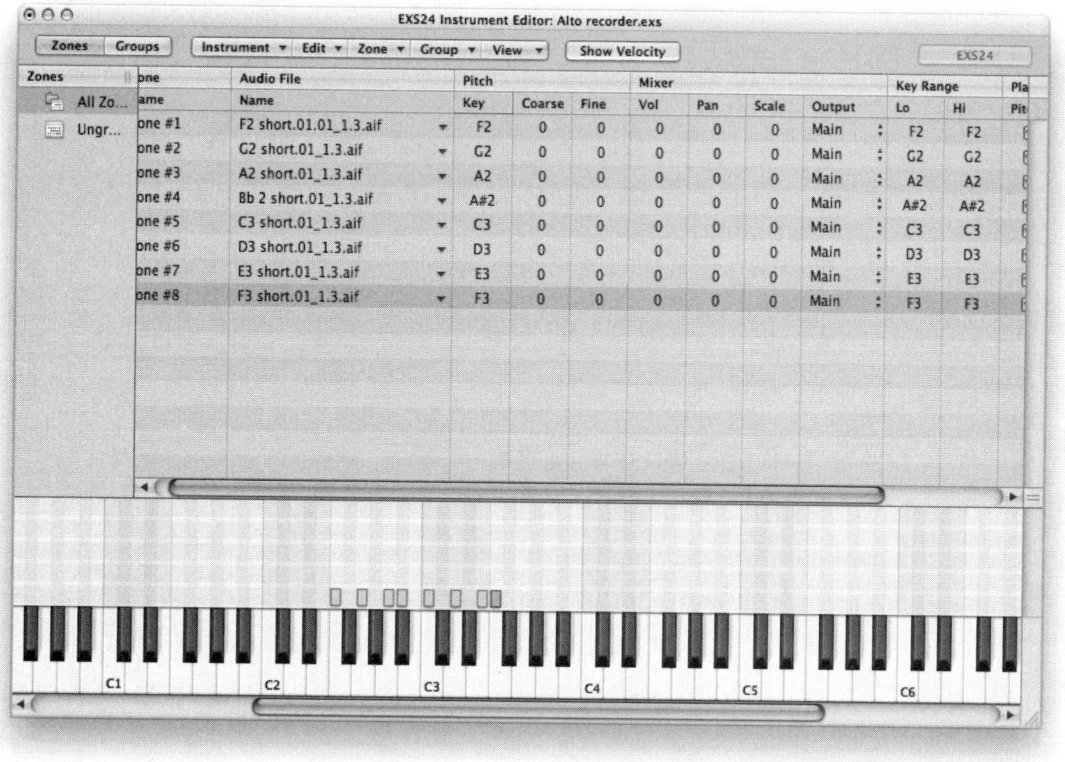

Figure 3.13 Dragged and dropped.

If you look at the list at the left side of the window, you can see that the EXS has created eight single-note Zones, which are note ranges within which a sample plays. We need to stretch the Zones to fill in the gaps where there are no samples, since we sampled every whole step rather than chromatically—if you play, say, a C#3, you won't hear anything.

Simply drag the mouse over gray blocks to select notes; when you reach the upper or lower Zone border, the mouse will change to a Length Change cursor so you can drag it over to stretch it up or down. We're going to stretch the Zones to the right. Figure 3.14 shows F2 stretched over so it plays on F#2 as well.

And here they've all been stretched. Note that you can select multiple notes at once and stretch them en masse—but also be aware that Zones can overlap and trigger multiple samples on the same key, an effect that's a feature when you want it but something to avoid in this case (Figure 3.15).

The samples are all pitch shifted correctly when you play a note that doesn't have a sample—in fact it would do that if you just used one sample across a single Zone spanning 88 notes of the keyboard.

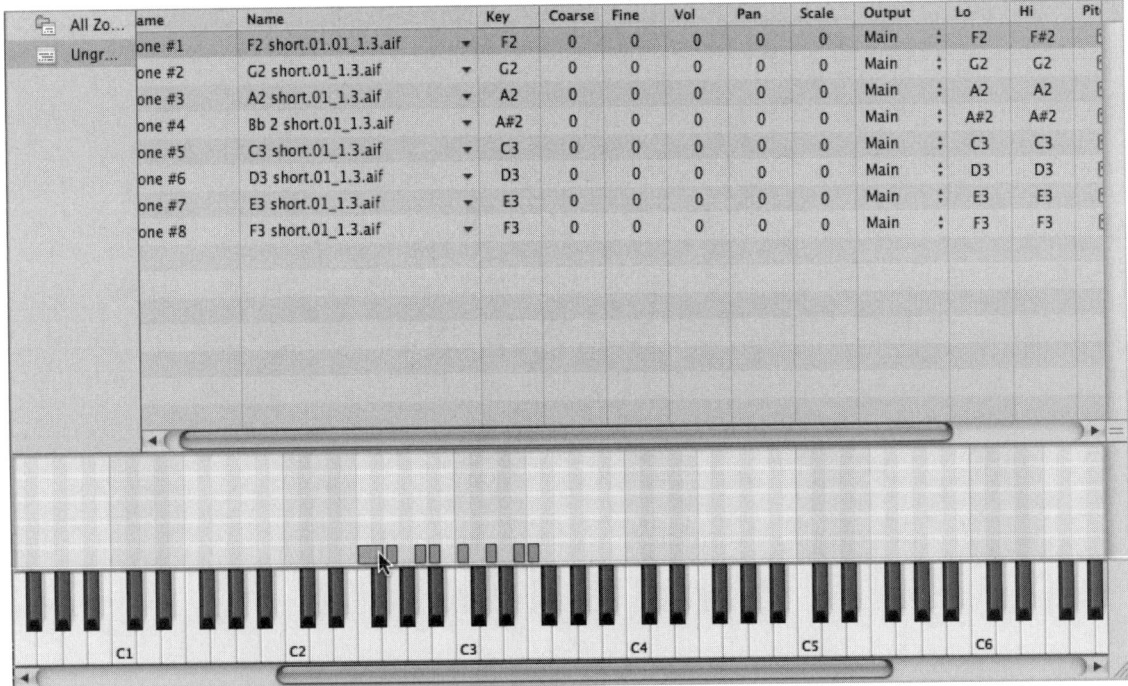

Figure 3.14   Stretching a Zone.

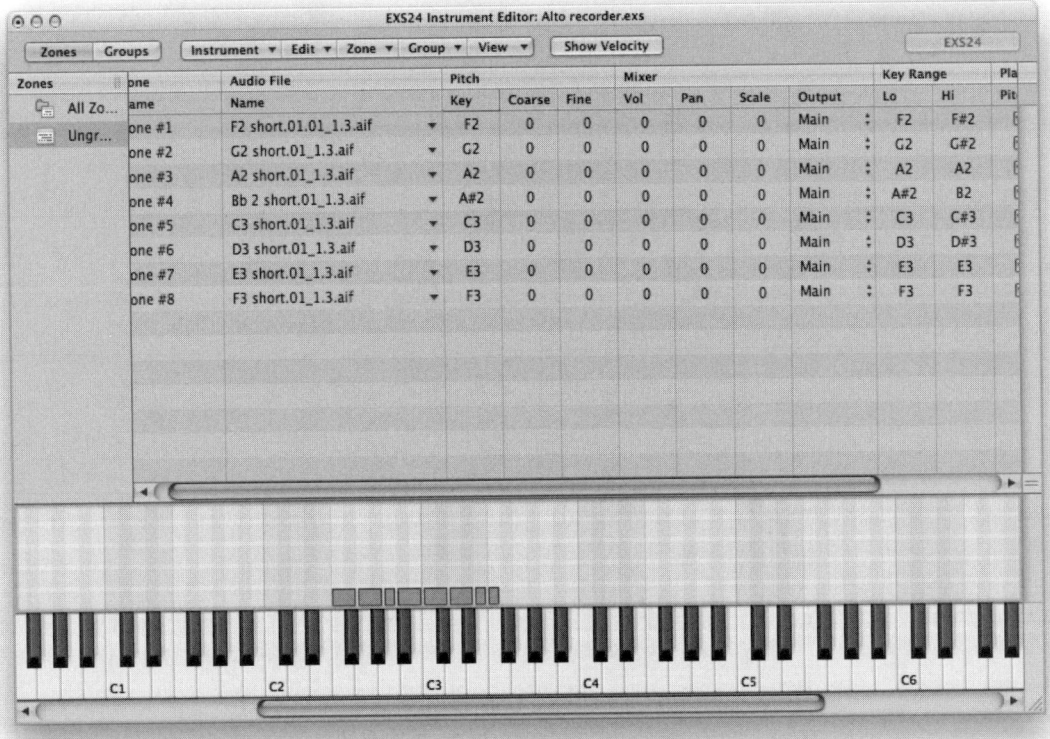

Figure 3.15   Stretched.

This is just a simple sample rate change, much like speeding up a tape recorder, so of course you'll hear the effects if you stretch too far.

Depending on whether the pitch shifting sounds okay, you might want to extend the top and/or bottom notes a few steps to increase the playable range of the instrument. For instance, the F2 Zone could go down to, say, D2 and the F3 to A3.

Under the Playback columns, be sure that 1Shot is not checked. 1Shot will play through the whole sample when you trigger it, rather than stopping when you release the key (Figure 3.16).

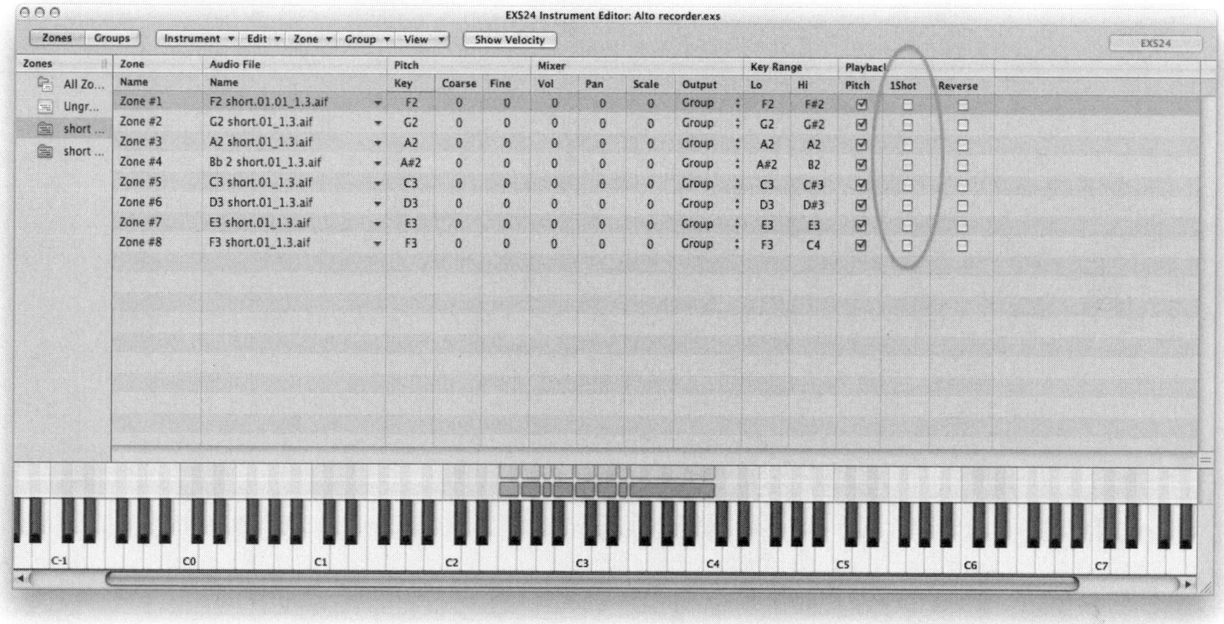

Figure 3.16 1Shot unchecked.

And at this point you've created a simple EXS instrument—a set of samples mapped to the keyboard that plays at all velocity ranges. These samples get louder at higher velocities; later we're going to limit the velocity range and have the staccato samples trigger in their place.

We're also going to add the vibrato and non-vibrato articulations and build a whole recorder instrument (the bottom octave of it, anyway).

Stage 2: Automatic Sample Alternation of Separate Performances

Sample-alternating is a common technique used for avoiding the dreaded "machine gun" effect that can make sampled instruments sound unmusical.

As an aside, it should be apparent that this is even better when you have more than the two alternate performances in this example. We're not going to go through the following process in this exercise, but you could easily go back to the sample editor and create an extra performance by copying one set of samples and pitch-shifting them up or down a short distance to change their sound in Logic's Pitch and Time Machine (accessed under the Factory menu in the sample editor). Alternatively, you might try Harmonic Correction; either way, the object of the exercise is to alter the formants slightly, which are the prominent frequencies that give sounds their unique character (Figure 3.17).

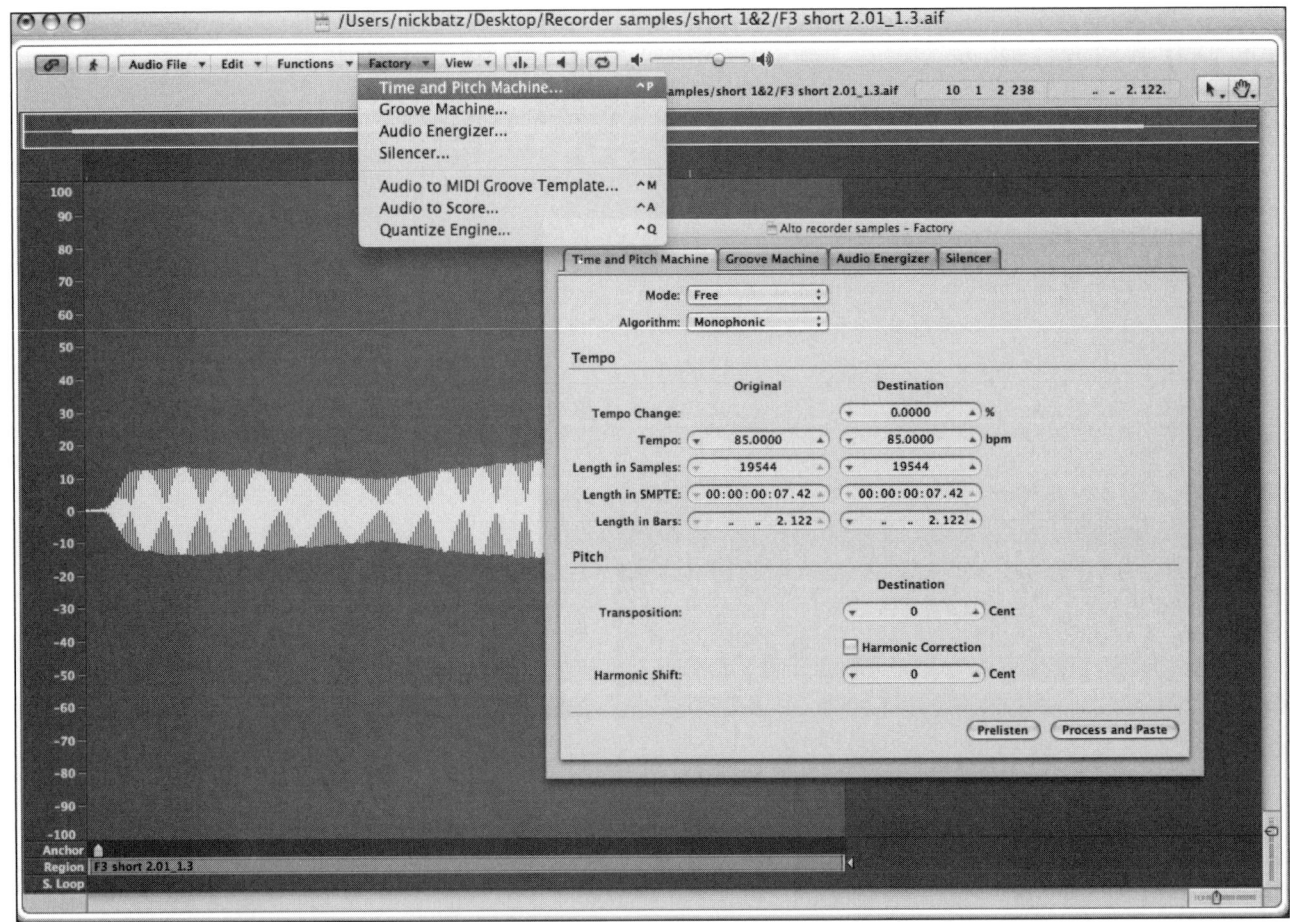

Figure 3.17 Transposing for a different sound.

Note that these changes are permanent, but the Pitch and Time Machine has a Prelisten button for auditioning the effects.

Unfortunately, the EXS24 doesn't allow you to randomize the order in which notes play—a feature known as round-robin. This means that the ear may yet detect a pattern, but at least we can set up a chain to play them in order. In any case, the procedure for setting up any number of alternate takes is the same as it is for two.

The first step in building a more advanced program like this is to organize the Zones into Groups. An EXS Group is simply a collection of Zones that share common programming settings, for example the velocity range over which it plays—and, salient to the program we're creating, the order in which it alternates with other Groups when you play repeated notes.

You can toggle between Zone and Group views in the editor by clicking on the button at the upper left.

Create a new Group (from the Groups menu) and double-click its generic default name so you can type in a meaningful one. We're going to call it "short notes 1" (Figures 3.18 and 3.19).

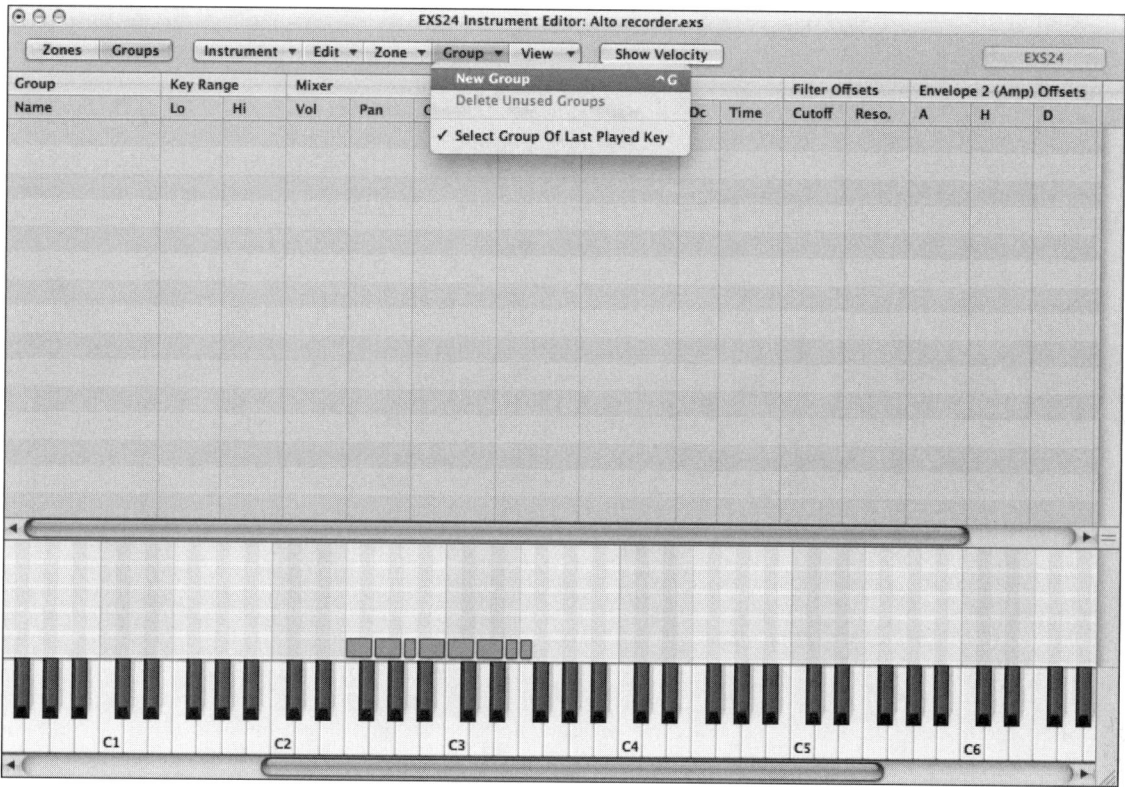

Figure 3.18 New Group.

Select all the Zones (the easiest way is to mouse over them all in the area above the keyboard) and then drag them from the list—not the keyboard area—into the "short notes 1" folder to assign them to that Group.

Create another new Group for the alternate sample performances, name it "short notes 2," and select it.

Drag all the short 2 samples into place just like you did with the short 1 samples (Figures 3.20 and 3.21).

Stretch the short 2 notes just as you did with the short 1 notes (Figure 3.22).

Toggle to the Groups view by clicking on the tab next to Zones view at the upper left. Under View, make sure Group: Select Group By is checked (so that it's visible), as shown in Figure 3.23.

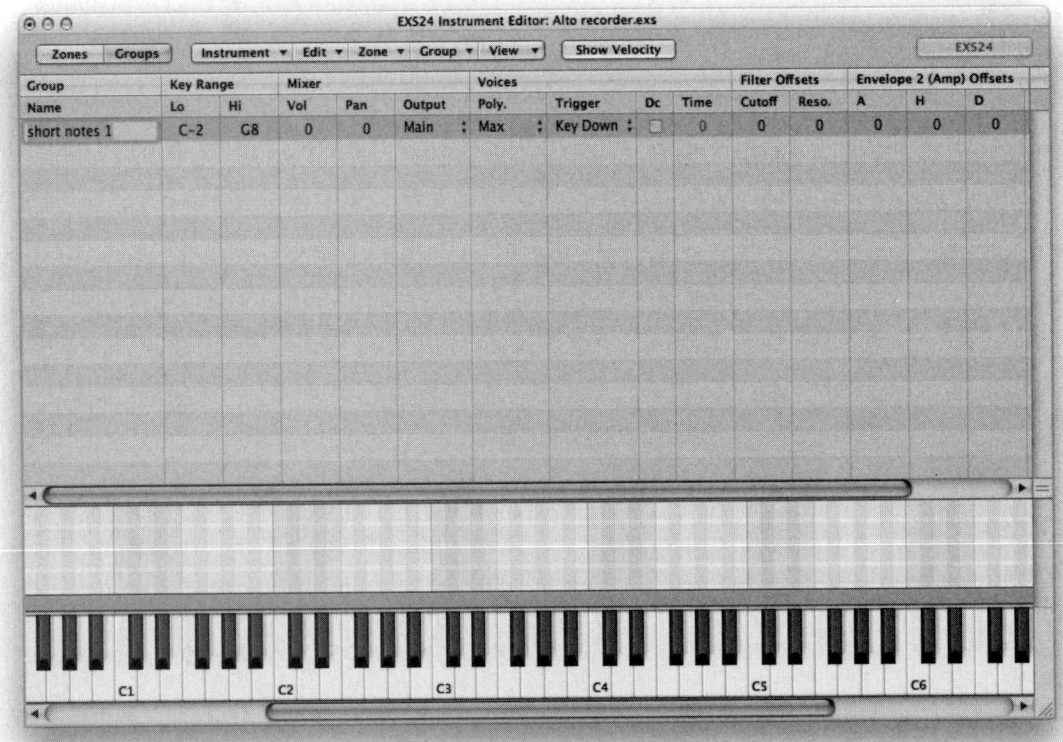

Figure 3.19 Naming the Group.

Zones		Zone	Audio File		Pitch			Mixer				Key Rang
		Name	Name		Key	Coarse	Fine	Vol	Pan	Scale	Output	Lo
	All Zones	Zone #1	F2 short.01.01_1.3.aif	▼	F2	0	0	0	0	0	Main	:	F2
	Ungrouped	Zone #2	G2 short.01_1.3.aif	▼	G2	0	0	0	0	0	Main	:	G2
	short	Zone #3	A2 short.01_1.3.aif	▼	A2	0	0	0	0	0	Main	:	A2
		Zone #4	Bb 2 short.01_1.3.aif	▼	A#2	0	0	0	0	0	Main	:	A#2
		Zone #5	C3 short.01_1.3.aif	▼	C3	0	0	0	0	0	Main	:	C3
		Zone #6	D3 short.01_1.3.aif	▼	D3	0	0	0	0	0	Main	:	D3
		Zone #7	E3 short.01_1.3.aif	▼	E3	0	0	0	0	0	Main	:	E3
		Zone #8	F3 short.01_1.3.aif	▼	F3	0	0	0	0	0	Main	:	F3

Figure 3.20 Drag samples into the Group.

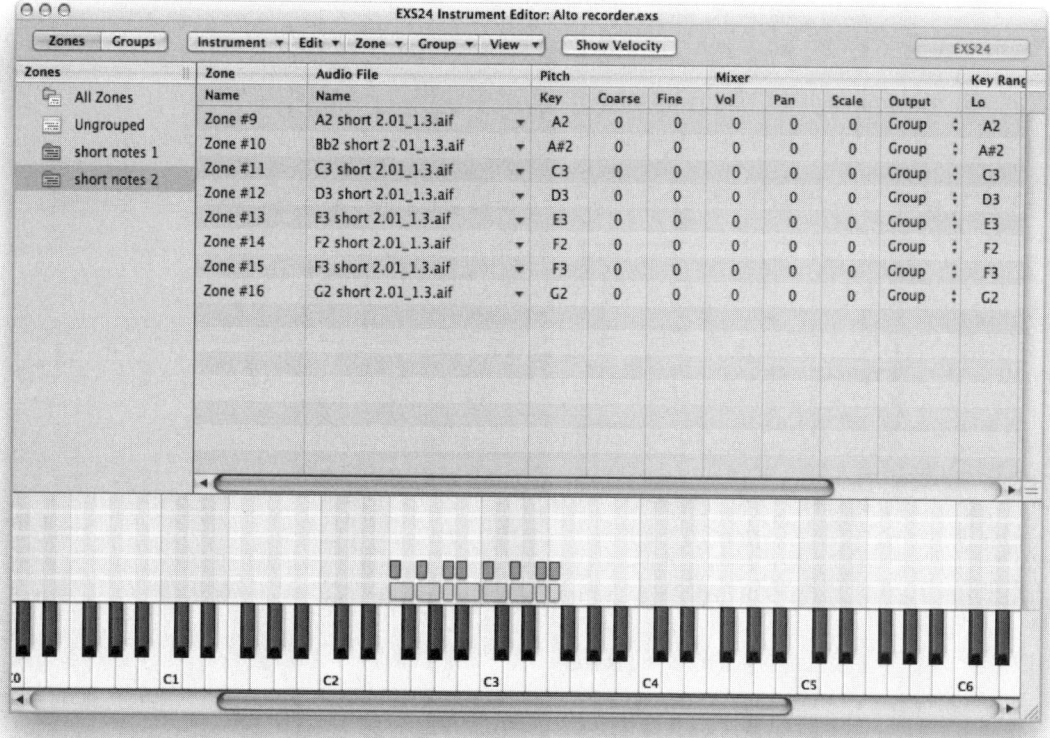

Figure 3.21   Short notes dragged in.

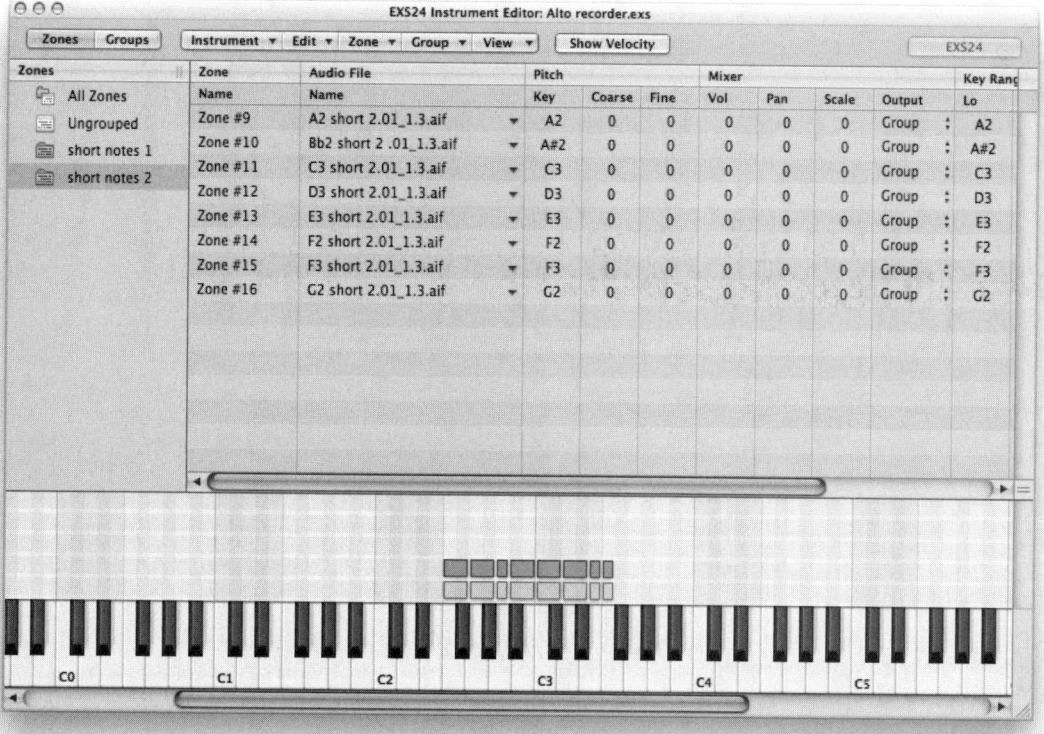

Figure 3.22   Short notes stretched.

Figure 3.23 Select Group By...

In the Select Group By column for the short notes 2 Group, choose Group short notes 1 (Figures 3.24 and 3.25).

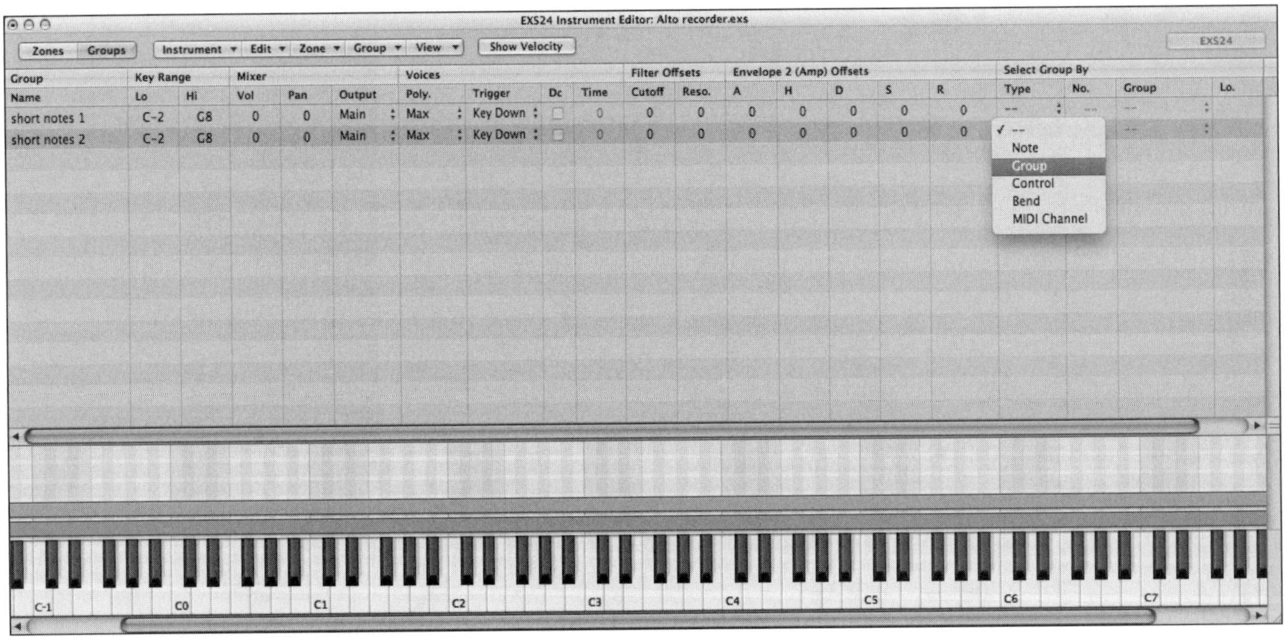

Figure 3.24 Select Group By Group.

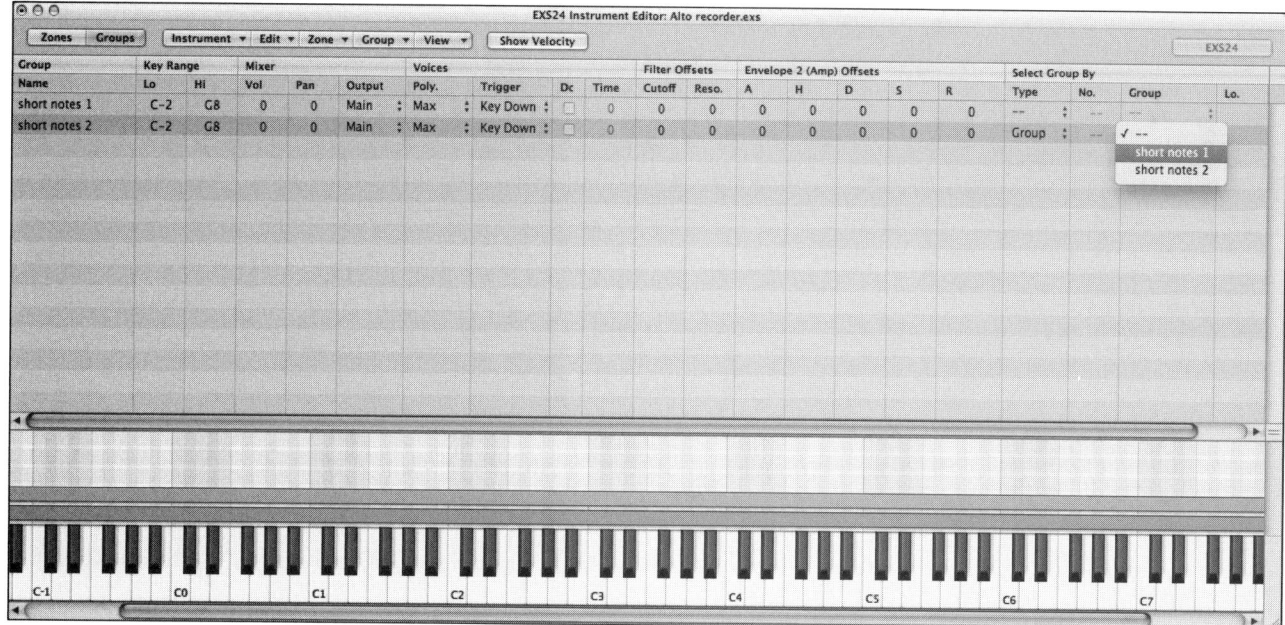

Figure 3.25 Select Group by the short notes 1 Group.

If you play repeated notes on the keyboard, you'll see that this means the short 2 samples alternate with—that is, follow—the short 1 samples. The short 1 samples are set to nothing (-- in the display); the way to picture this is that you're creating a chain.

This effect can sometimes be subtle, since the same player will tend to play notes the same way every time (especially when sampling, outside the context of real music), but if you listen to the B♭ in this program, it'll be very obvious.

Stage 3: Bringing in the Staccato Notes and Setting Velocity Ranges

Now we're going to add the two staccato variations to the program. They're going to trigger at lower velocities, and the regular short notes will trigger at higher ones.

The process of bringing in the new sets of samples and setting them up to alternate is exactly the same as what we just did with the regular short notes. Create a stacc 1 Group and drag in the stacc 1 samples, create a stacc 2 Group and drag in the stacc 2 samples, and then select the stacc 2 Group by stacc 1.

Your program should now look like this (Figures 3.26 and 3.27).

Setting the Hi and Lo points for the velocity range in which a Zone is to trigger couldn't be simpler, although adjusting the ranges to taste can be a little finicky.

Probably the easiest way to adjust the velocity range is from the Groups view.

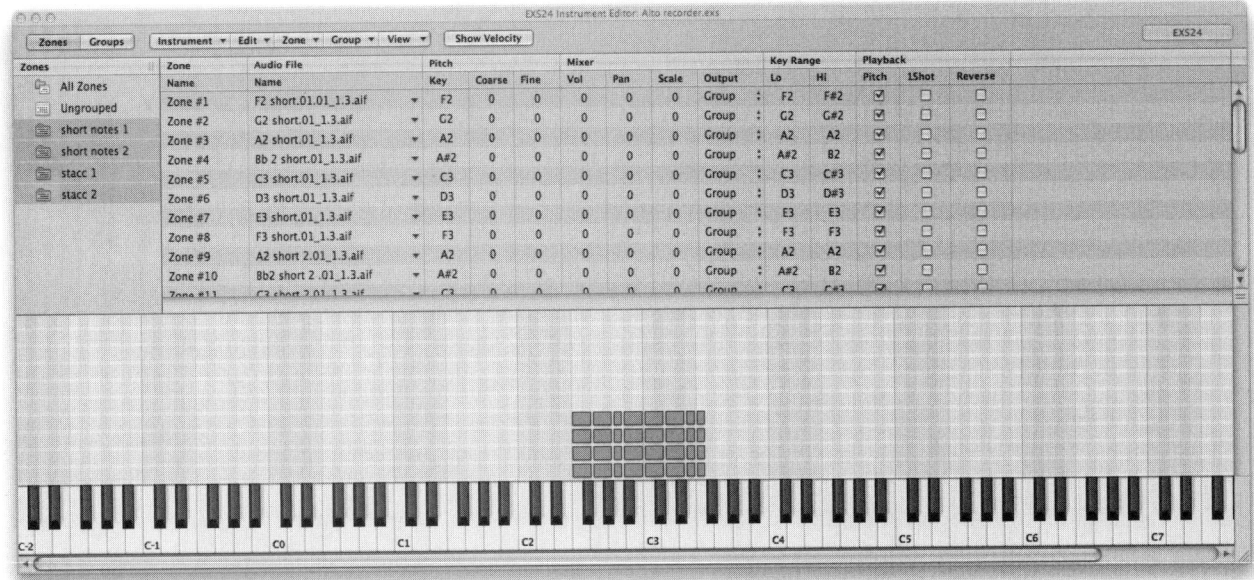

Figure 3.26 With the staccato notes added (Zones).

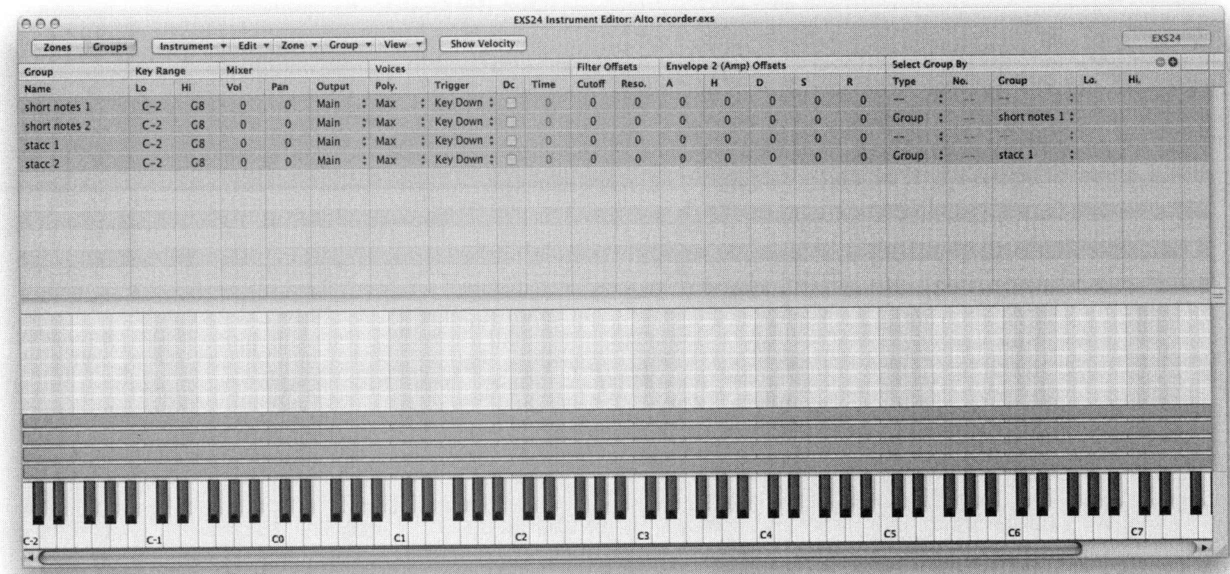

Figure 3.27 With the staccato notes added (Groups).

Under View, make sure Group: Velocity Range is checked. There's also a prominent button to toggle between showing and hiding the velocity (in the upper right of Figure 3.28).

A middle pane will appear, showing a light blue velocity graph. But it's easier just to enter the values in the Group window.

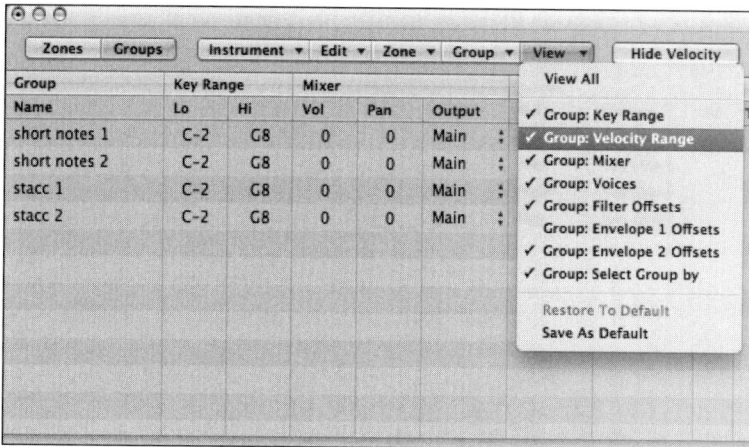

Figure 3.28 Show Velocity Range.

Set short notes 1 & 2 to trigger from velocities 80–127 and staccs 1 & 2 to trigger from 1–79 (Figure 3.29).

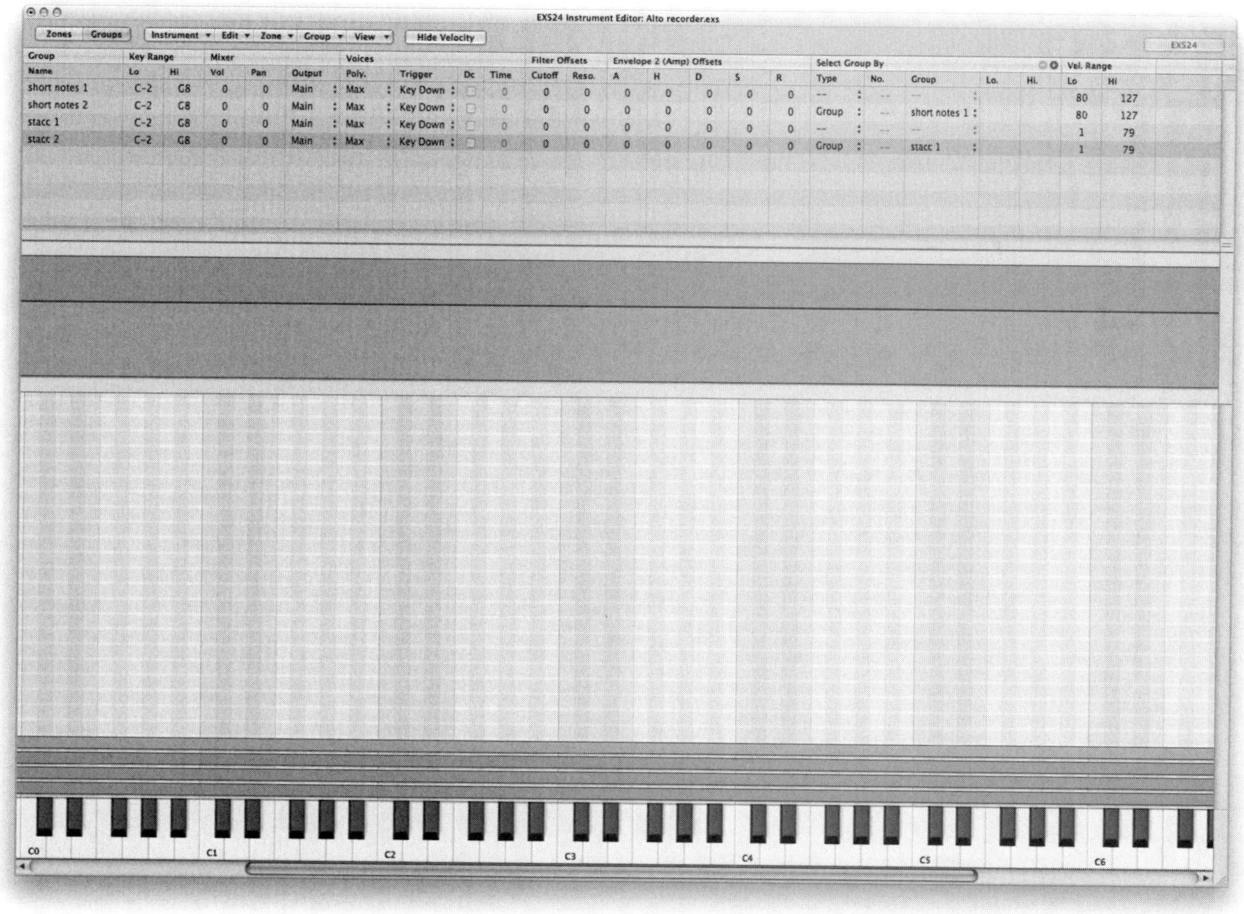

Figure 3.29 With the Velocity Ranges set.

Try playing this, and you'll see how musical it feels to switch to the more pronounced short notes when you play harder. You may want to adjust the velocity switch point to taste (and to work well with your controller keyboard's velocity response). While it's not necessary in this case, you can also adjust velocity ranges independently for each Zone (in Zones view). In other words, you can adjust each sampled note independently.

Stage 4: Adding the Long Notes

Adding the two long note articulations is more of the same, only the Select Group By parameters will be more complicated for this program. What we're going to do is have the non-vibrato notes trigger only when the mod wheel is on less than half way (1–63) and the notes with vibrato sound when it's over half way (64–27). If the wheel is all the way off—0—then the short and staccato notes will play as before; the mod wheel brings in the long notes.

As an aside, note that it's easy to copy and paste Groups between EXS programs, so you may find it convenient to create separate programs in addition to all-in-one programs like this one. While memory access isn't really much of an issue these days, why deal with a combination program if you only need the short notes?

Bringing in the long note samples should be familiar by now.

Create "Long vib" and "Long nonvib" Groups and map the samples to the keyboard. Turn off that 1Shot feature that is so annoying when you don't want it.

Your EXS editor will look like this (Figure 3.30).

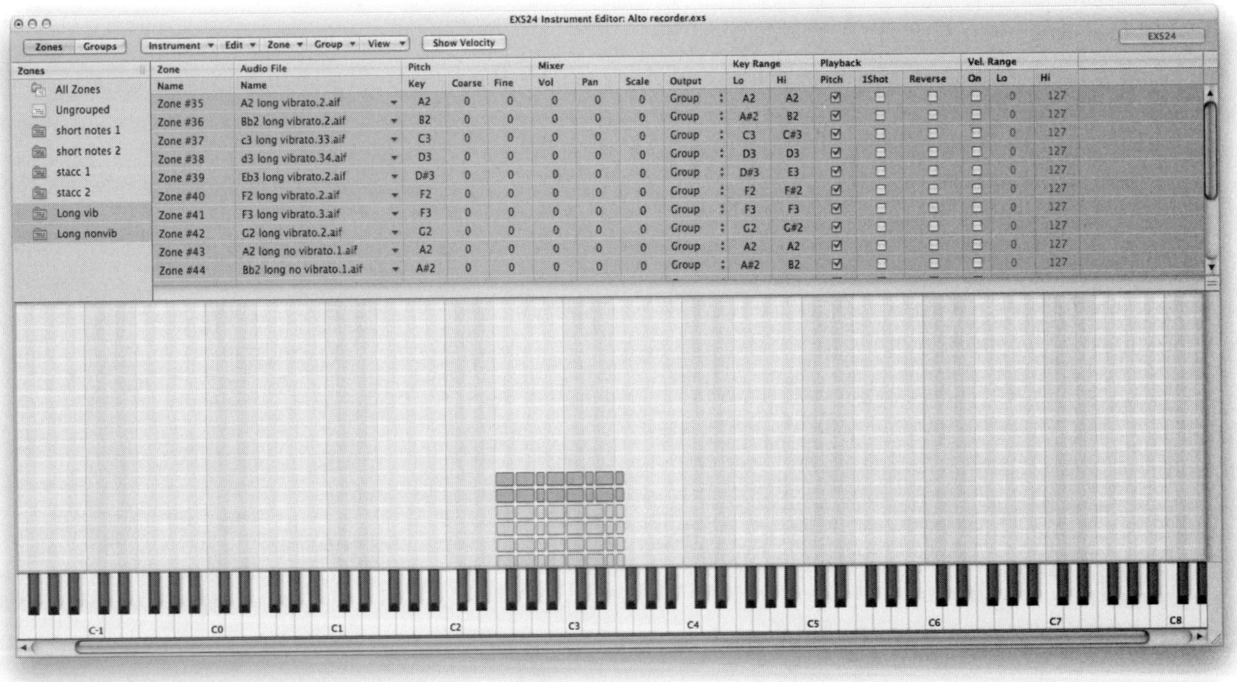

Figure 3.30 The long notes are in.

Now we're ready to re-do the Select Group settings, which are a little quirky when you're setting up more than one condition. The MIDI controller being used to select a Group has to come first in the list.

The first thing is to set MIDI Continuous Controller #1—the mod wheel—as the first Select Group By type (Figure 3.31).

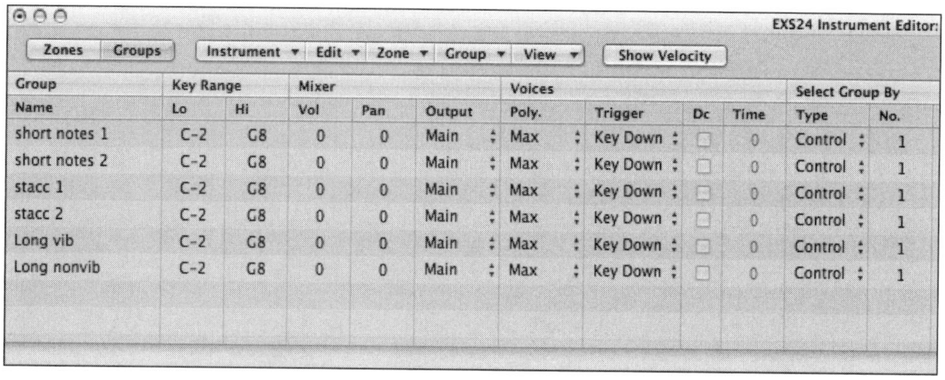

| Group | Key Range | | Mixer | | | Voices | | | | | Select Group By | |
Name	Lo	Hi	Vol	Pan	Output	Poly.		Trigger		Dc	Time	Type	No.
short notes 1	C-2	G8	0	0	Main :	Max	:	Key Down :		☐	0	Control :	1
short notes 2	C-2	G8	0	0	Main :	Max	:	Key Down :		☐	0	Control :	1
stacc 1	C-2	G8	0	0	Main :	Max	:	Key Down :		☐	0	Control :	1
stacc 2	C-2	G8	0	0	Main :	Max	:	Key Down :		☐	0	Control :	1
Long vib	C-2	G8	0	0	Main :	Max	:	Key Down :		☐	0	Control :	1
Long nonvib	C-2	G8	0	0	Main :	Max	:	Key Down :		☐	0	Control :	1

Figure 3.31 Select Group By the mod wheel.

Next we're going to set the mod wheel range within which each Group will sound.

Short notes 1 & 2 and staccs 1 & 2 should sound only when the mod wheel is off, so their Lo and Hi ranges get set to 0. The Long nonvib Group gets triggered when the mod wheel is between 1 and 63, and the Long vib Group is to sound when the mod wheel is between 64 and 127 (Figure 3.32).

Notice that the Vel Range settings for the short and stacc settings are the same as they were before; i.e., short notes 1 & 2 trigger at high velocity settings.

Now we need to set up alternating between the two sets of short articulations just like before. Click on the little + next to Select Group By to bring up Select Group By (2), meaning the second set of parameters. Short notes 2 is selected by short notes 1, and stacc2 is selected by stacc1. It should now look like Figure 3.33.

You may notice that both long note articulations cut off rather abruptly, so as a quick fix let's lengthen the release of the envelope just a little (we'll discuss release samples later). The front panel controls apply to the entire program, but this is a very subtle tweak, and it doesn't make any difference to the sound of the short articulations. Had that been a problem, we could simply have entered a negative value in the Envelope 2 (Amp) Offsets column in the Groups view.

Go to the EXS front panel and set ENV2's release to somewhere around 108 milliseconds (the pop-up indication of the exact setting when you click on it isn't shown in this screen grab, but you can see where the mouse pointer is). Too long a decay and it will sound horribly synthy; much shorter and you won't hear any difference (Figure 3.34).

The only thing remaining is to claim the mod wheel from its default assignment in the front panel mod matrix (LFO 1).

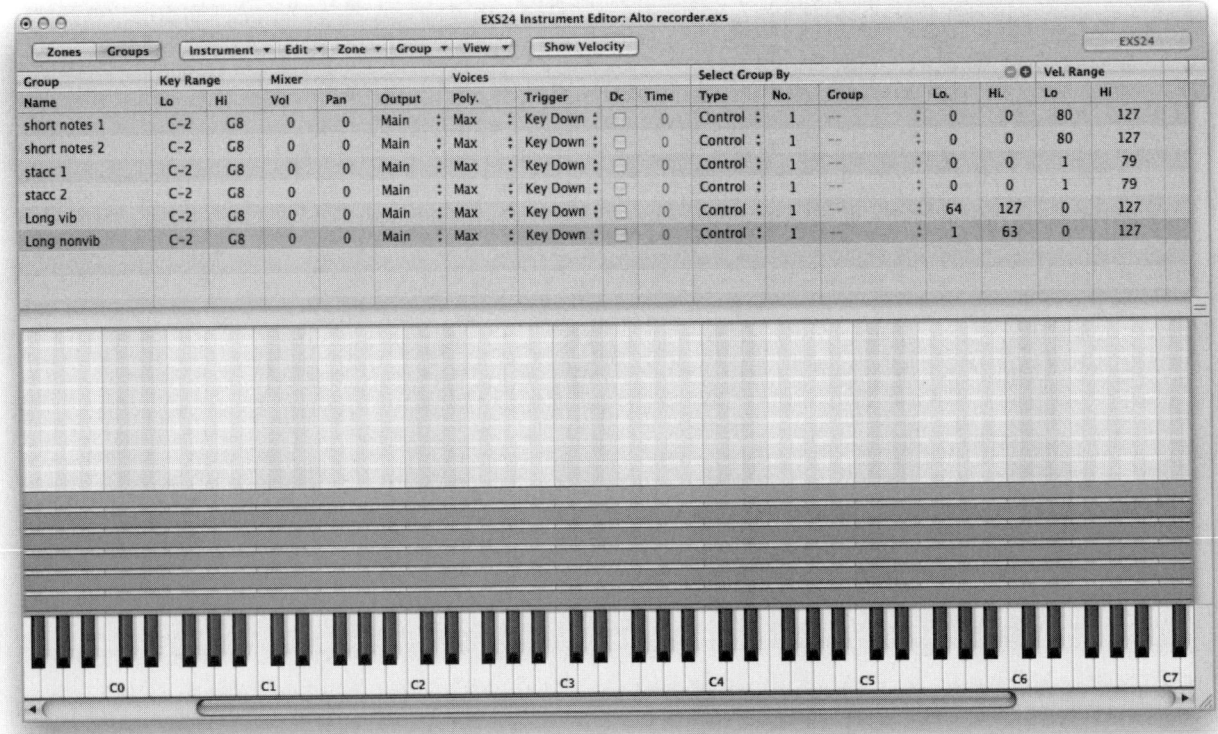

Figure 3.32 Setting the mod wheel ranges.

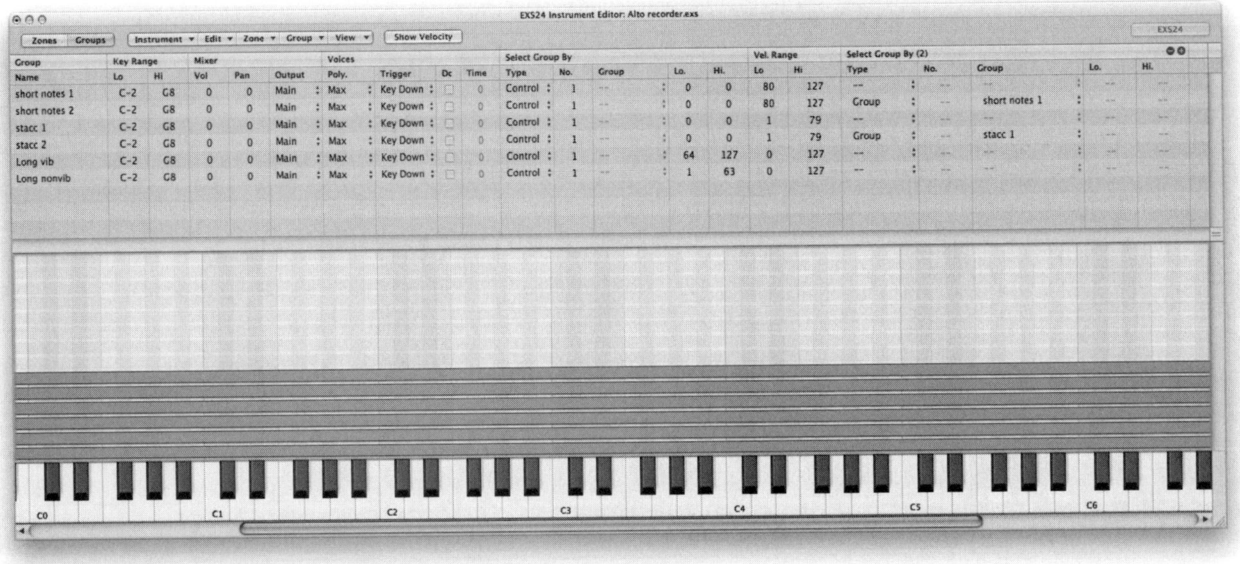

Figure 3.33 Finished alto recorder program.

Figure 3.34 Adding some release.

In the second block, move Ctrl #1 (the mod wheel) to -— (nothing). Translation: nothing is triggering LFO 1 (Figures 3.35 and 3.36).

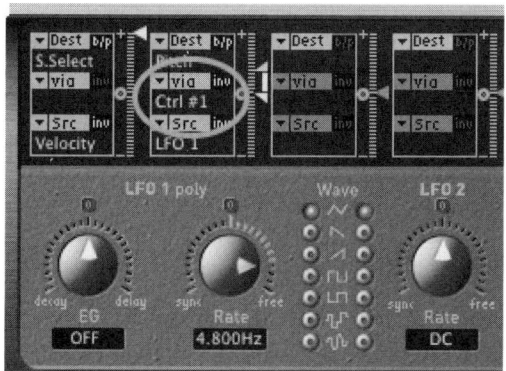

Figure 3.35 Claiming the mod wheel for our own devices.

In order to preserve the natural dynamics and character of the instrument, we're not going to adjust the volume levels or tune the notes. Had we wanted to do that, however, it's probably worth pointing out that the Pitch and Mixer fields are in plain sight in the editor.

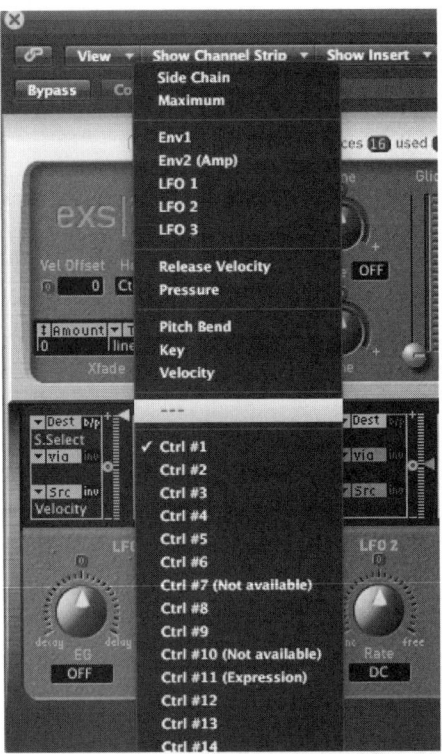

Figure 3.36 Set mod wheel to — (nothing).

So we're done. The completed front panel should look like this (Figure 3.37).

Figure 3.37 Done.

4 Building Programs in Native Instruments Kontakt

Native Instruments Kontakt has become the most widespread sampler format for commercial libraries, and it's the most advanced sampler available. For example, every sampler lets you set up a loop; Kontakt lets you set up eight of them.

In this book we're taking a direct path to creating custom sample libraries, so it's appropriate to focus on the essential features toward that end. Kontakt has a remarkable number of additional tricks up its sleeve for you to explore, however, and they're quite accessible (with the caveat that its controls are very small, even for those of us fortunate enough not to need reading glasses). Inside its Instrument Edit mode is a rack of modules, where you map samples, edit waveforms, set up modulations, insert effects, edit scripts, and so on.

But the feature that throws it over the top is KSP, its custom scripting language, which allows any MIDI command to be manipulated and twisted inside out to trigger any internal parameter. There are public scripts available for all kinds of things, from switching articulations based on the speed of your playing to generating pretty impressive legato transitions using subtle pitch bends and varying the sample start position. Writing scripts from scratch is a separate skill, but using public or included ones is very easy, and we will go over that in a later chapter.

As with the EX24, we'll work with one octave of an alto recorder instrument. We have the four most common recorder articulations: very short ("tick" and "ka"), short ("toot"), long notes with vibrato, and long notes without vibrato. These long note articulations can actually work for shorter notes, too; the important difference is the vibrato.

The recorder's dynamic range is quite limited—and the bottom octave can only be played quietly—so we only sampled one dynamic layer. However, the way recorder players create a louder feel is by articulating more heavily; the very short "ticka tick" notes tend to have a lighter feel than the regular "toot" ones, so we'll use velocity to switch between the two. We're also going to set up two variations of each short note to alternate automatically. This will help avoid the repeated note effect that gives away the secret that you're using samples right away.

Then to illustrate an example of a useful performance setup, we'll bring in two other multi-sampled programs—long notes with and without vibrato—that will trigger instead of the short notes when the mod wheel is on. The vibrato layer will sound when the mod wheel is over half way, and the non-vib when it's below.

Stage 1: A Basic Playable Instrument

In this tutorial we'll create a basic instrument; the figures show Kontakt 4. Please open the "short 1 & 2" folder; we're going to use the short 1 samples—the first of the two short note variations—to create our first program.

Create a new instrument from under the floppy disk icon (Figure 4.1).

Figure 4.1 New instrument.

Save it. You can place Kontakt samples and programs anywhere you like (Figure 4.2).

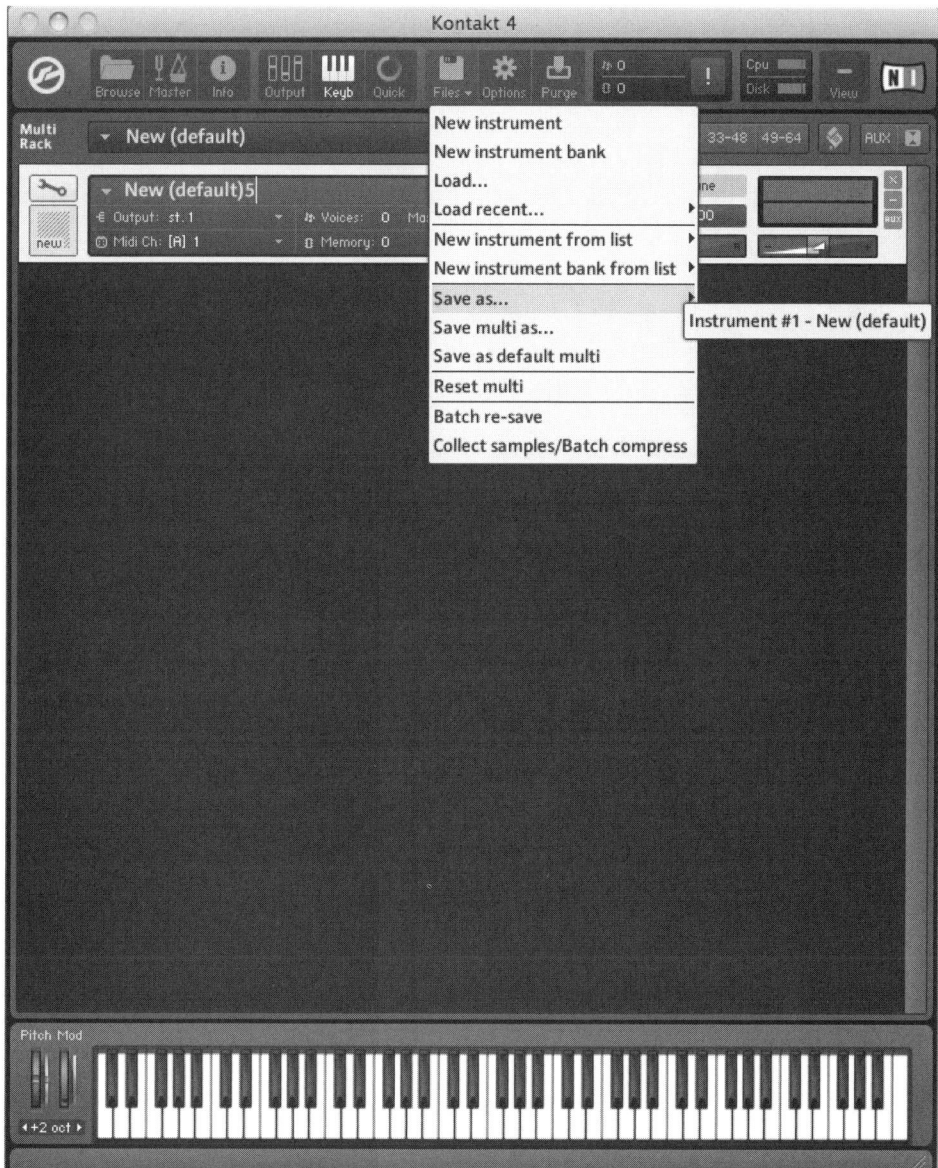

Figure 4.2   Save As.

Click on the wrench icon to go into Edit mode. Some of the Kontakt modules will appear (Figure 4.3).

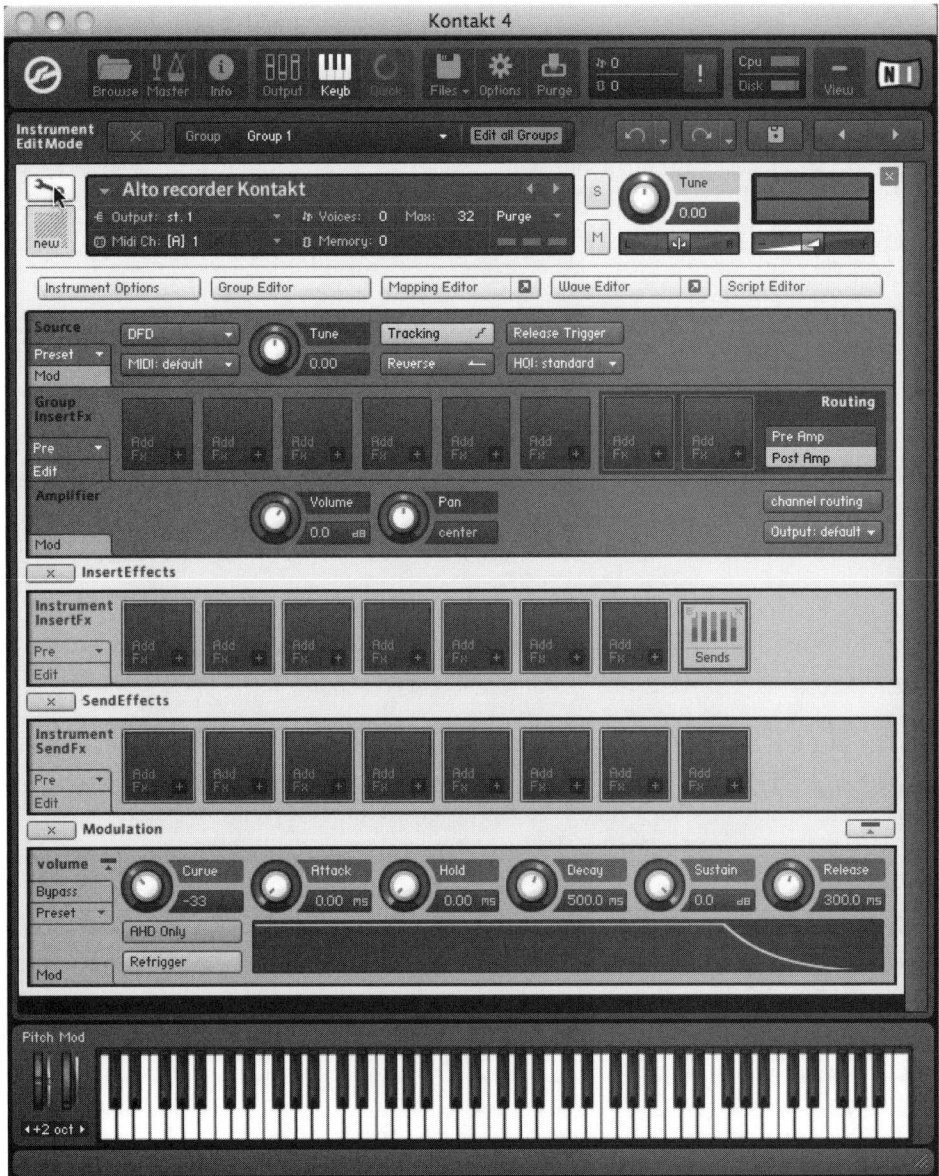

Figure 4.3 Click the wrench.

The module we need to build our programs is the Mapping Editor, so click as shown to open it (Figure 4.4).

Drag the samples in one by one (Figure 4.5). Here the F2 short 1 sample is being dropped onto F2.

Like other samplers, Kontakt has other ways that attempt to automate the process of assigning samples to Zones. But bringing them in manually always works the first time.

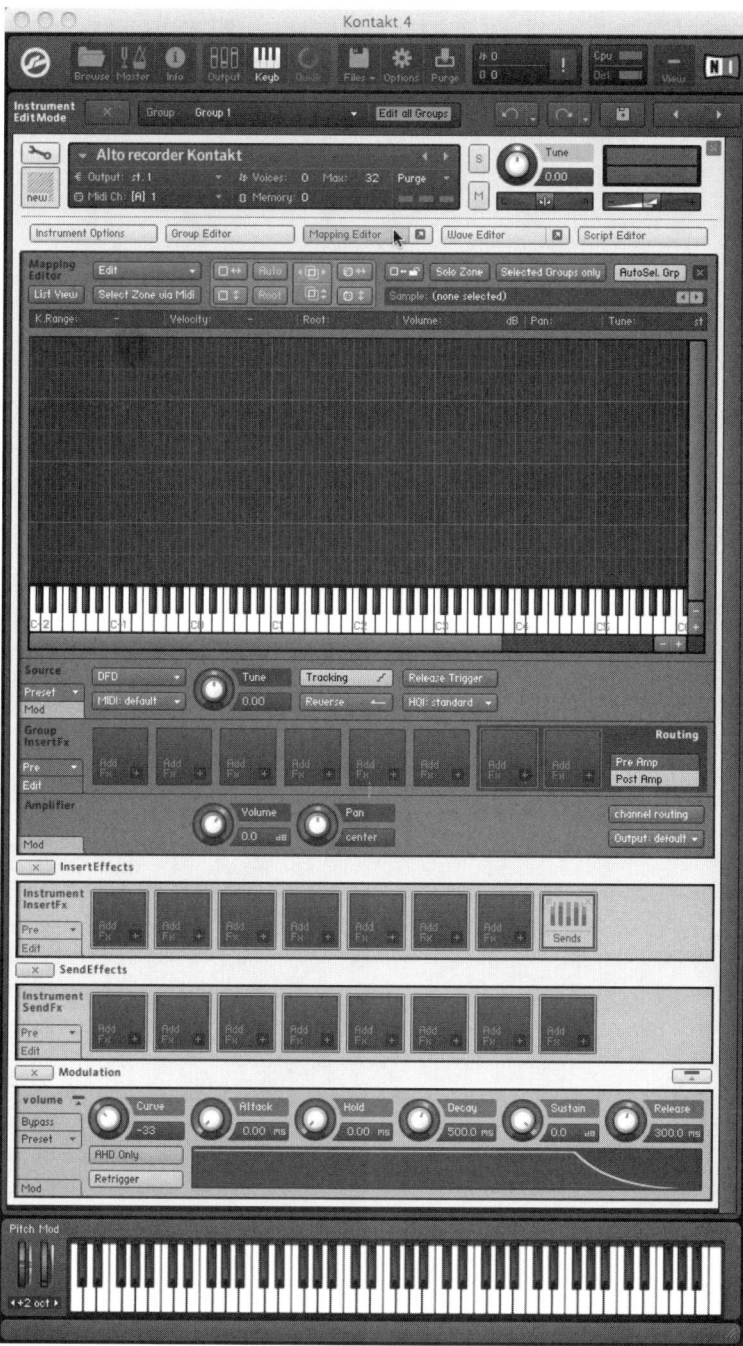

Figure 4.4 Open the Mapping Editor.

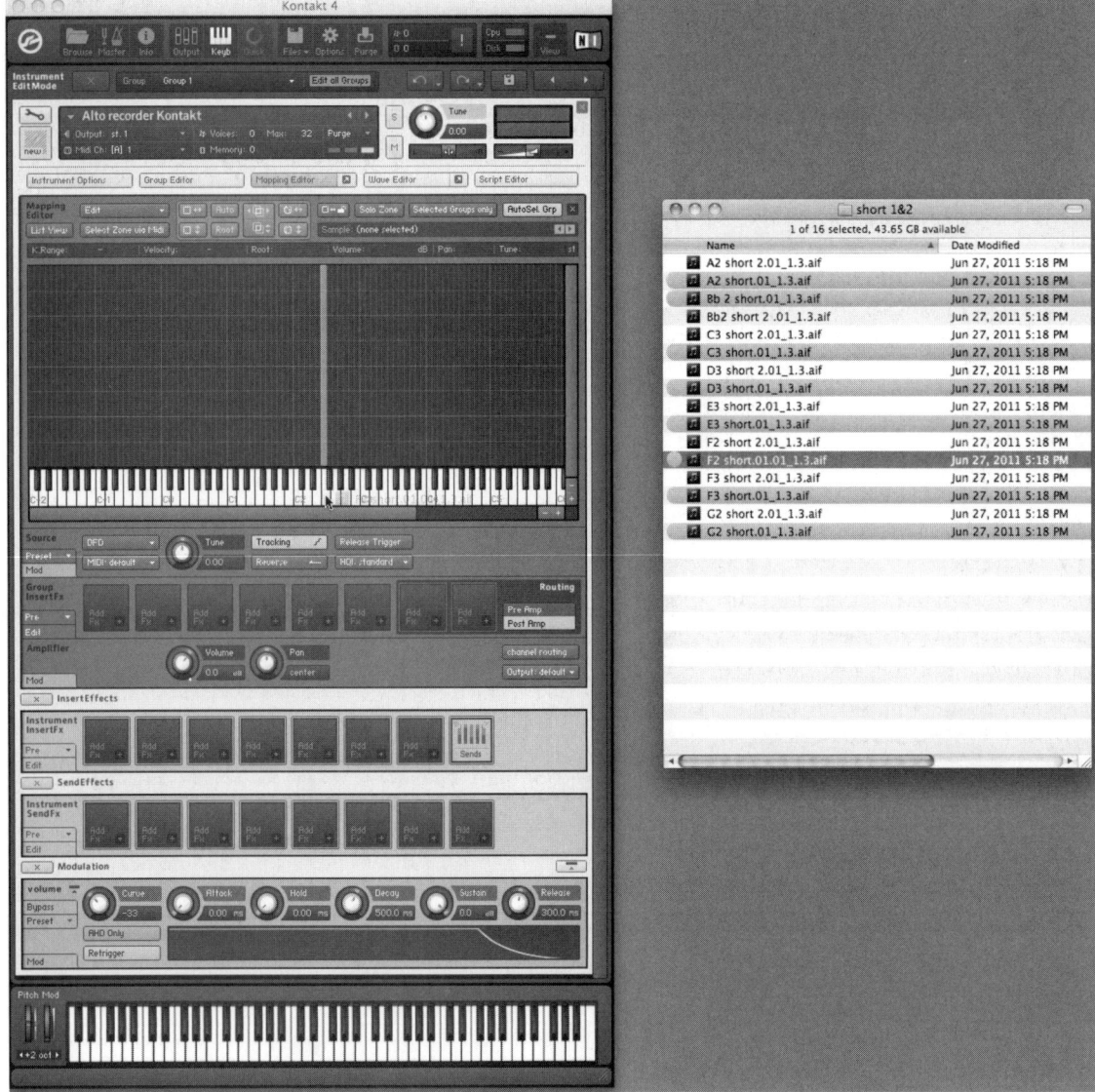

Figure 4.5 Dragging in the short 1s.

Your program should look like Figure 4.6; be sure to save.

Since we didn't sample every note, there are keys where nothing will sound, for example F#2. So we're going to stretch the range of the sample below each gap to fill it in, and of course the sampler will handle the pitch shifting automatically. We could also stretch the higher samples lower, but in this case it's six/half a dozen which one sounds better.

You can shift multiple samples together when they need stretching the same amount, for example F2 and G2 (Figure 4.7).

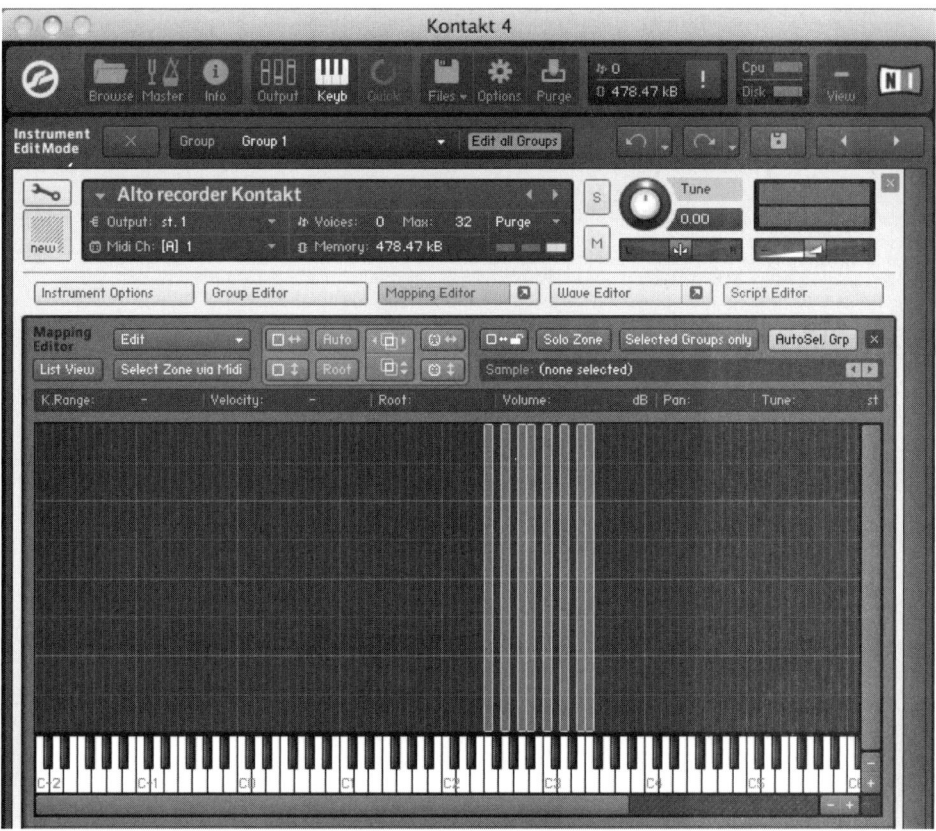

Figure 4.6 Short 1s dragged in.

Figure 4.7 Stretching the ranges.

At this stage, we've created a simple Kontakt instrument that plays at all velocity ranges, meaning the "harder" you play, the louder the instrument sounds (Figure 4.8).

Figure 4.8   The basic program.

Later we're going to limit the bottom of the velocity range and have the staccato samples trigger at lower velocities.

We're also going to add the vibrato and non-vibrato articulations and build a whole recorder instrument (the bottom octave of it, anyway). And we'll eventually cut release samples for more natural note endings. That will fix the problem of the short samples sounding a little synthy if they're not held to the end.

Stage 2: Automatic Sample Alternation of Separate Performances

Now we're going to bring in the short 2 samples and set them up to alternate with the short 1 samples when the same note is played.

Every sampler has slightly different terminology and ways of explaining how programs are organized, but the concept is the same. As in the EXS24, as soon as you put a sample on the keyboard in Kontakt, it becomes a Zone; the Zone is simply the key range over which this sample is triggered.

Zones are then organized into Groups, which are collections of one or more Zones set up to trigger under prescribed conditions. The most obvious condition is the incoming velocity level, but the condition we're setting up here is that the same note in the short 1 Group has just played (Figures 4.9, 4.10, 4.11). (We only have two alternate takes, but the process of setting up lots more is the same.)

Open the Group Editor.

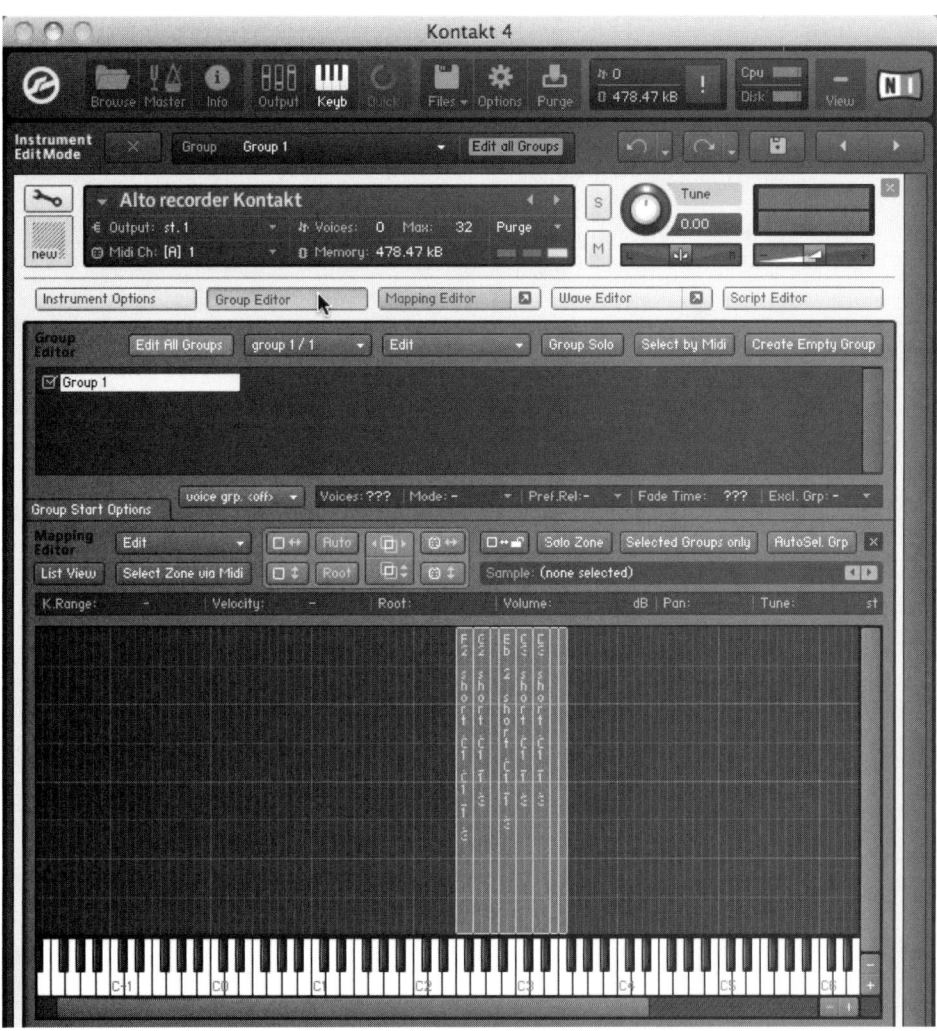

Figure 4.9 Open the Group Editor.

Create a new Group.

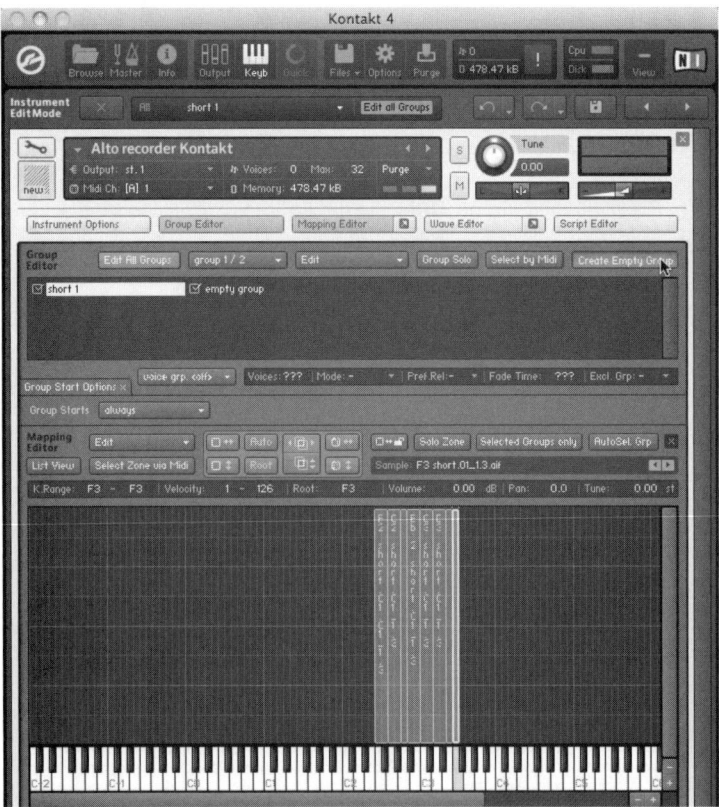

Figure 4.10 Create a new Group.

Name it "short 1."

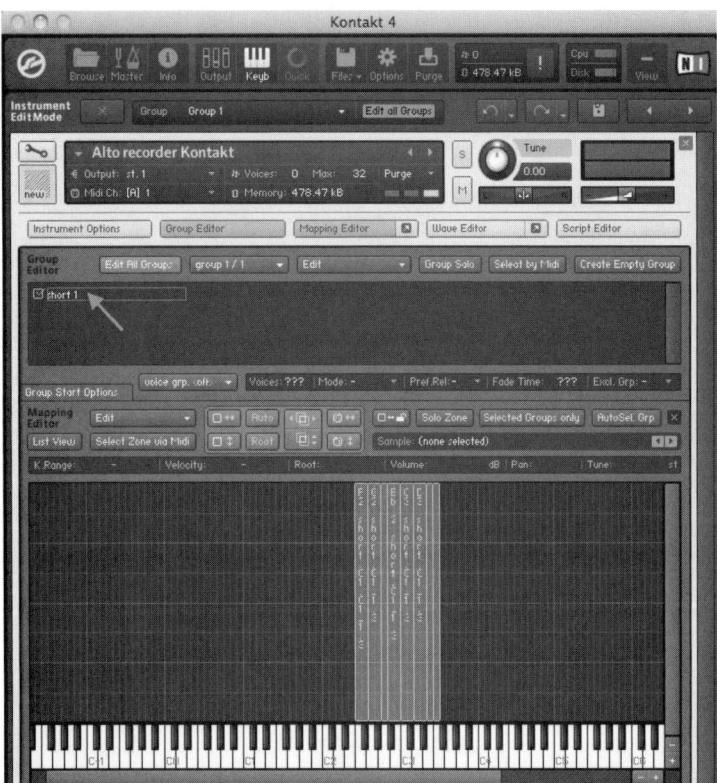

Figure 4.11 Name the Group.

Now create another new Group for the short 2 samples, name it "short 2," and click on the Selected Groups Only button. This will keep the short 1 samples out of the view so we can see what we're doing (Figure 4.12).

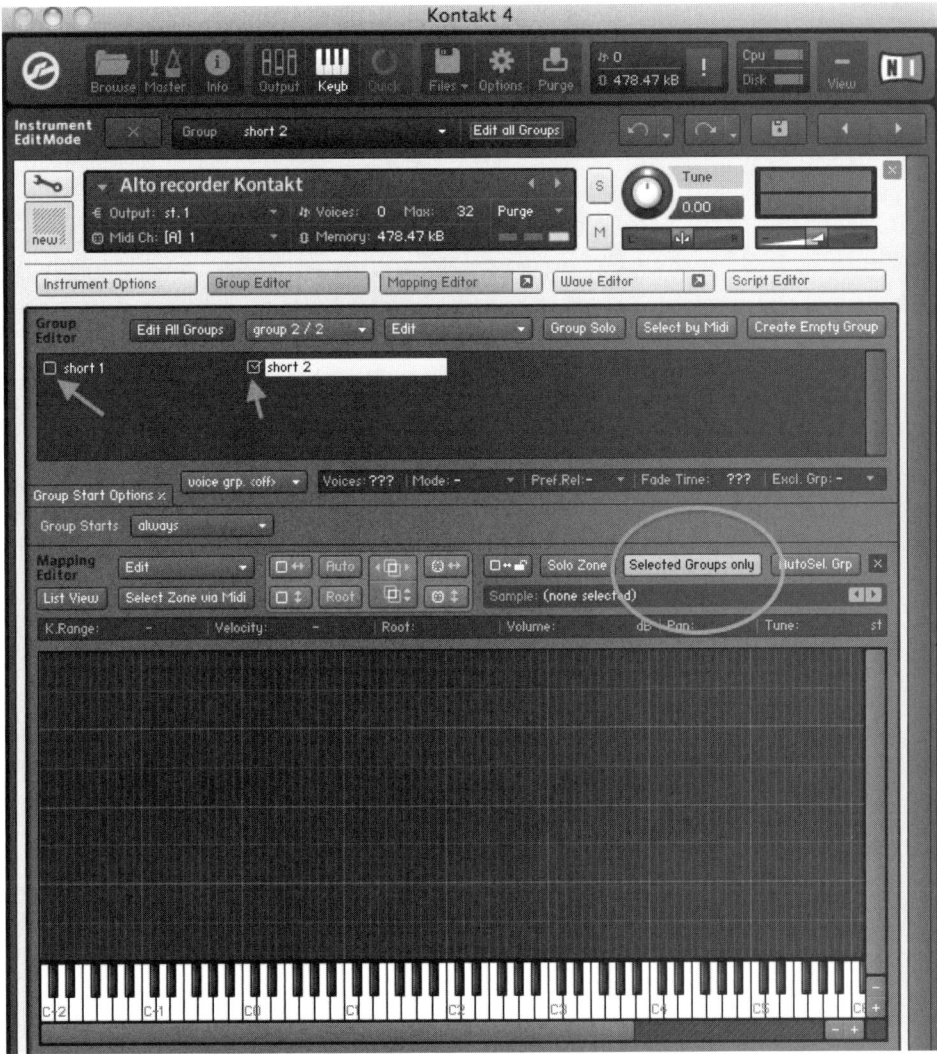

Figure 4.12 Selected Groups Only.

Drag in and stretch the short 2 samples just like we did with the short 1s (Figure 4.13).

The Group Start Options drop-down allows you to set all kinds of exclusive conditions (in addition to the key and velocity ranges) under which the Group will trigger.

Select the short 1 Group and click on the Group Start Options button (Figure 4.14).

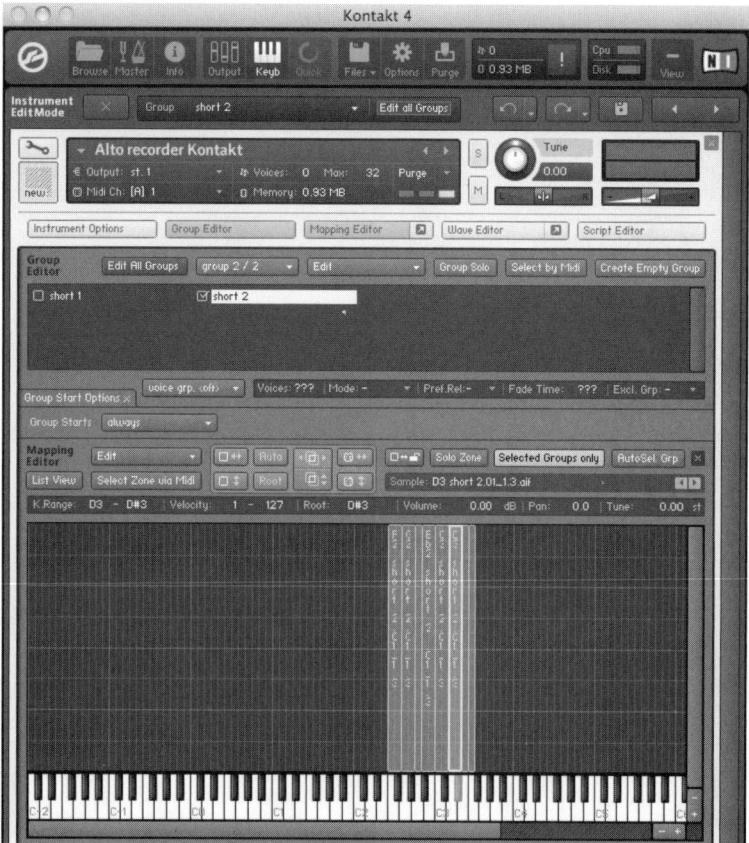

Figure 4.13 Dragging in the short 2 samples.

Figure 4.14 Short 1 Group Start Options.

Figure 4.15 Cycle round robin.

Select "cycle round robin" (Figure 4.15).

The short 1 samples will occupy the first position in the chain (Figure 4.16).

Do the same for the short 2 Group, but set it for the second position in the chain (Figure 4.17).

Done. Now you'll see the Group holding the current note highlighted in yellow (short 1 in the following figure) when you play repeated notes. You'll also see a little red horizontal line superimposed over the Zone border that's tracking the note and velocity of your playing (Figure 4.18).

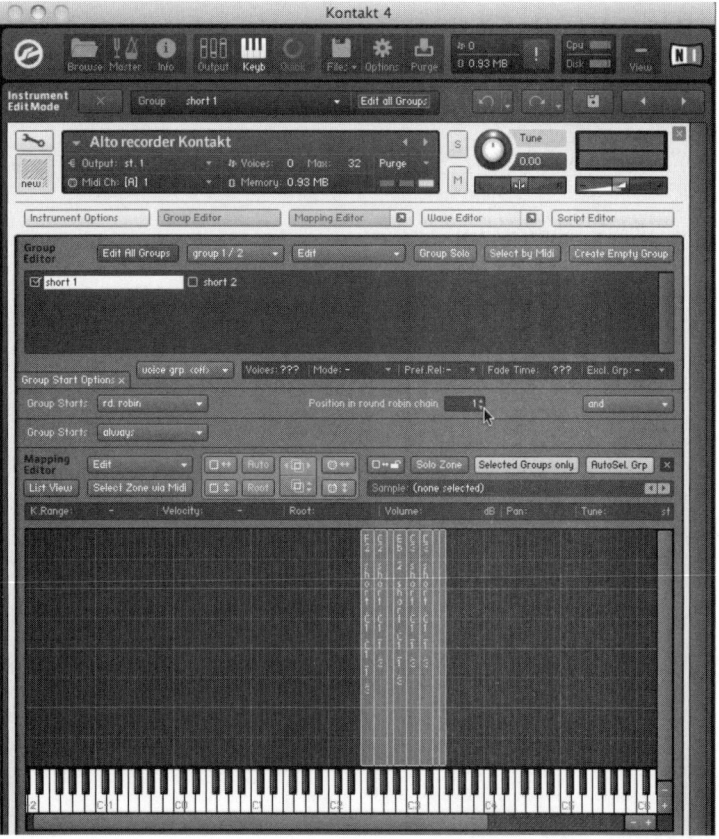

Figure 4.16 Setting the position in the round-robin chain.

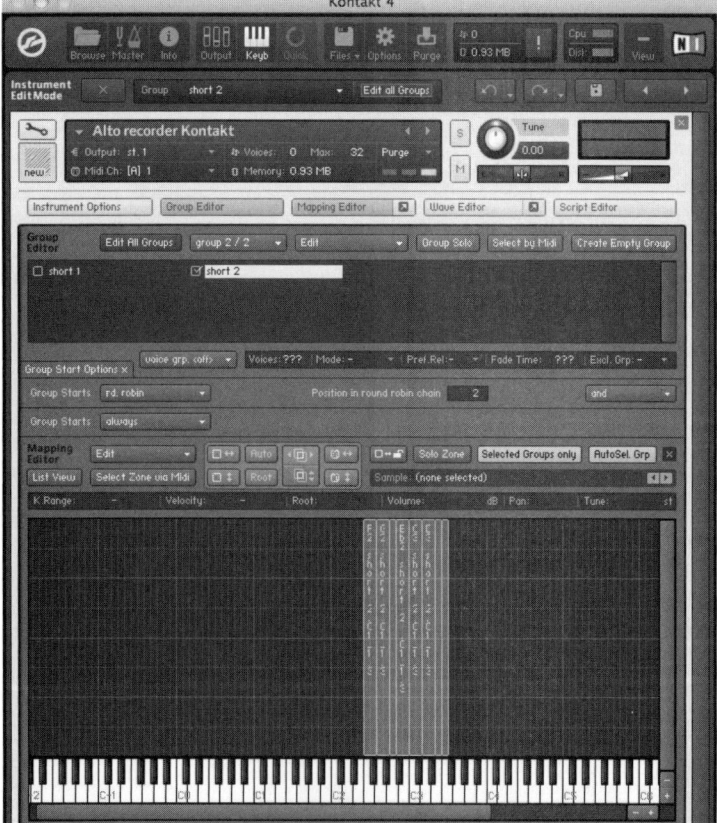

Figure 4.17 The second position in the chain.

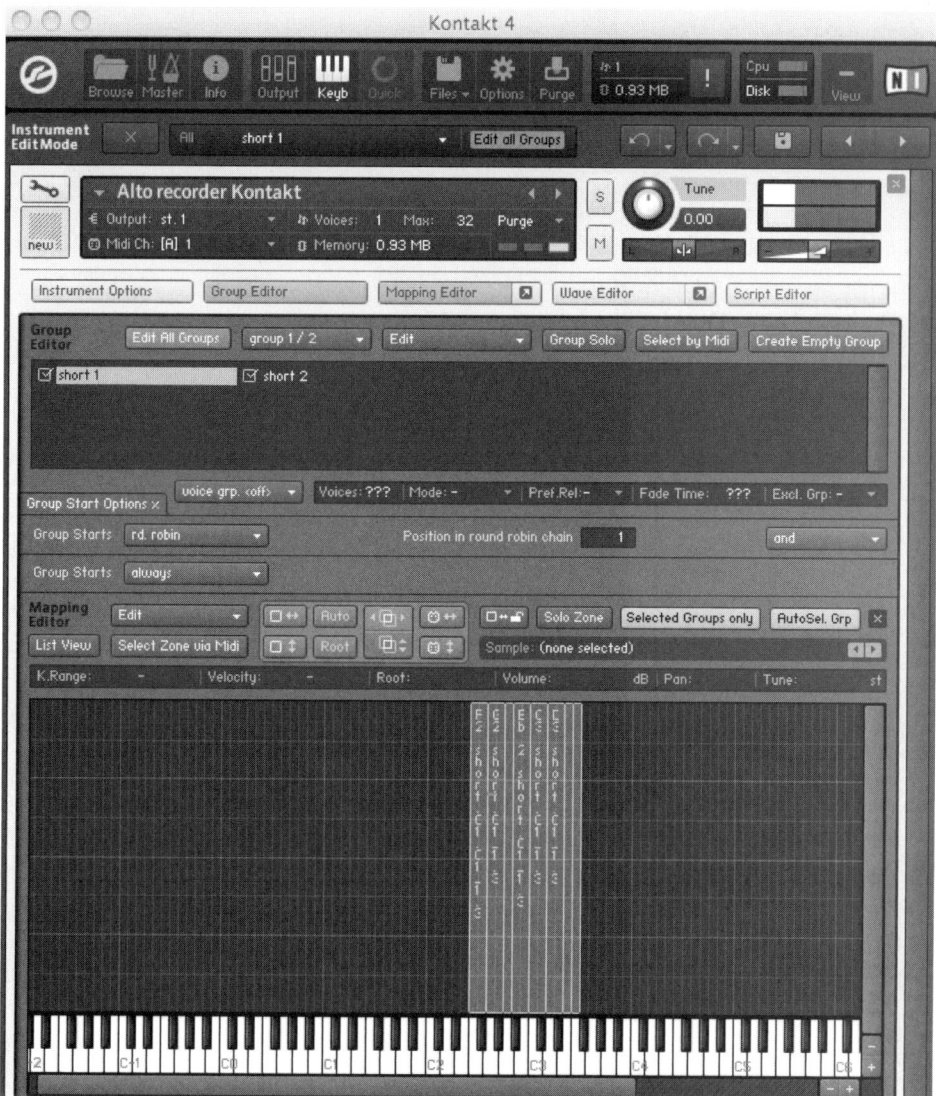

Figure 4.18 Yellow indication of the Group.

This works better with more than two samples, because the ear will notice it less (play the B♭ and you'll hear this very clearly). With three or more alternate takes, you may want to try "cycle random" instead of "cycle round robin" as the Group Start option. Actually, random cycling doesn't sound bad with just the two takes in this example.

Stage 3: Bringing in the Staccato Notes and Setting Velocity Ranges

Now we're going to create two new Groups for the stacc 1 and 2 samples, bring them in, and set them up to round-robin just as before (Figure 4.19).

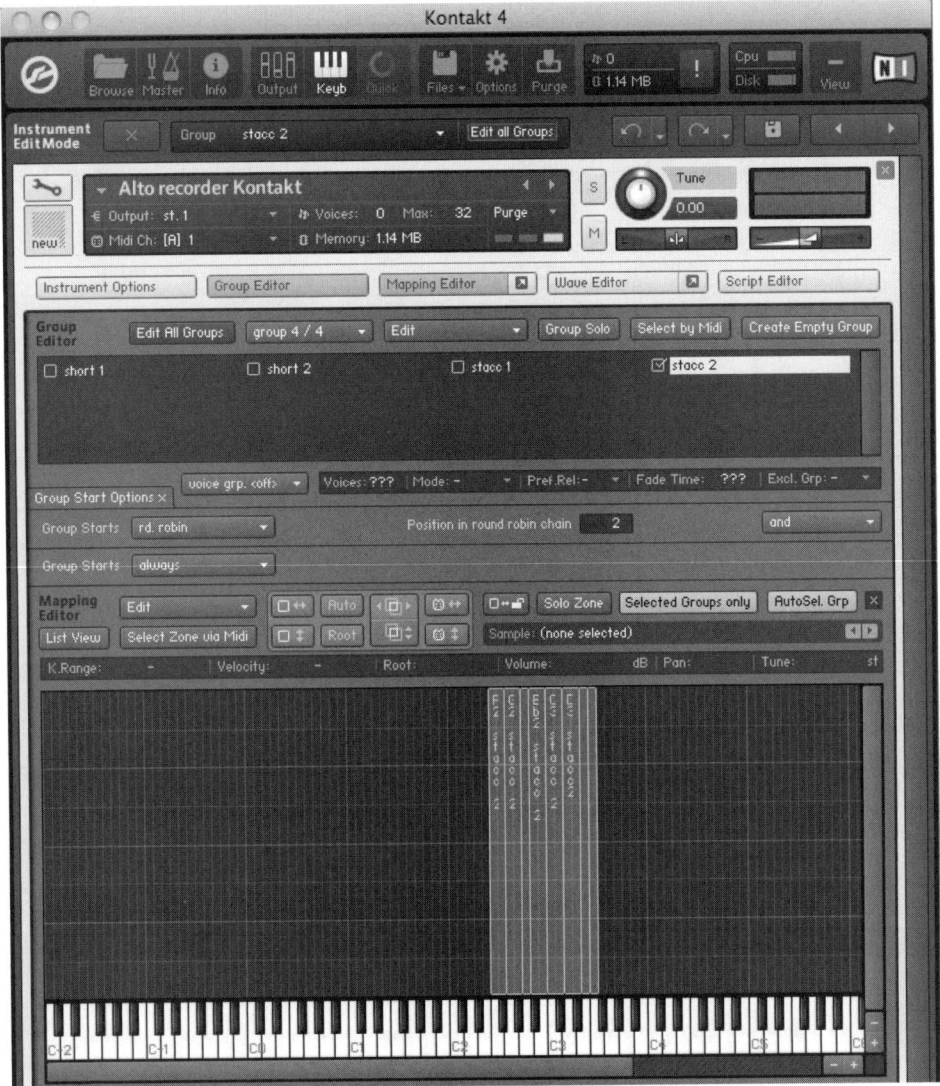

Figure 4.19 The staccato samples dragged in and set to round-robin.

You may want to tweak these settings for your MIDI keyboard and playing style, but let's set the staccs to trigger at velocities below 80 and the shorts at velocities from 81 and higher. Setting the velocity ranges for a Group is as easy as selecting its samples and typing in the numbers.

Select the first stacc 1 Group and enter **80** as its maximum velocity (Figure 4.20).

Repeat for stacc 2. You'll see that as soon as you hit the Enter key, the light blue sample container graphic shortens to indicate the velocity range (Figure 4.21).

Now set the short 1s and 2s to trigger from 81–127 (Figure 4.22).

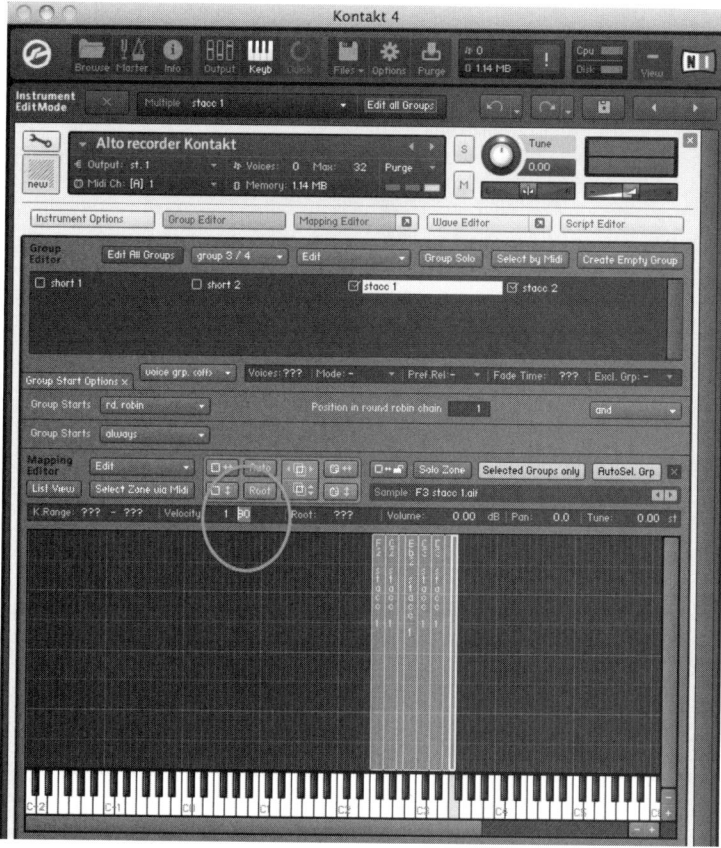

Figure 4.20 Max velocity 80.

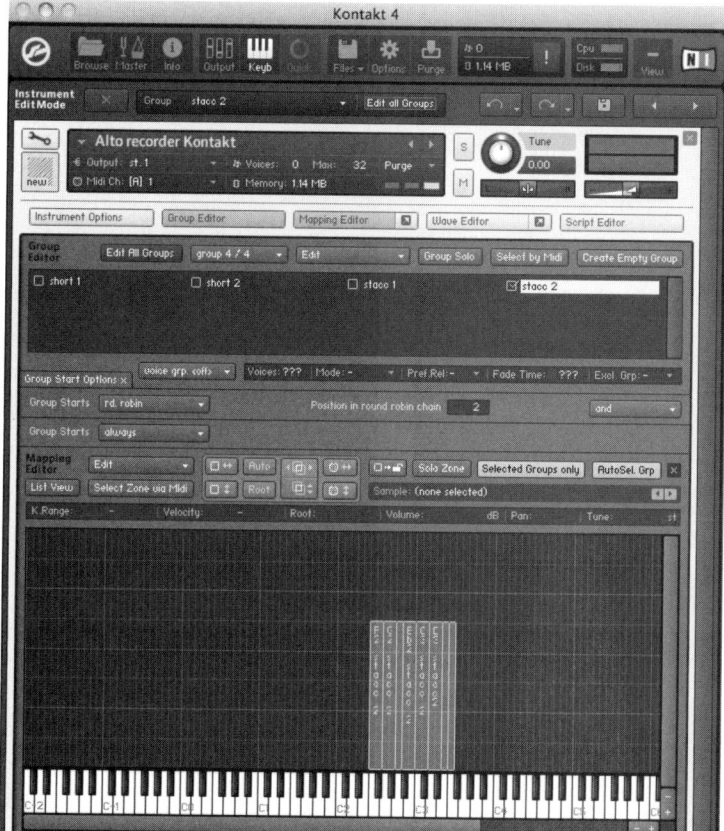

Figure 4.21 The velocity bar shows the range graphically.

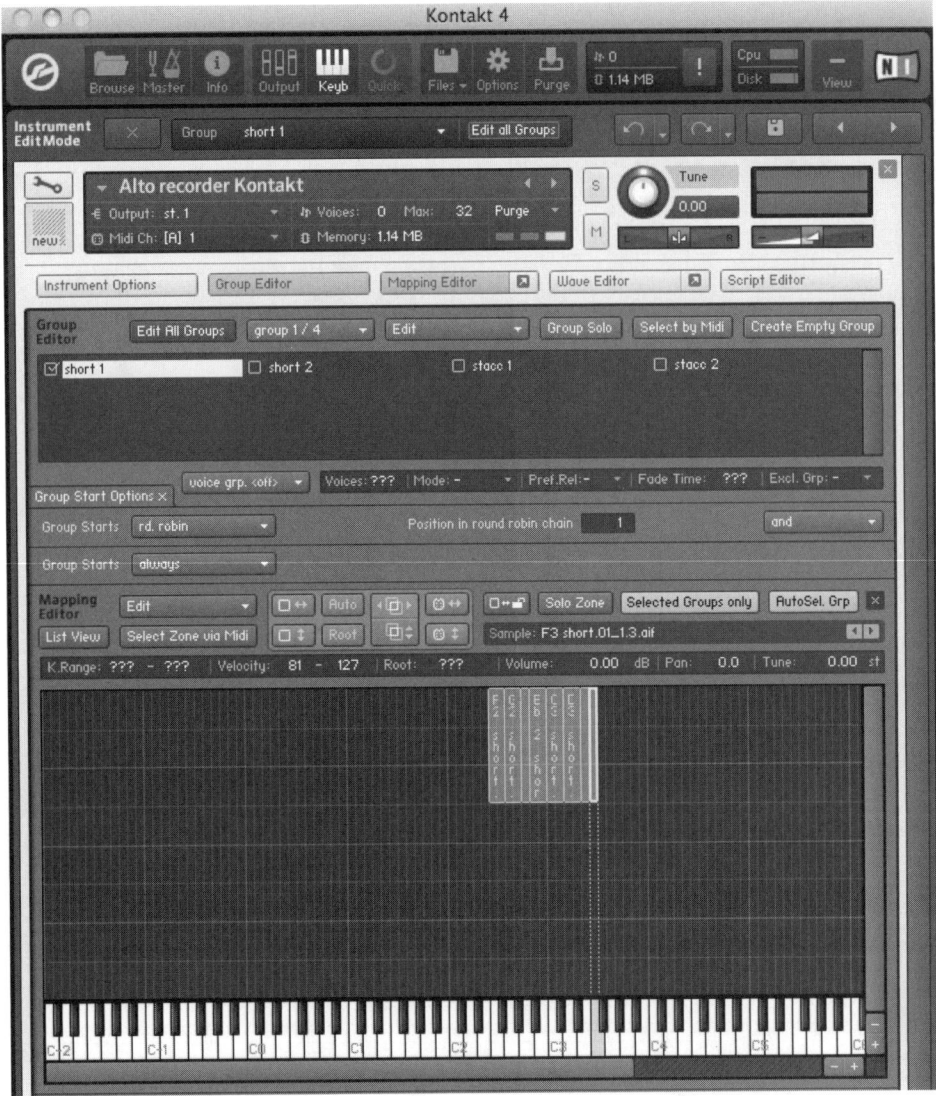

Figure 4.22 The short notes trigger from 81 to 127.

And you're done.

Stage 4: Adding the Long Notes

Adding the two long note articulations is more of the same procedure, only the Group Start parameters will be different. What we're going to do is have the non-vibrato notes trigger only when the mod wheel is on less than half way (1–64) and the notes with vibrato sound when it's over half way (65–27); when the mod wheel is off (0), then the round-robin staccato and short notes will trigger as before.

Create new Groups called "long no vib" and "long vib (Figure 4.23)."

Drag in the two sets of samples (Figure 4.24).

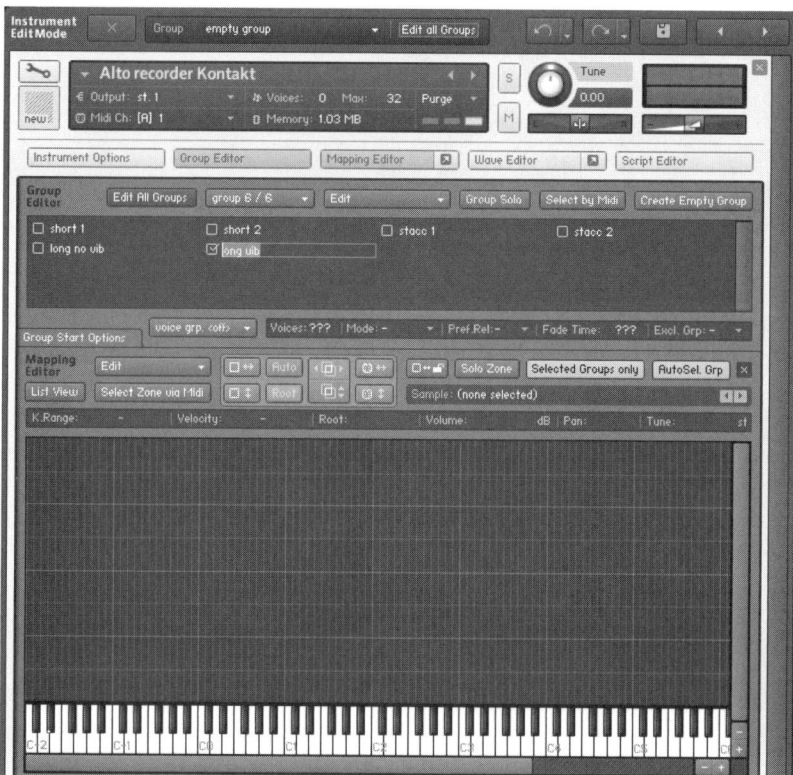

Figure 4.23 New Groups for the long notes.

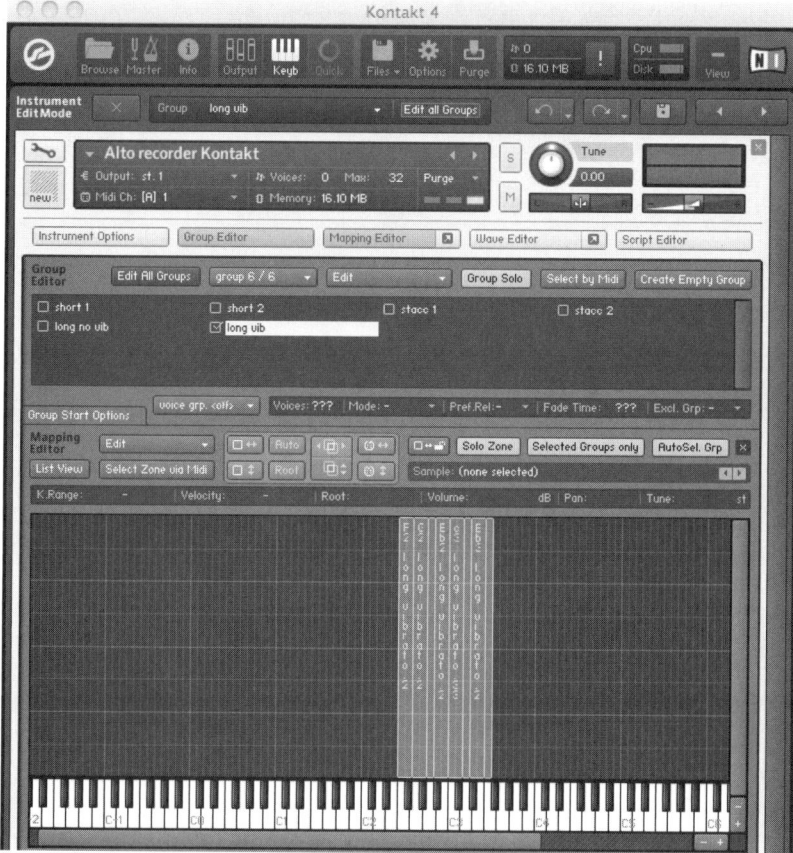

Figure 4.24 The long notes are in.

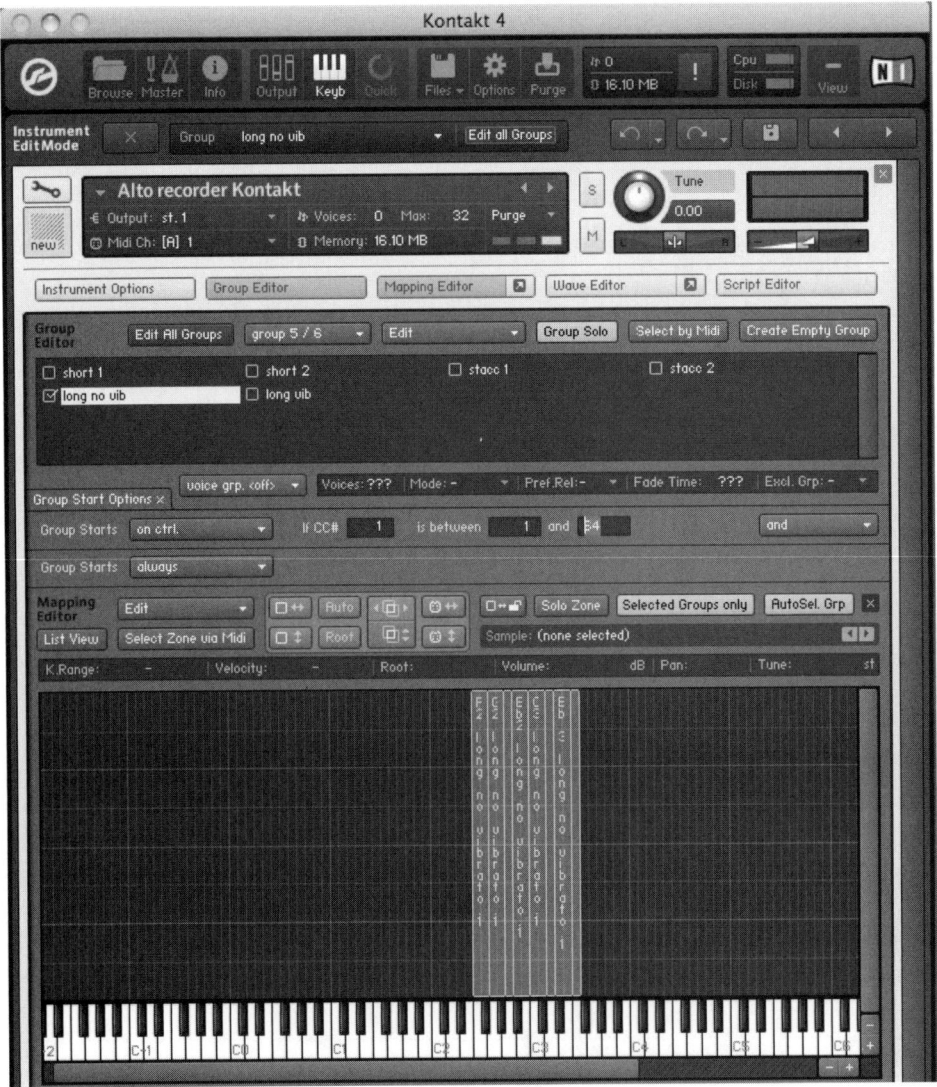

Figure 4.25 The long notes sound when the mod wheel is 65 and over.

Now we have to set the long no vibs to start when the mod wheel (MIDI CC#1) is between 1 and 64 and the long vibs start when it's between 65 and 127. This is just a different Group Start parameter (Figures 4.25 and 4.26).

Try playing the alto recorder program with the mod wheel all the way off. You'll hear the short notes behaving just as before, with the stacc notes at low velocities and the short notes at high ones.

Now move the mod wheel up somewhere below halfway. The long no vib sounds. Move the mod wheel over half way, and the long vib sounds, except that the short notes are also sounding at the same time. We need an additional Group Start setting.

Set up a second Group Start condition: Group Start on ctrl. CC# 1 is between 0 and 0. This has to be done for each of the four Groups—stacc 1, stacc 2, short 1, and short 2 (Figures 4.27, 4.28, 4.29).

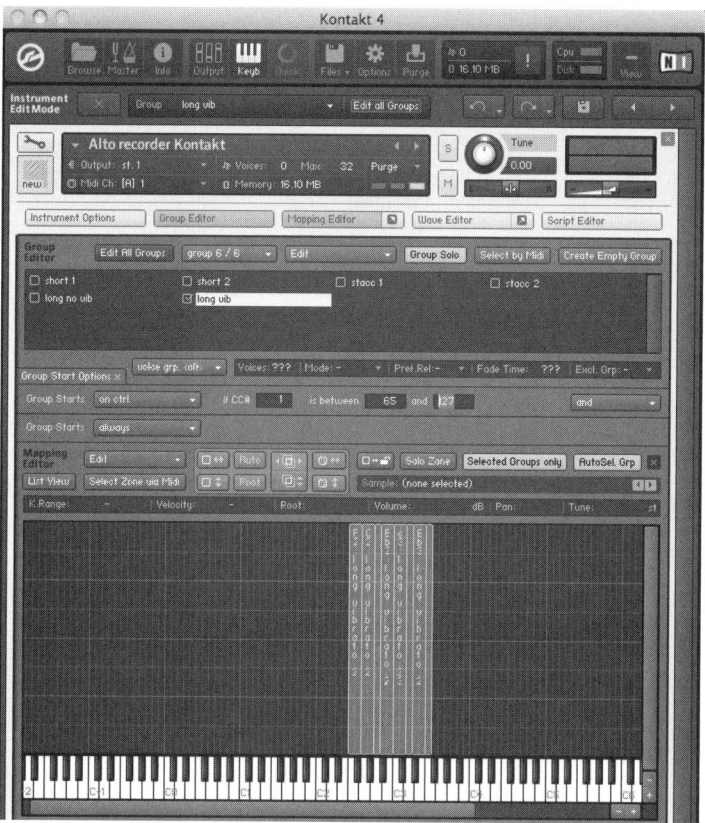

Figure 4.26 The long notes mod wheel setting.

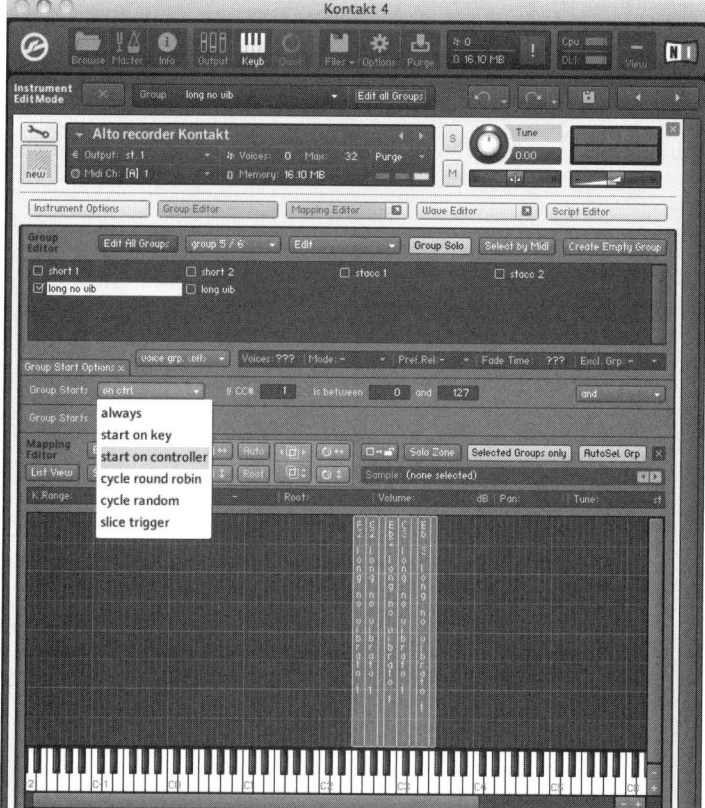

Figure 4.27 Group Starts condition: the mod wheel is off.

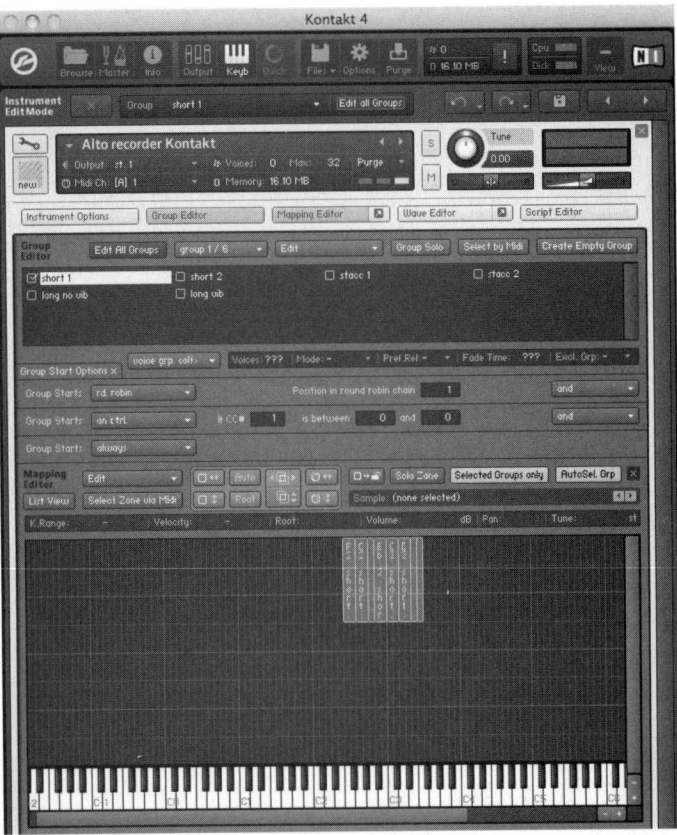

Figure 4.28 Other Groups start only when the mod wheel is off.

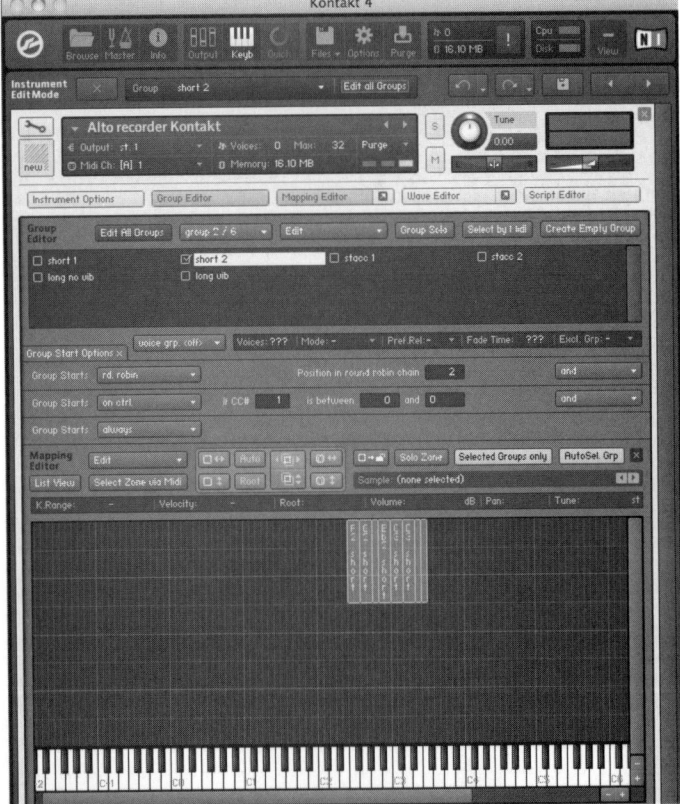

Figure 4.29 Completed alto recorder program.

And now the program works correctly.

5 Building Programs in the Propellerhead Reason (and Record) NN-XT Advanced Sampler

Propellerhead Reason is a popular, highly efficient, self-contained music production program that includes a variety of synthesizers and effects processors, presented as virtual hardware devices. It's been around for over a decade, yet it's still totally current. Recently Propellerhead merged its features with the audio recording/production ones in Record, which makes complete sense. However, the name "Reason" approaches generic status in the same way that "auto-tuning" means vocal pitch correction and "to Pro Tools" means to edit audio.

Among Reason's instruments are two "hardware" samplers you can put in its rack: the very simple NN19 Digital Sampler and the slightly fuller-featured NN-XT Advanced Sampler, which we'll take a look at here. (If you know the NN-XT, then you know the NN19.)

To be blunt, the NN-XT Advanced Sampler is actually not advanced by modern standards. It loads samples into memory rather than streaming them, and its collection of features is limited to just the essential ones. But then none of Reason's devices is intended to be the last word in its category; the program is designed to provide as direct a path as possible to making music, while putting a large quantity of interesting sounds within immediate reach. And the NN-XT follows that approach—it's unintimidating and relatively quick to use, as long as you're dealing with relatively small numbers of samples like we are here.

What NN-XT does is allow you to set up overlapping or crossfaded velocity layers and create round-robin programs with alternating samples to avoid the machine gun effect. What it doesn't allow you to do is select layers or articulations with a MIDI CC (control change). So instead of using the mod wheel to change from the two short to the two long alto recorder articulations in our demonstration samples, we'll set up separate programs for each.

There's another point to be made with carefully chosen words: Reason is more of an electronic music program than a high-fidelity audiophile one. We're just going through these exercises to learn the program, but in reality it's probably not the first choice for pure acoustic alto recorder programs like we're creating.

Yet Reason is a great program that doesn't need to apologize for its limitations, which is why so many professional users have it on their hard drives. It's not necessary to use it as a self-contained program; you can trigger it from and stream its output into your main sequencer using the built-in ReWire protocol, taking advantage of its devices as another tool in your arsenal.

Stage 1: A Basic Playable Instrument

First we're going to build an alto recorder instrument with just the Long No Vibrato samples. In Stage two we'll add the Vibrato samples and assign the two articulations to separate velocity ranges, and then in Stage three we'll set up a two-layer round-robin program for the short articulations.

Create a new Song and save it (Figure 5.1).

Figure 5.1   Create a new Song.

Drag an NN-XT Advanced Sampler onto the rack (or set one up from the Create menu) as shown in Figure 5.2.

Figure 5.2 Create an NN-XT Advanced Sampler.

It will connect to the mixer automatically, and if you press the Tab key the rack will spin around and you can see the patch cables move! Then Tab to spin it around to the front again (Figure 5.3).

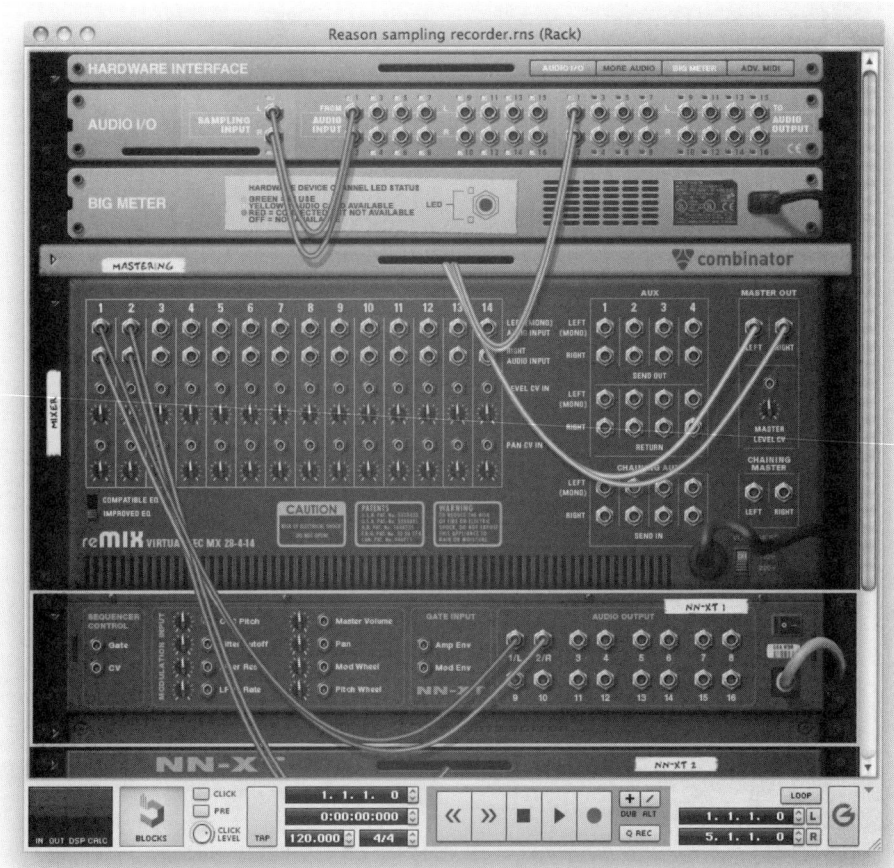

Figure 5.3 It's automatically patched in.

Since the NN-XT comes loaded with a piano that we don't want, right-click or Control-click to bring up the contextual menu and initialize the Patch (Figure 5.4).

Save the Patch (Figure 5.5).

You'll probably want to organize the Reason screen; here we've gone to the Windows menu, detached the sequencer window, and put it on the dock (if this were an MS Windows machine, it would be the task bar). Then click on the Remote Editor triangle to get under the NN-XT's hood (Figure 5.6).

Figure 5.4   Initialize the Patch.

Figure 5.5   Don't forget to save!

Figure 5.6 Detach the sequencer for convenience.

You must open the samples from the dialog box, as shown; unlike other samplers, you don't just drag samples in from the desktop. But you can select them all, and by the way Reason lets you audition samples from this dialog (Figures 5.7 and 5.8).

Figure 5.7 Opening the samples from the dialog.

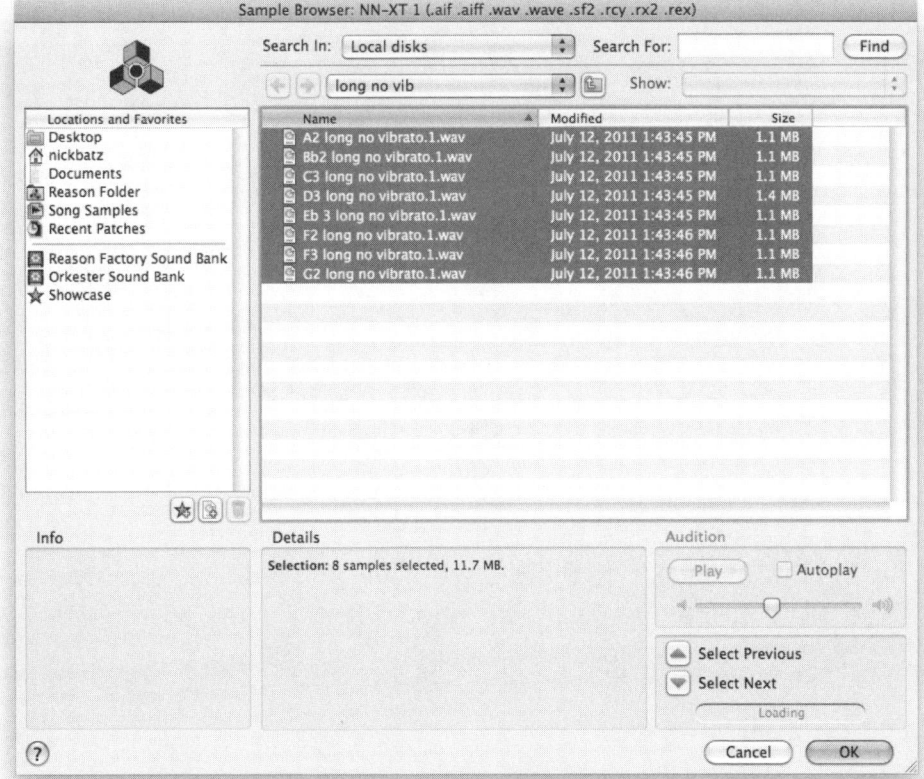

Figure 5.8 Loading the samples.

The samples will be layered on top of one another, all of them stretched across five octaves.

It can be a nuisance hearing all eight (in this case) samples at once when you play any key while you're creating the program, so click on the Solo Sample button. In this case the F2 Long No Vibrato, selected at the left, will be the only one you'll hear when you play within its keyboard range (which we haven't set yet). This is shown in Figure 5.9.

Figure 5.9 Solo for convenience.

Now we're going to set the F2's range by dragging its handles graphically, and then we're going to tell NN-XT that its root note is F2 by turning the onscreen knob shown here (Figure 5.10).

Repeat the same process for the other samples. It will look like Figure 5.11.

We now have a basic playable instrument.

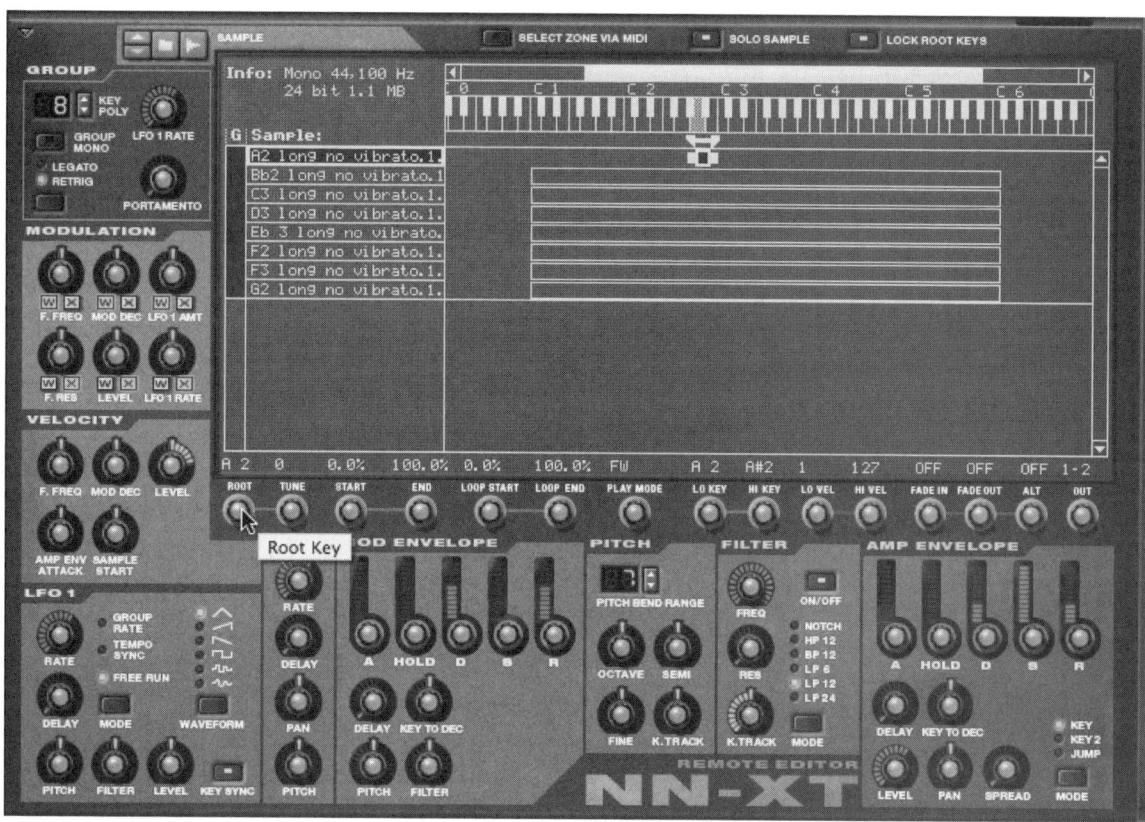

Figure 5.10   Dragging the Zone borders.

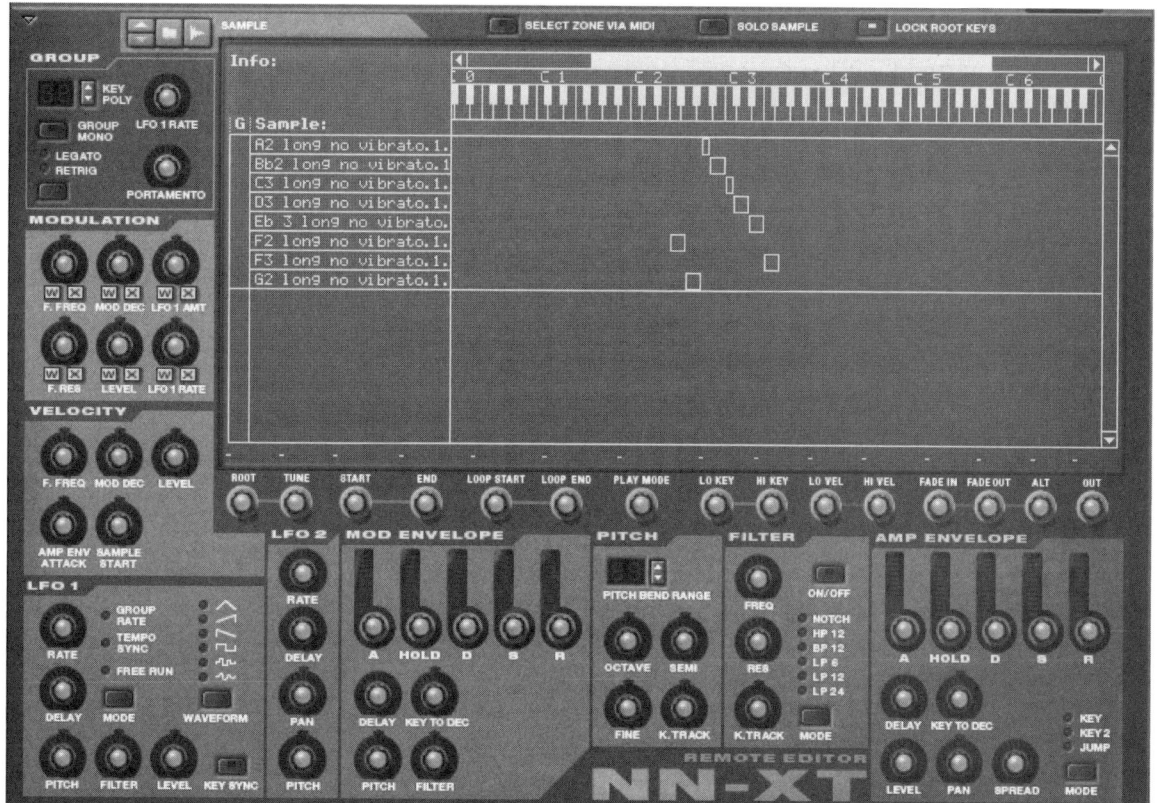

Figure 5.11   The basic instrument.

Stage 2: Bringing in the Vibrato Samples

Now we're going to add the Vibrato samples and make them respond to velocities over 80.

First select all the No Vibrato samples; then go to the Edit window and select Group Selected Zones (Figure 5.12).

Figure 5.12 Group Selected Zones.

As with any sampler, grouping makes it easier to manage related samples all at once.

Now set the No Vibrato samples to trigger at velocities between 0 and 80 with the HI VEL knob (Figure 5.13).

Figure 5.13 Setting the velocity range for the long notes.

Bring in the Long Vibrato samples and group them as before (Figure 5.14).

Set their Zone ranges as before and set their velocity response range from 81 to 127 (Figure 5.15).

Figure 5.14 Bringing in the Long Vibratos.

The one thing we haven't done is set the root note for the Vibrato samples, and there's a reason: to point out that while it's worth a try, Reason's Set Root Notes from Pitch Detection feature may not have the result you want. In this case, it thinks everything is an octave higher than we want, so we're back to doing it manually (Figure 5.16).

And here's the completed program (Figure 5.17).

Note that velocity ranges can overlap, so for example you could set the Long No Vibratos to trigger from 0 to 100 and the Long Vibratos from 65 to 127. The Fade In and Fade Out knobs (to the right of the velocity knobs) let you set the balance between the two in the crossover range. You can also blur the velocity boundaries with the Fade knob even if the ranges don't overlap. Just for fun, try it, and you'll see that it's actually not what we want to do here.

Figure 5.15 Set the velocity range from 81–127.

Figure 5.16 Automatic pitch detection almost works.

Figure 5.17 The completed long notes program.

Stage 3: Creating a Round-Robin Staccato/Short Notes Program

Now let's create a short notes program with the staccato samples at low velocities and short notes at higher ones, and let's have the NN-XT alternate between the two sets of samples in each articulation automatically. The process is more of what we've just done, except that you turn on the Alt button. But there are a couple of quirks to be aware of.

Create an NN-XT, right-click or Control-click to bring up the context menu, initialize the patch to get rid of the default piano samples, and import the short 1 samples (Figure 5.18).

Set each short 1's root note to the correct pitch and map it to the correct keyboard Zone. Save the program (Figure 5.19).

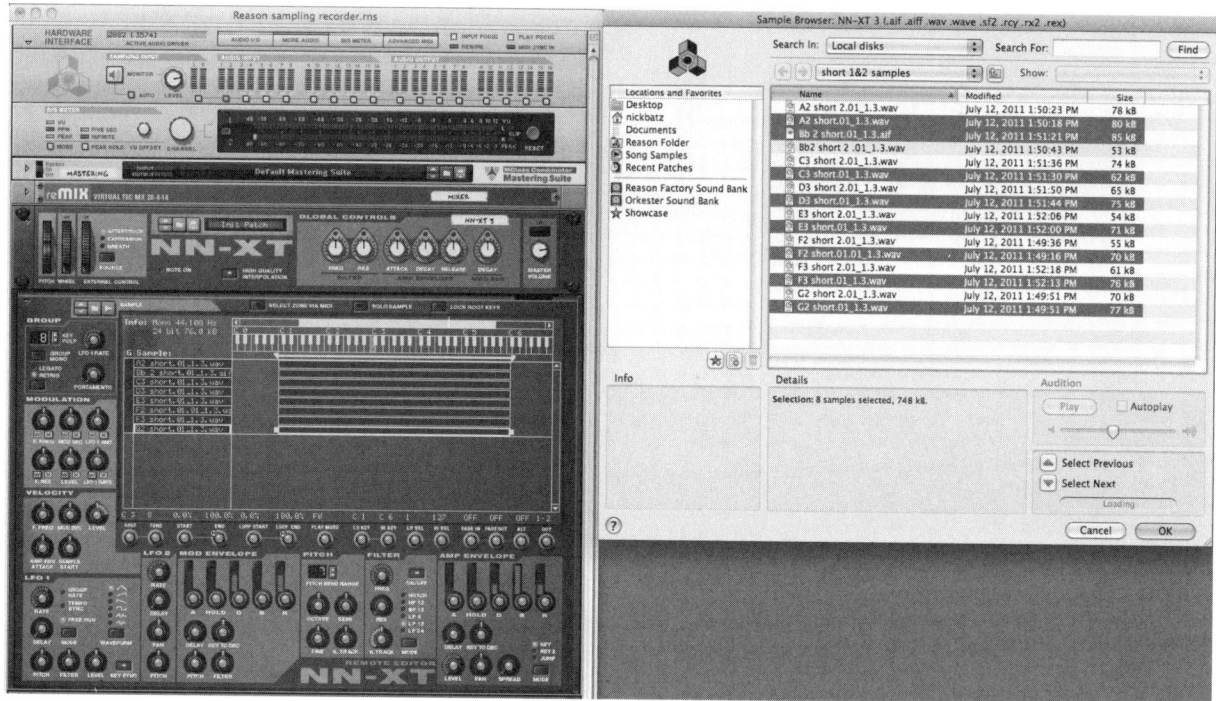

Figure 5.18 Initialize the Patch and import the short 1s.

Figure 5.19 Short 1s mapped.

Do not group the samples yet, because NN-XT can sometimes get confused a couple of steps hence.

Now bring in the short 2 samples (Figure 5.20).

Figure 5.20 Bring in the short 2 samples.

Set their root notes and Zones (Figure 5.21).

You'll hear two recorders play each note in unison at this point. We want them to alternate between each one.

Select each pair of samples (e.g., F3 short 1 and F3 short 2), and turn the Alt knob to On. Repeat for each of the eight pairs (Figure 5.22).

Figure 5.21 The short 2 samples mapped.

You should now hear alternating short notes. If it's hard to hear, play the B♭2 sample, and it should be obvious what's happening.

Note that NN-XT alternates between two or more Zones, not two or more Groups. Also note that the Zones have to be the same. You can't alternate between, say, two C3s and have one cover a minor third and the other a half step. (If you needed to do that—and it's not uncommon or even a problem for there to be a duff note here or there in a library—then you'd simply make copies of the stretched note and use each one over a shorter range.)

Figure 5.22 Alternating Zones.

Anyway, now you can create a Group of the short 1 & 2 samples.

Time to bring in the stacc 1s and stacc 2s (Figure 5.23).

Set their root notes and Zones in the familiar way (Figure 5.24).

Now if you play a note repeatedly, you'll hear three layers (both staccs plus the currently alternating short note 1 or 2). This is a useable sound on its own. But we'll continue.

Figure 5.23 Add the staccatos.

Select each pair of samples, pair by pair, and turn the Alt knob on for each one (Figure 5.25).

All that's left is to set the velocity ranges. Select all the stacc 1 & 2 samples and set their range from 0 to 80 (Figure 5.26).

Select all the short 1 & 2 samples and set their velocity range from 81 to 127 (Figure 5.27).

And we're done here.

Figure 5.24 Map the staccatos.

Figure 5.25 Layered round-robin is a useful sound.

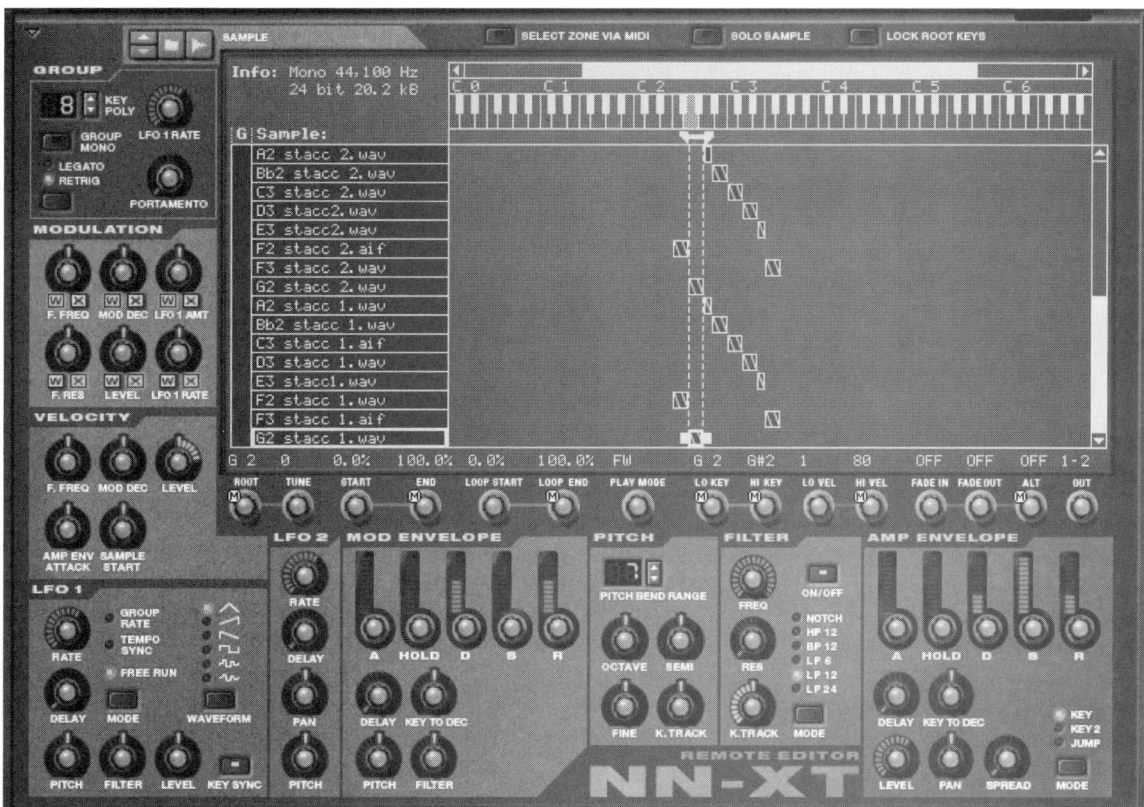

Figure 5.26 Staccato velocity ranges set.

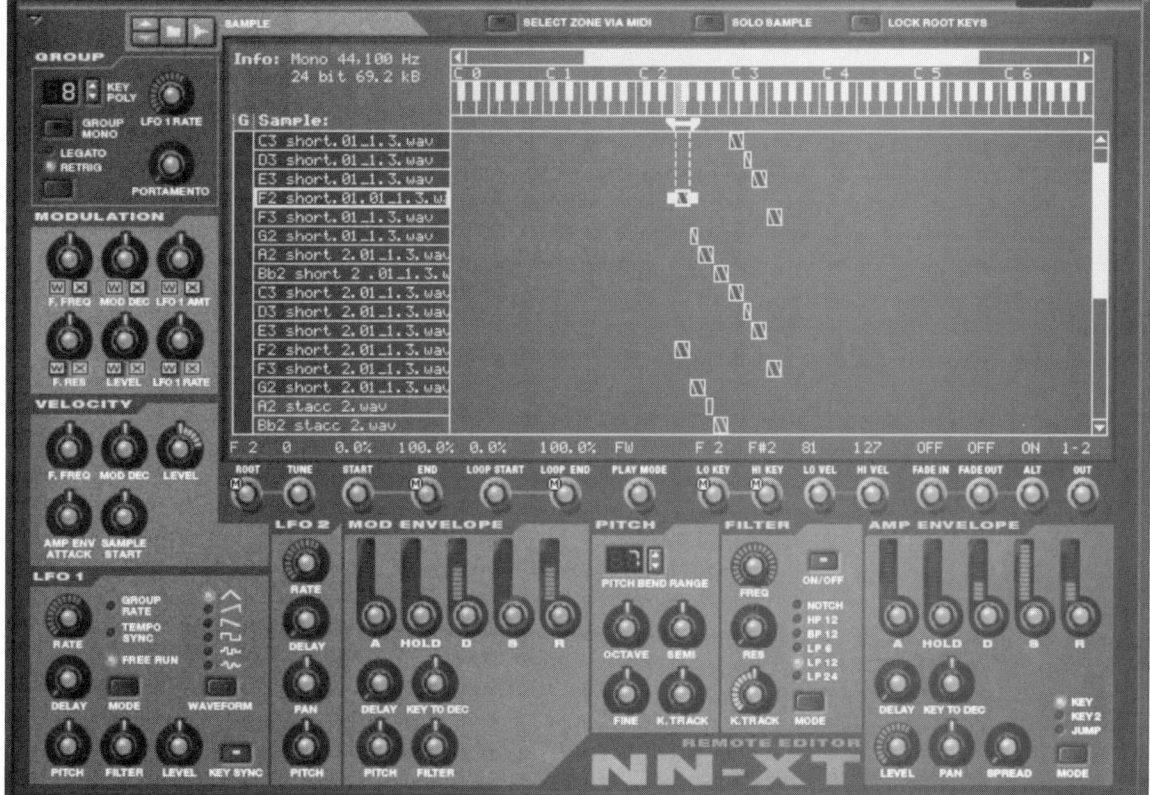

Figure 5.27 Short note velocity ranges set.

6 Building Programs in Avid (Formerly Digidesign) Structure

Structure is an RTAS format instrument, which means it runs exclusively in Pro Tools. It is the newest sampler of any we're covering, and it has all the advanced features you're likely to think of. The only thing Structure doesn't have is the custom scripting language that Kontakt has, but then most of the features you'd need a custom script for are already included (in the form of Parts). If you need a set of samples to trigger only when you're playing fast, for example, that's a built-in feature with bells on it; not only does it not require a custom script, but it's quite straightforward to program.

If there's a downside it's that the RTAS format is inherently less efficient than VST and AU, and it's still 32-bit, so the memory access is limited. As of this writing, however, Avid is in the process of replacing this creaky standard with their new AAX Native plug-in format, and that will almost certainly address these issues. Structure is a very impressive sampler in all other ways.

As with the EX24 and Kontakt, we'll work with a single octave of an alto recorder, having sampled the four most common articulations: very short ("tick" and "ka"), short ("toot"), long notes with vibrato, and long notes without vibrato. These long note articulations can also work for shorter notes, but the "toot" notes are different.

The recorder's dynamic range is very limited (which is why the flute took over back in the day), and the bottom octave can only be played quietly, so we sampled only one dynamic layer. Now, you know how the feel of a groove gets slower when drummers play backbeats on the toms instead of the snare, even though the tempo hasn't changed? Well, recorder players create the illusion of dynamics the same way. You can simulate a louder feel by articulating more heavily, while the very short "ticka tick" notes tend to have a lighter feel than the regular "toot" ones.

Because of that effect, it makes sense to use velocity to switch between the two. We're also going to set up two variations of each short note to alternate automatically, a controlled randomizing technique that disguises the fact that we're using samples.

Then as with the EXS24 and Kontakt, we'll create a performance program with the long notes triggering instead of the short notes when the mod wheel is on. Also, the vibrato layer will sound when the mod wheel is over half way, and the non-vib when it's below.

After that, we'll create a variation: switching articulations using playing speed.

Stage 1: A Basic Playable Instrument

As in the other tutorials, let's start by building a basic playable program and then build upon that. Please fetch the Long No Vibrato samples; we're going to start by building a basic program.

First, the basics.

Create a new 24-bit Session in Pro Tools (Figures 6.1 and 6.2).

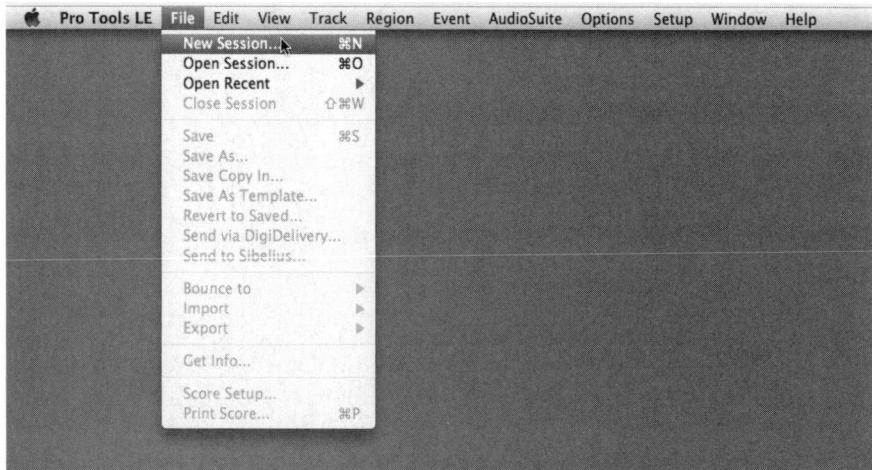

Figure 6.1 Create a new Session.

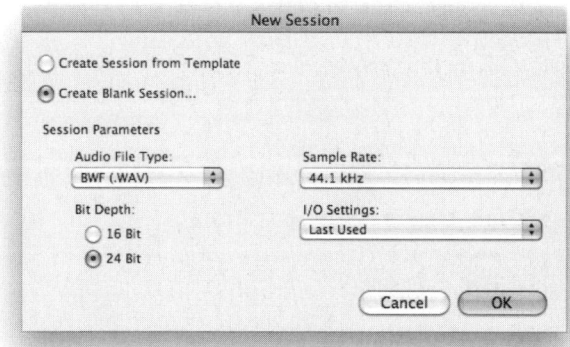

Figure 6.2 Appropriate Session settings.

Create a stereo Instrument track (Figure 6.3).

Insert a Structure instrument as shown in Figure 6.4 (Pro Tools 8, before Digidesign became Avid, is shown).

Figure 6.3 New stereo Instrument track.

Figure 6.4 Insert a Structure sampler.

Structure opens with a default sine wave program just so it makes a noise when you play it. We don't need this Patch, and while it appears in some of the subsequent figures, this is as good a time as any to get rid of it (Figure 6.5).

Now we're ready to build the program.

Figure 6.5 Remove the default sine wave program.

Drag the Long No Vibrato samples in as shown, and let Structure create a new Part for them (Figures 6.6 and 6.7).

"Part" is Structure's name for a multisampled group of samples, and also for some other types of objects (effects, MIDI processing modules, and so on).

It should look like Figure 6.8.

Click the Edit button (Figures 6.9 and 6.10).

You'll probably find it easier to work if you zoom in (Figure 6.11).

Drag each sample to its root key. Here the G2 sample has been dragged over the G2 key (Figure 6.12).

Figure 6.6 Drag in the Long No Vibrato samples.

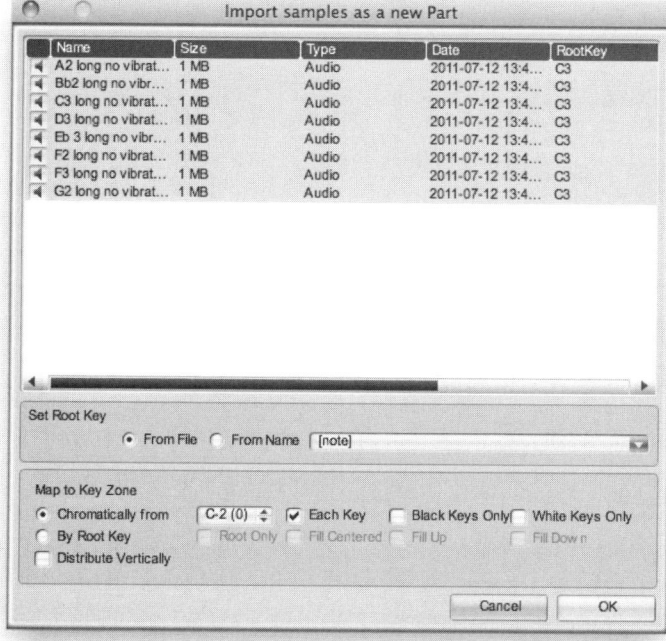

Figure 6.7 Import samples as a new Part.

Figure 6.8 After importing.

Figure 6.9 Click the Edit button.

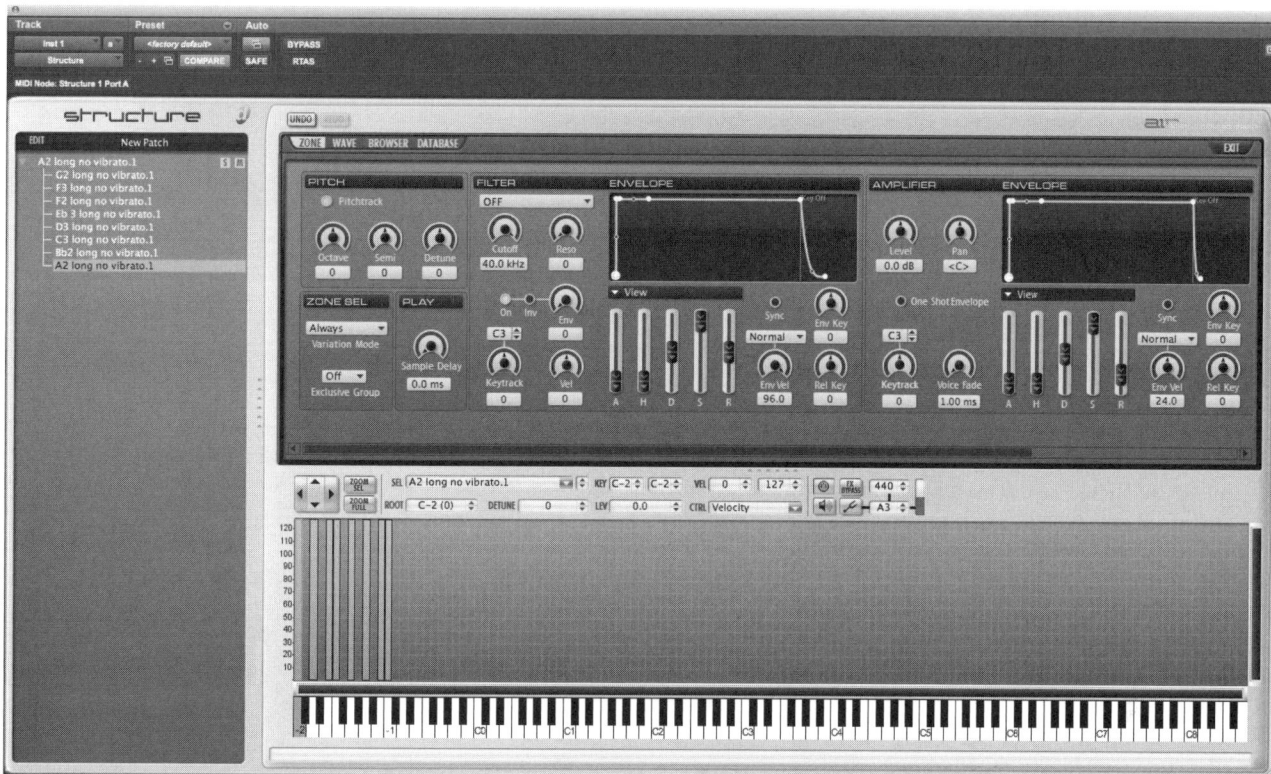

Figure 6.10 Edit mode.

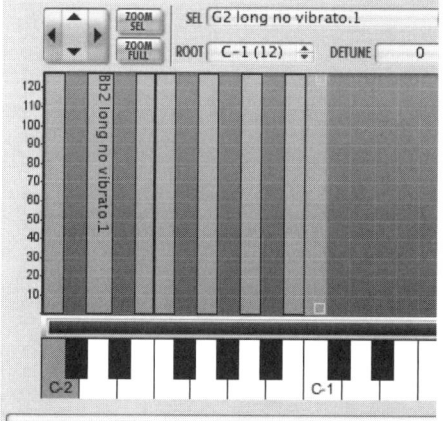

Figure 6.11 Zoom in.

When all eight samples have been moved, it should look like Figure 6.13.

Stretch each sample to cover the full range over which it's going to play. That is, stretch the samples so they're pitched up when you play notes with no recorded sample.

It should look like Figure 6.14.

Note that we could just as easily have stretched the zones to cover the notes below rather than above the recordings. With the recorder, the difference in sound quality between pitch-shifting up or down a half step is insignificant at best, but with more complicated sounds they might not sound the same; it's important to experiment.

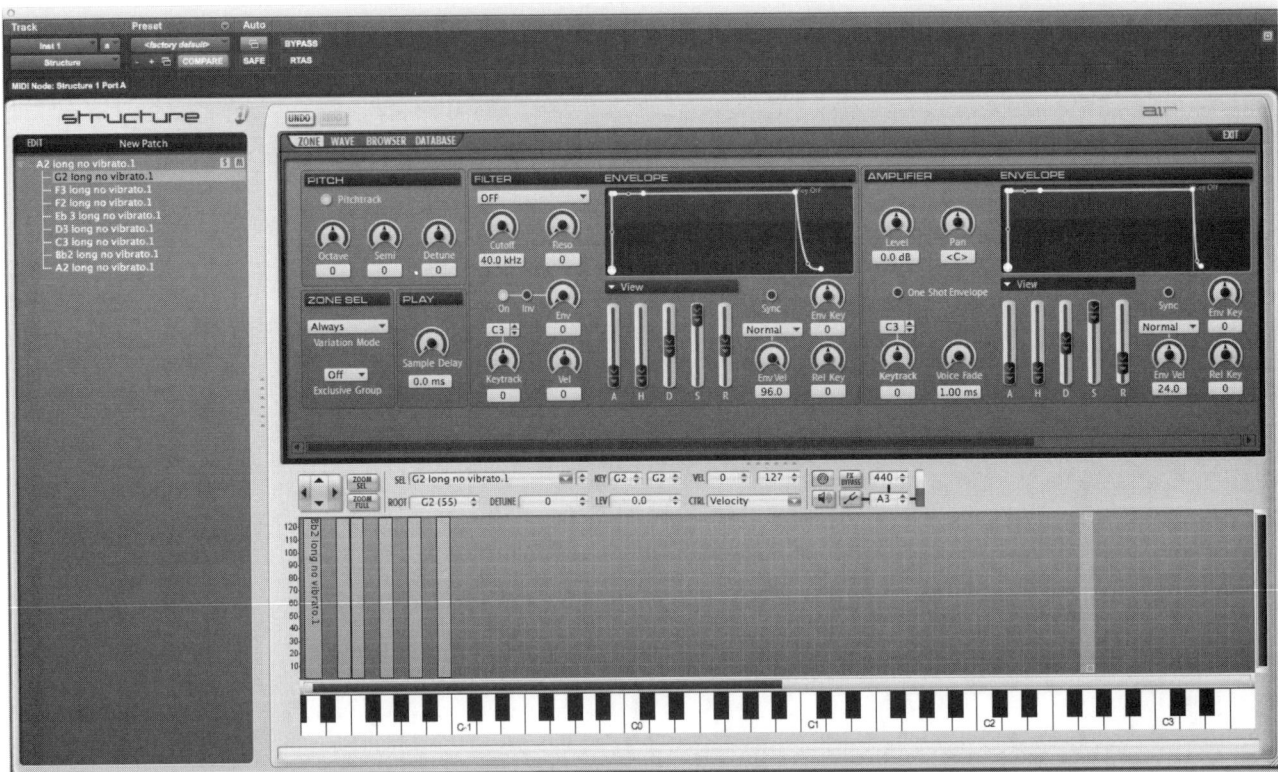

Figure 6.12 Drag the samples in.

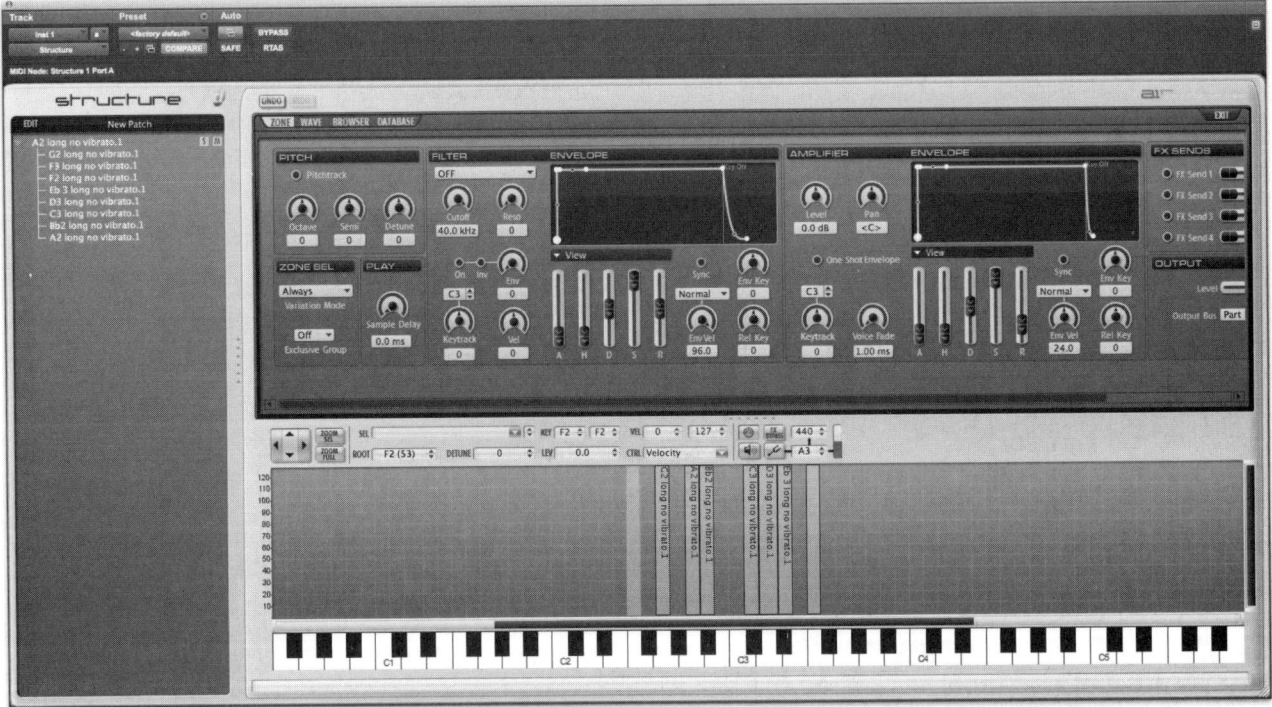

Figure 6.13 The samples dragged in.

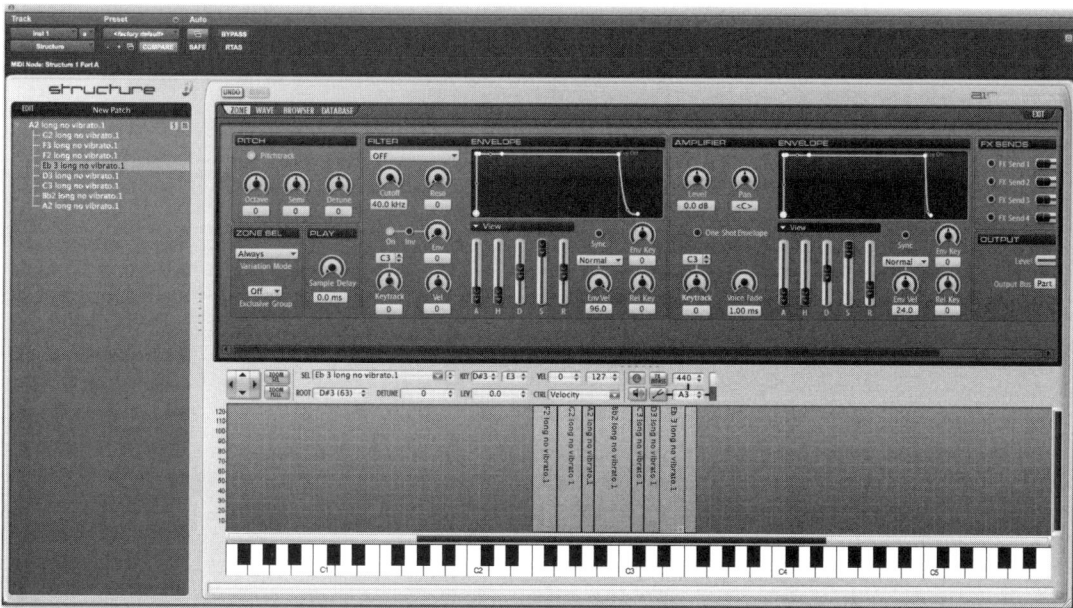

Figure 6.14 Stretch the samples across its range.

Save the Part as "Alto recorder long no vibrato" (Figures 6.15 and 6.16).

And now we have a playable program.

Figure 6.15 Save the Part.

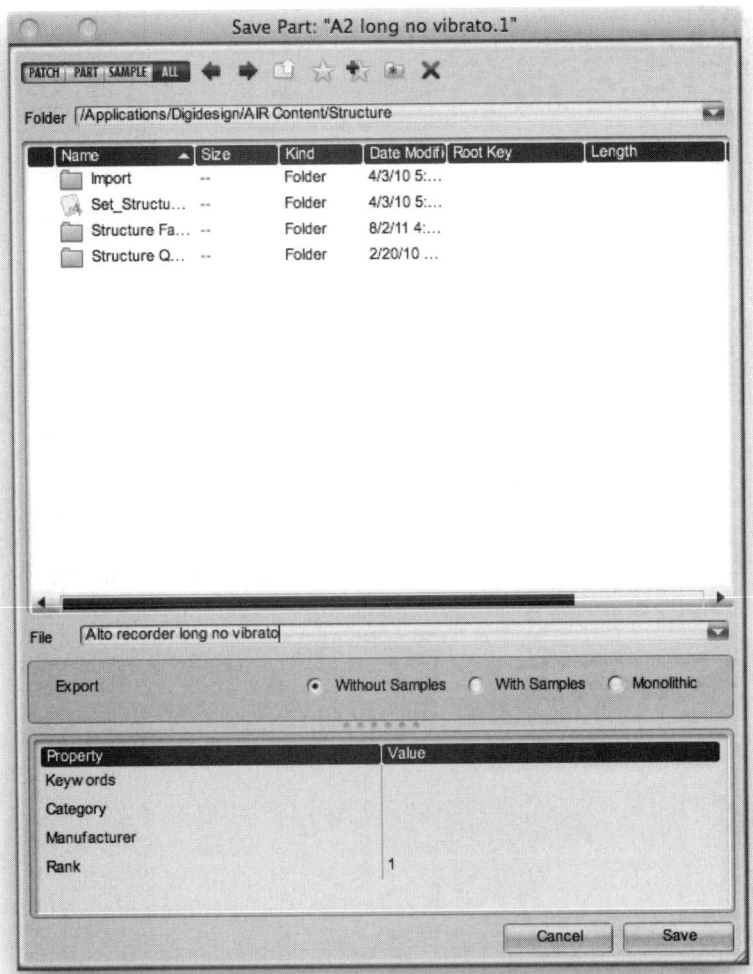

Figure 6.16 A basic playable program.

Stage 2: The Vibrato Samples

Now let's add the vibrato samples to our Patch and program them to play only when the mod wheel is over halfway on, and the non-vibrato samples to play only when the mod wheel is on but less than half way. (Later we'll set up the short note articulations to play only when the mod wheel is all the way off.)

The first steps are identical to what we've just done.

Drag in the Long Vibrato samples as a new Part (Figures 6.17 and 6.18).

Map the Long Vibrato samples to the appropriate keyboard Zones and stretch the Zones to cover all notes as before (Figure 6.19).

Figure 6.17 Drag in the Long Vibrato samples.

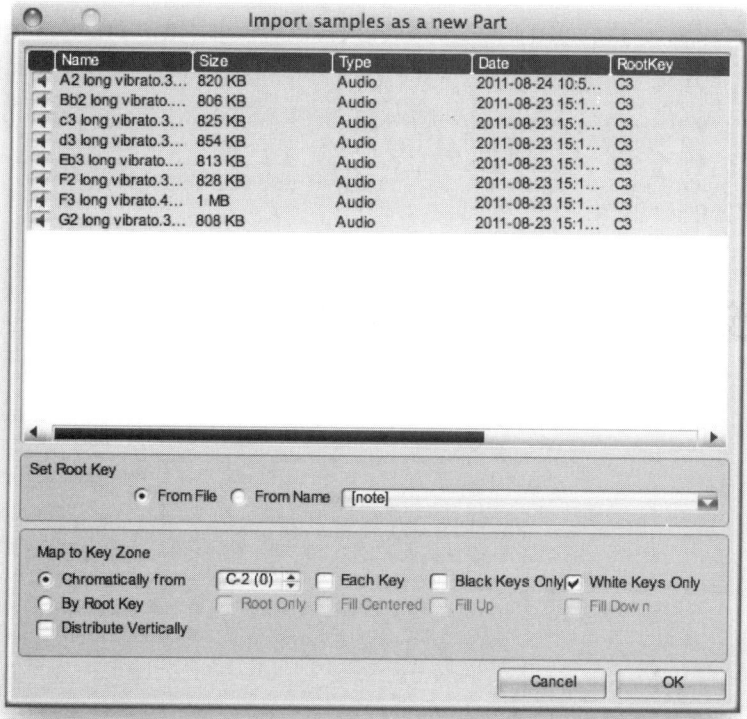

Figure 6.18 A new Part is created.

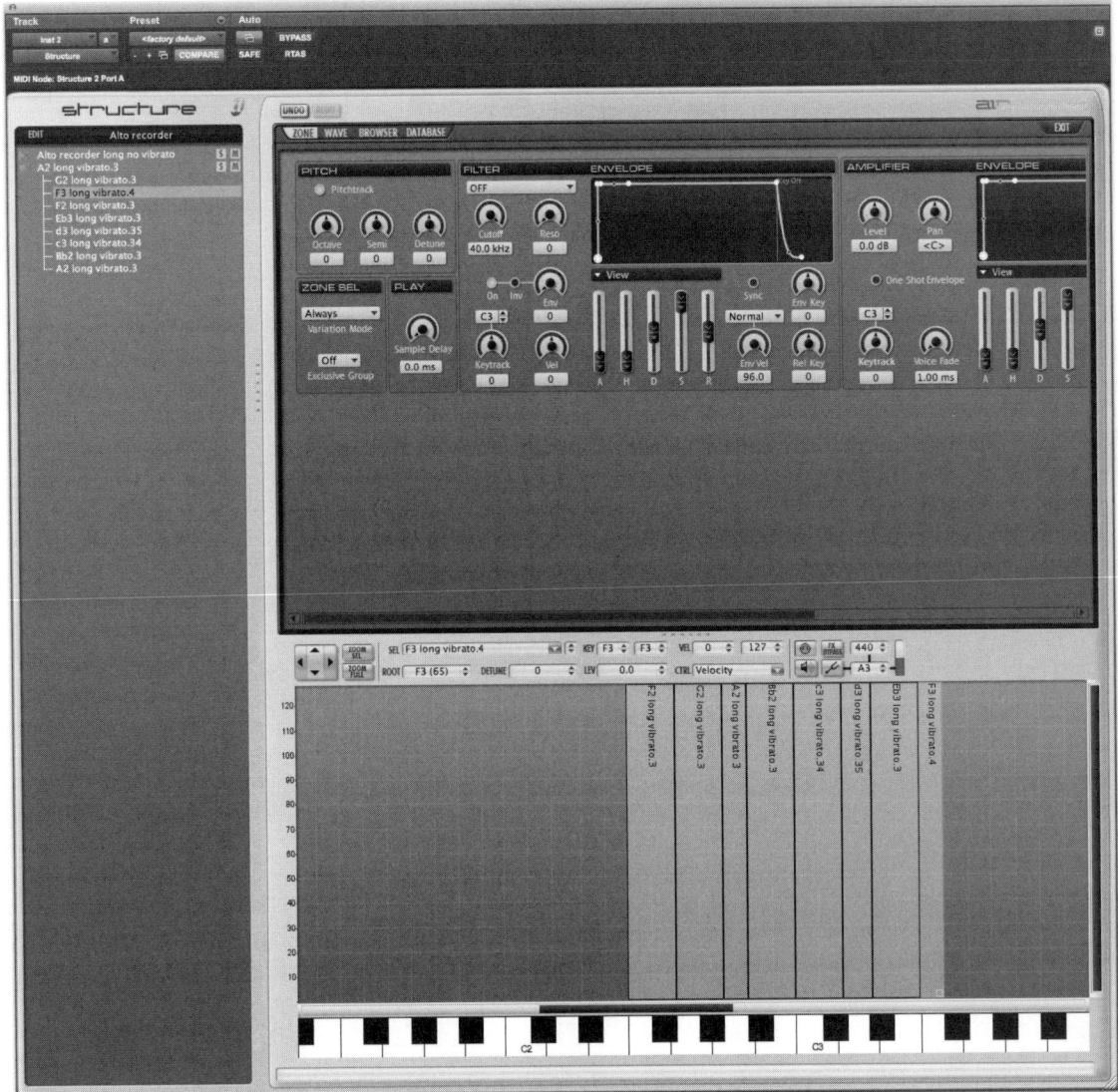

Figure 6.19 Stretch the samples.

Figure 6.20 shows how Structure should look at this point.

Both the Non-Vibrato and Vibrato samples will play in unison now. This stacked Patch itself is useful, so you could save it as an alternative. But we're going to stick a MIDI data filter in front of each articulation that causes it to play only while the mod wheel is in the desired position.

Add a Sub-Patch from the Patch menu (Figure 6.21).

Since Structure's logic about where it puts objects in the list is tricky to predict, odds are that the Sub-Patch isn't where we want it to be. Drag the Sub-Patch above the Long No Vibrato samples (Figure 6.22).

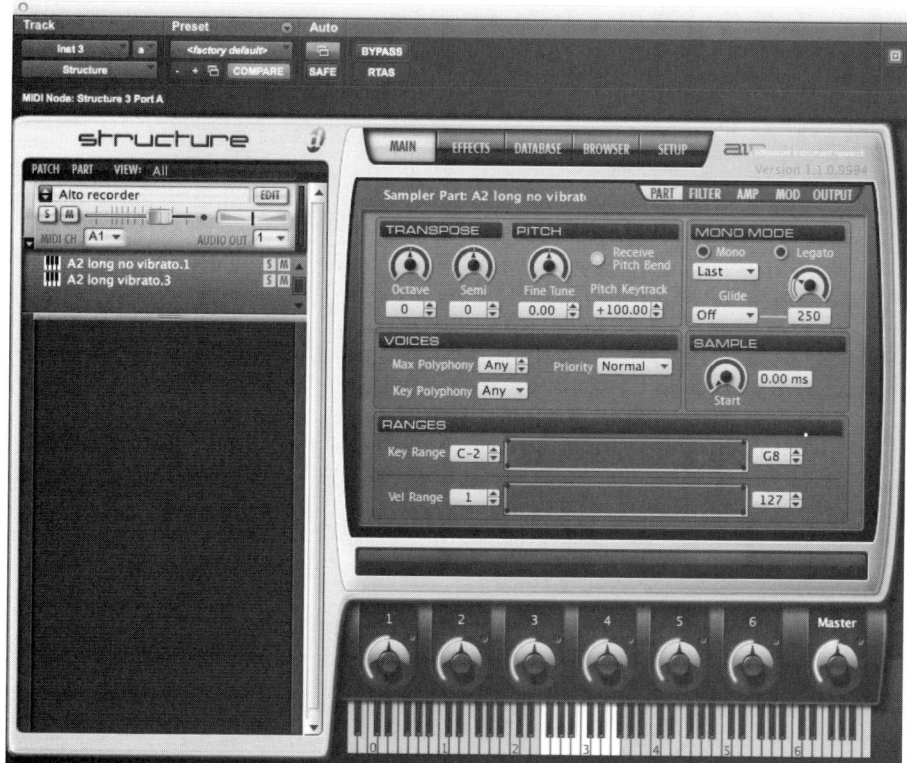

Figure 6.20 Progress so far.

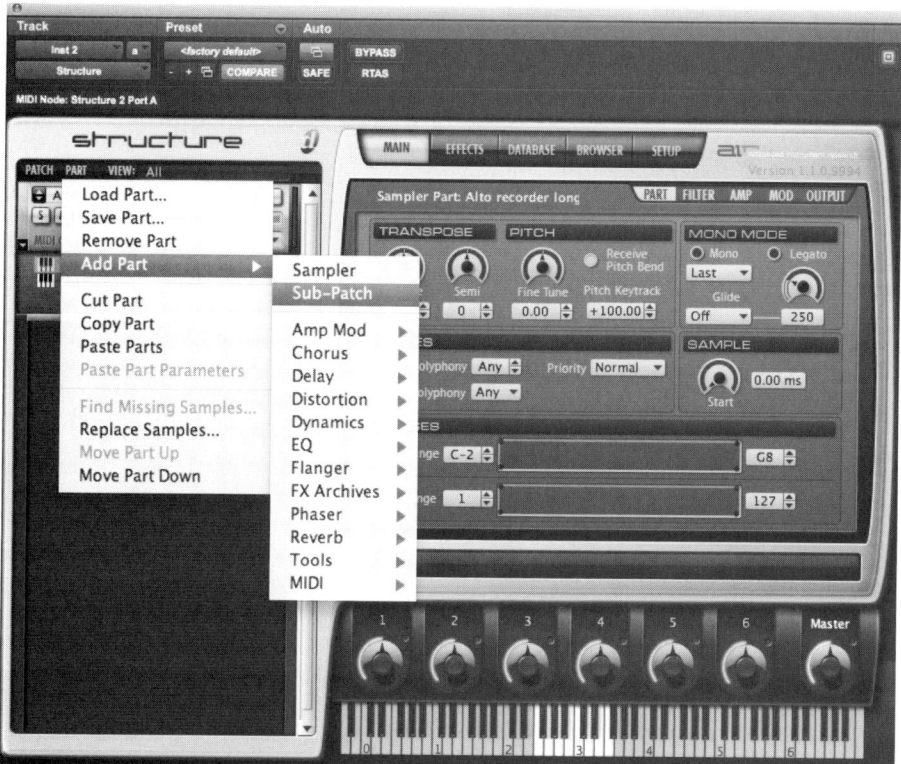

Figure 6.21 Add a Sub-Patch.

Figure 6.22 Move the Sub-Patch into position.

Drag the Long No Vibrato Part onto the Sub-Patch so that it attaches as shown in Figure 6.23. The flow makes sense if you think of the Sub-Patches as being MIDI data filters.

Click on the Sub-Patch and set the condition to ModWheel, the Range to 1 to 63, and be sure the two yellow radio buttons are on—the ones to the left of Condition and ModWheel.

At this stage, you'll get both sets of samples when the mod wheel is between 1 and 63 and just the Vibrato samples when it's between 64 and 127. We need another Sub-Patch to tell the Long Vibrato Samples not to play between 1 and 63.

Set up another Sub-Patch, attach the Long Vibrato samples to it, and set its Condition to Mod-Wheel, Range 64–127 (Figure 6.24).

The long notes are happening. Let's add the two short articulations.

As always, save.

Figure 6.23 Condition: ModWheel between 1 and 63.

Figure 6.24 Another new Sub-Patch, set to play when the ModWheel is between 64 and 127.

Stage 3: The Short Notes

The staccato and short note articulations are going to trigger only when the mod wheel is off (at 0). We're going to switch between the two using velocity: at velocities below 64 we'll get staccatos, and at 65–127 we'll get the regular short notes. (Actually, a switch point around 80 works better on most keyboards, but that's just a matter of entering different values.) Both of these short note articulations are going to alternate between two separate takes—the 1s and the 2s.

First let's bring in the staccato 1s and 2s and set up an alternation control Sub-Part.

Bring in the staccato 1 samples as a new Part. Note the red labels (a Mac feature); neat housekeeping makes a happy sample library man or woman (Figures 6.25, 6.26, 6.27).

Figure 6.25   If you're on a Mac, using the Finder labels for organization.

Figure 6.26   Drag in the staccato 1 samples.

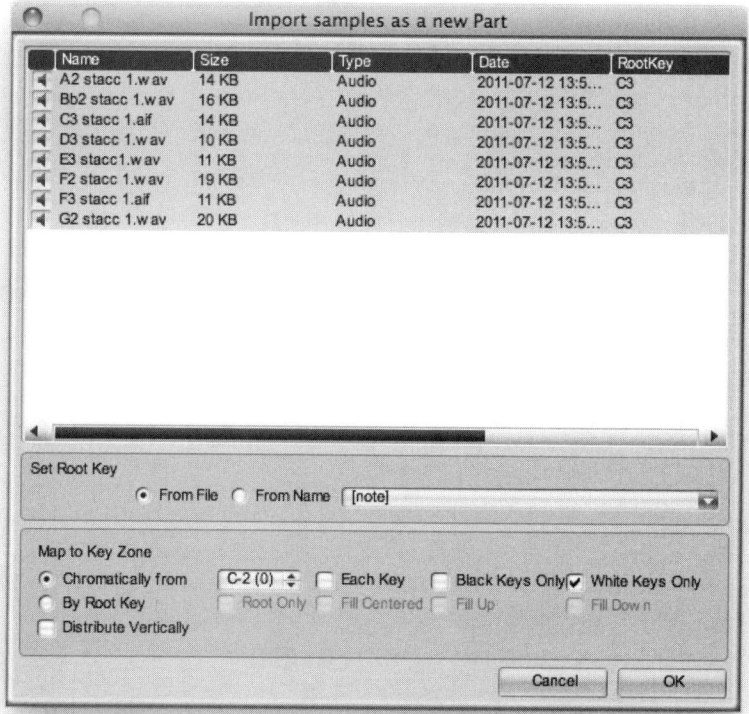

Figure 6.27 Create a new Part automatically.

Oops. By mistake you dragged the samples below the gray dividing line below the blue area belonging to the Patch we're working on, and they automatically attached themselves to a new Patch. This kind of thing is pretty easy to do in Structure, but all you have to do is drag them up in the list and select Remove Patch from the Patch menu, but be sure you've saved your work first, because you'll get really annoyed if you accidentally delete the wrong one (Figure 6.28).

Map the stacc 1 samples (Figure 6.29).

Bring in the stacc 2 samples and map them (Figure 6.30).

Try playing the program now with the mod wheel off. Staccatos 1 & 2 play in unison, another useful stacked program that might be worth saving along the way.

Making them alternate is simple.

Add an Alternation Control Sub-Part (in the MIDI hierarchical menu) as shown in Figure 6.31.

Drag the short staccato 1s and 2s to attach them to the Alternation control (Figure 6.32).

Click on the Alternation control and set it to alternate between the two Parts (Figure 6.33).

Play. The notes now alternate between the two staccato takes; if it's hard to hear, listen to the B♭.

Figure 6.28 Changing the hierarchy and removing the Patch if you goof.

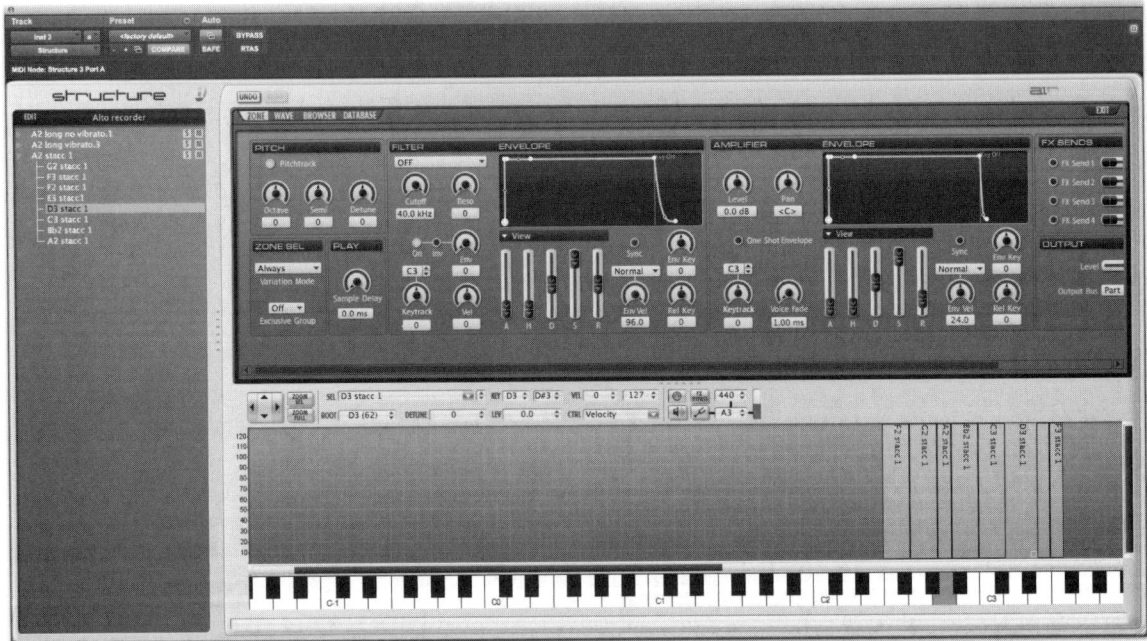

Figure 6.29 Map the stacc 1 samples.

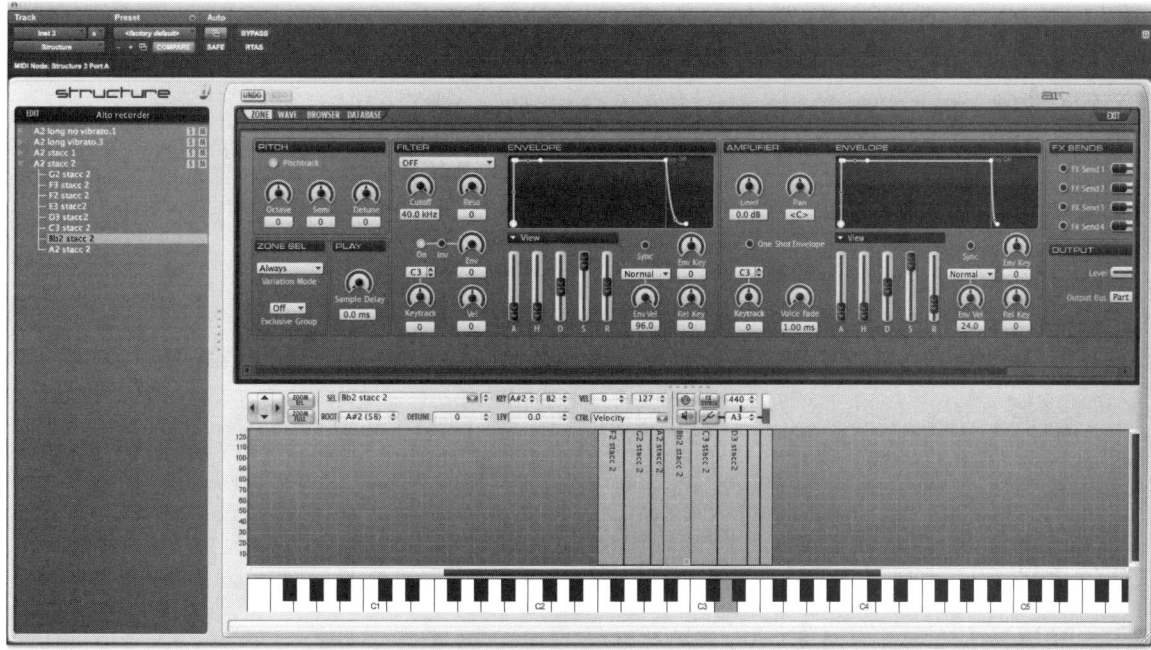

Figure 6.30 Drag in and map the stacc 2 samples.

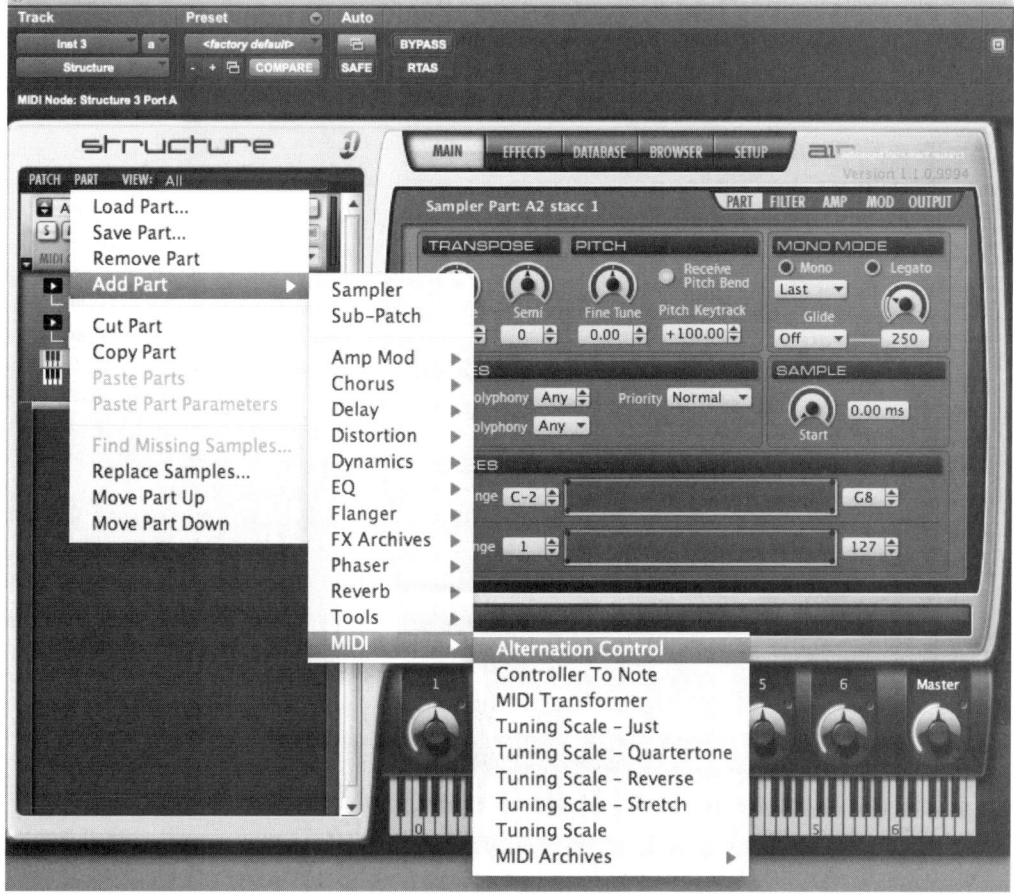

Figure 6.31 Add an Alternation Control Sub-Part.

Figure 6.32 Attach the staccato samples to the Alternation Control.

Figure 6.33 Destination: Parts.

Now we're going to add the short notes 1 & 2. This is all familiar.

Drag in the short note 1 samples as a new Part, and map them. Ditto the short note 2 samples (Figure 6.34).

Figure 6.34 Bring in and map the short 1&2 samples.

Setting the short 1s to play at velocities between 64 and 127 is as easy as selecting all the samples and entering the values as shown in Figure 6.35.

Do the same for the short 2 samples.

Set the staccato 1s and then the staccato 2s so they both trigger at velocities between 1 and 63 (Figure 6.36).

Again, setting the velocity switch to 80 is probably better.

Insert an Alternation control for the short 1 & 2 samples, and as before set it to alternate Parts (Figure 6.37).

The Patch should now look like Figure 6.38.

All that remains is to set up filters so the short notes trigger only when the mod wheel is off.

Add Sub-Patches above the two Alternation controls for the staccato and short note samples, drag the Parts to attach them, and set the Conditions to ModWheel value 0 (Figure 6.39).

And we're done (Figure 6.40).

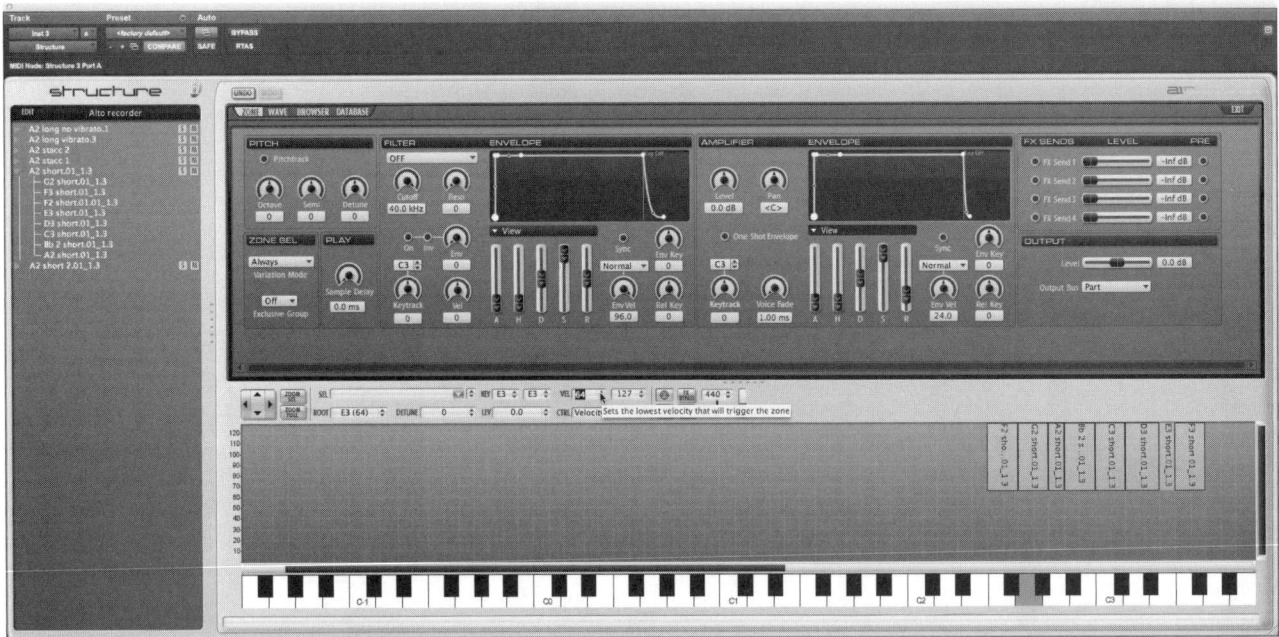

Figure 6.35 Set the short 1 velocity range for 64 to 127.

Figure 6.36 Same for the short 2 samples, velocity 1 to 63.

Figure 6.37 An Alternation control for the short samples.

Figure 6.38 The Patch so far.

Figure 6.39 Add another Sub-Patch, attach the staccato samples, set the Condition to ModWheel 0.

Figure 6.40 The completed alto recorder program.

Alternative: Switching Short Notes by Playing Speed

Instead of using velocity to switch between the staccato and short note samples, let's try setting it up so faster playing triggers the "ti-cka" staccato notes and slower playing causes the regular "toot" short notes to play. We're still going to leave the previous mod wheel programming intact so it switches between the two short note articulations when the wheel is all the way down and two long note ones, depending on how far it's raised.

There is an unavoidable limitation here: the Playing Speed Sub-Patch parameter measures the time since the last note you played to determine which articulation to play, so the first note can be unpredictable, and it has no way of knowing your intention if you try to play one or more staccato 16th notes followed immediately by a regular short note. But we'll explore a couple of workarounds.

Go back and set the four short note Parts (staccato 1 & 2, short notes 1 & 2) to play over the full velocity range (Figure 6.41).

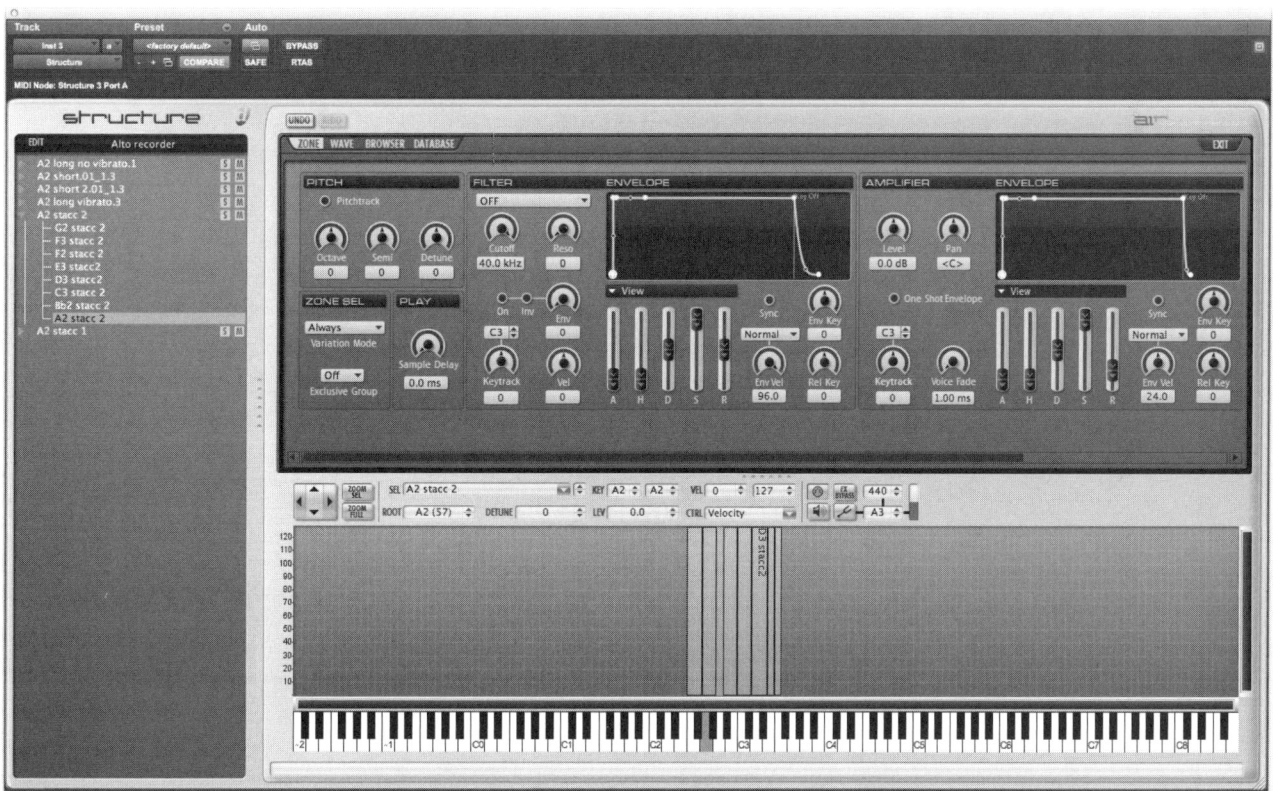

Figure 6.41   Return the staccato and short notes to the full velocity range.

As before, the two short articulations will play only when the mod wheel is all the way down (0). You'll hear both notes in unison now, but of course we're going to change that.

Click on the staccato Sub-Patch and add a second Condition: Playing Speed. Set its range to 0.01 to 0.19 (Figure 6.42).

Figure 6.42 New Condition: Playing Speed 0.01 to 0.19.

Click on the short notes Sub-Patch add a second Condition: Playing Speed. Set its range to 0.20 to 100.00.

These values appear to be arbitrary; in other words, they have no discernible relationship to actual time.

Now play while watching the yellow cursor travel across the Playing Speed lane. Notice that it resets to the beginning—resets the timer—every time you play a note. If you're watching the short notes Sub-Patch, you'll see that the short notes sound while the yellow cursor is over the dark blue range, while the staccato notes play while it's over the light gray range (or vice versa if you're watching the staccato notes Sub-Patch).

As a practical matter, it sounds fine if the first note in a passage is intended to be staccato, but instead you just let the key up early while playing a regular short note. But what if you want to play one or more staccato 16th notes followed by a regular short note? Similarly, the easiest answer is just to raise the mod wheel before the regular short and substitute a regular Long No Vibrato note, releasing it early. Nobody will know the difference.

But let's pretend that we're playing a different instrument, and it is important to play the correct articulation at the beginning of a phrase. If you set up a third Condition to tell Structure which articulation you intend, that condition has to be "true" for it to play, and there goes the whole point of switching by playing speed.

The solution is to duplicate both short note articulations and set them up to play only under new Conditions.

7 Looping

Looping means two things when applied to sampling. One is "beats," as in "creating an ostinato out of repeated sampled grooves." Here we're concerned with the other: finding a section of an instrument sample to repeat over and over—as inaudibly as possible—in order to extend its length while you hold the note. This kind of looping has been a basic feature of sampling since its dawn in the early '80s, when the very limited memory available made it mandatory; it wasn't anywhere near possible to sample every note as long as a player would hold it.

A digression: for some historical perspective, the first popular samplers such as the Ensoniq Mirage, Emu Emulator, Akai S9000, and Sequential Prophet 2000 started with as little as 128k—that's k as in kilobytes, not megabytes (1000k) or gigabytes (a million k). A single sampler allowed just under 15 seconds of 12-bit recording at a 16kHz sampling rate. And yet that didn't stop skillful developers from getting a whole lot of mileage out of that tiny amount of memory, nor did those mediocre audio specs prevent them from making their instruments sound good.

A further aside: part of the reason instruments like the Prophet 2000 sounded good had to do with the character of their analog electronics. For example, converted Prophet 2000 samples—which are on floppy disks—can lose a lot of their magic when played back on modern samplers with much better audio specs. Having said that, sampling technology is still a whole lot better today.

One more quick historical tidbit: Digidesign's SampleCell II card for the Mac II came out a few years later with up to 32MB of onboard RAM (remember, a $5 USB flash drive these days is 4000MB—4GB). People were amazed at that; it was possible to fit an unlooped piano into one of those cards! It would have been very difficult to imagine the sampled piano libraries of today: with maybe 16 velocity layers of pedal down and another 16 of pedal up, separate layers of hammer noise, alternate takes to avoid repeated notes, samples may be half a minute long to capture the whole decay.

Anyway, previous restrictions are water under the bridge now that we have essentially unlimited recording time at any sample rate and bit depth we want to use (the example files are 48kHz/24-bit). And yet there are times when it's necessary and desirable to loop samples. Human beings can't sustain a loud tuba note for very long, for example, but you can loop the note and create a musician with lungs the size of New Jersey.

Looking at the empty half of the glass, the two essential rules of looping are these:

1. Don't do it if you can help it. If possible, record notes that are longer than you'll ever need and/or see if your DAW's time-stretching feature sounds good enough on your recordings to act as a substitute. More about this later.

2. If you need to do it, try to use a program that does it for you (or that at least gets you very close, such as Redmatica Keymap).

The reason for these rules is that finding inaudible loop points can be difficult, time consuming, and sometimes suboptimal. Yet there's also a half-full side of the glass: loops can work very well, and they're a standard part of sampling.

Looking at Edit Points

Automatic looping software will find what it thinks are the best loop points. But if you're doing it manually, the first tool to use is your eyes, because it's easy to look at a waveform display and get a rough idea where beginning and ending points have a chance of working.

This loop shown in Figure 7.1 isn't going to work.

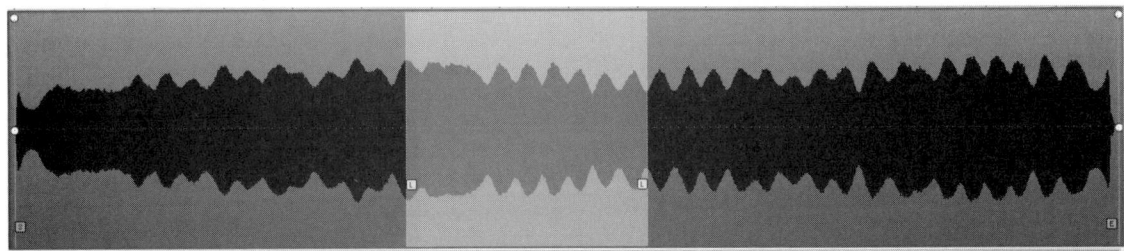

Figure 7.1 This is unlikely to work.

It's clear that both sides of the edit don't match (a loop is just an edit that gets repeated). For openers, the right loop marker is positioned where the audio is much louder. If you look just a little more closely, it's in a trough in the waveform, and the left marker is in a peak; even if everything else were right, that would have to create a nasty bump.

The one shown in Figure 7.2 looks like it might work.

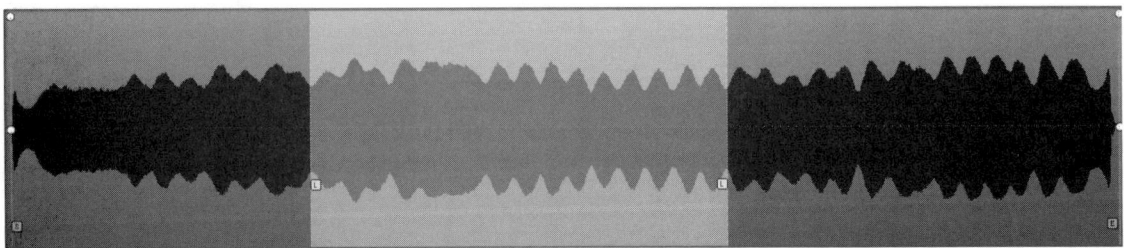

Figure 7.2 This might work.

The wave is at a similar amplitude on both sides of the loop, and the markers are in the troughs on both sides. So far so good. Now let's zoom way in on the sample.

The left marker is shown in Figure 7.3.

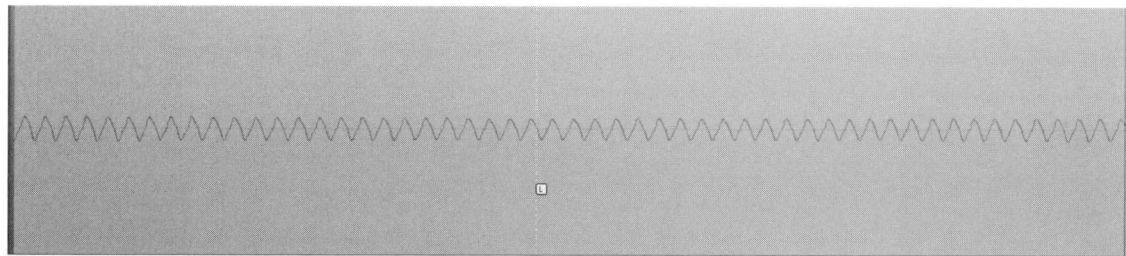

Figure 7.3 Zoomed in on the left loop marker.

And the right one is shown in Figure 7.4.

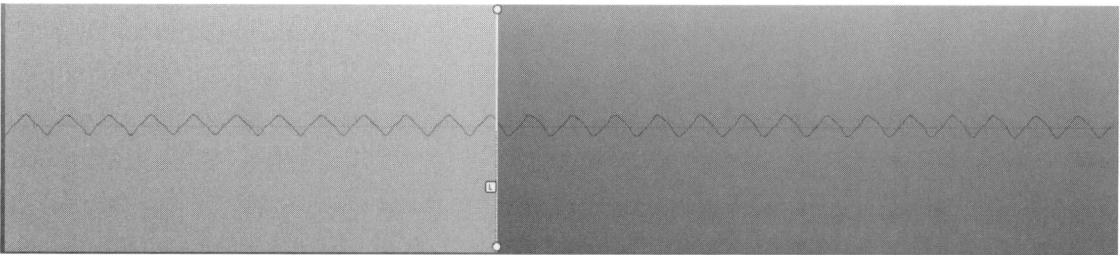

Figure 7.4 Zoomed in on the right loop marker.

These screenshots are looking at individual cycles of the waveform. Each cycle is 1/48,000 of a second at a 48kHz sample rate—a pretty small slice of time.

Incidentally, this happens to be a long vibrato alto recorder sample. Recorder is a very pure-sounding instrument, just a little edgier than a pure sine wave, which is rounded (Figure 7.5).

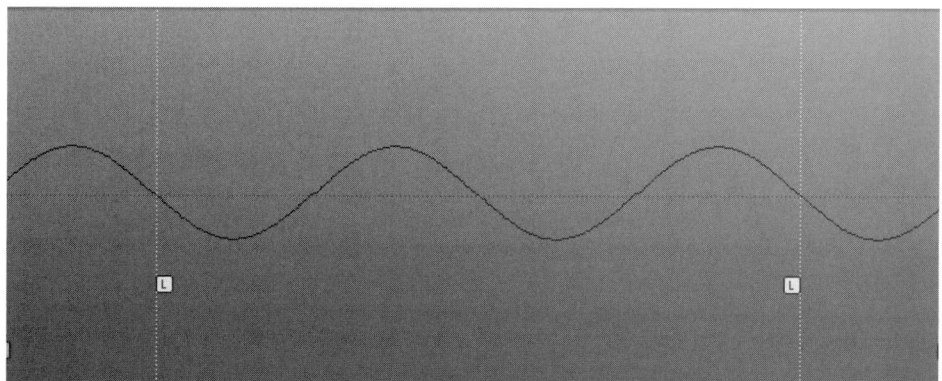

Figure 7.5 A pure sine wave.

The loop markers in the recorder sample (and for that matter in the sine wave, but let's leave that aside) are both placed on zero crossings. These are the points in the wave's oscillation at which it is neither positive nor negative; if this were a vibrating string, it would be where it passes its resting position, or if it were a loudspeaker, the cone wouldn't be on either the negative or positive point of its excursion.

The conventional wisdom is that one should try to cut audio on a zero crossing. That makes perfect sense, except that we've just seen that there's nothing magical about zero crossings—it's easy to make terrible-sounding loops or edits on them. Ditto if you cut at the corresponding point in the waveforms on both the in and out (or loop start and end) points: that doesn't tell the whole story.

In practice it's usually necessary to put in a quick crossfade at the loop point, even if you're using automatic looping software. Most samplers do that easily, as we'll see shortly.

But we're still not home free, even if the loop is crossfaded so it doesn't glitch. Let's take another look at the loop we think may work (Figure 7.6).

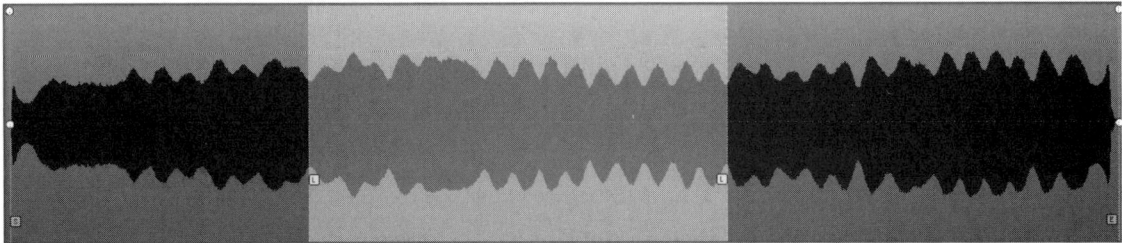

Figure 7.6   Will this work?

We're getting very close to the point at which it's necessary to put this in a sampler and actually listen. You can't tell by looking whether the note is in tune on both sides of the loop, and if it's not, no crossfade will fix that.

But first there's one more issue. This is a vibrato sample, and you can see from the waveform shape that the oscillations become more frequent as time goes on. That's intentional; good players will often do that to make held notes more interesting, just as they will with trills in some styles.

This loop jumps from stable and fast vibrato oscillations to slower and less stable ones. That's not going to sound good. In fact, this sample isn't all that easy to loop, as we'll see.

Setting Loop Points

Time to load a couple of samples into your sampler so we can play around with loop points. Please use the two F3 samples (with and without vibrato) in the Setting Loop Points folder on this book's companion Web site (which can be found at www.courseptr.com/downloads).

As in the following chapter on release samples, we're using only two samples so that we don't have to be distracted by having to deal with mapping a full set; the process is exactly the same when you have lots of samples. We'll also stretch these single samples across the keyboard just to give us a wider keyboard range for playing. Who cares if it sounds like the wrong end of a horse?

Loop Points in Structure

1. Insert a Structure sampler on an instrument track in Pro Tools. Remember to remove the default Sine Wave program (Figure 7.7).

Figure 7.7 Insert a Structure instrument.

2. Drag the F3 long vibrato sample in to create a Patch. It should stretch across all octaves, but stretch it across the keyboard it if it doesn't (Figure 7.8).

3. Click on Edit, go to the Wave tab, use the navigation arrows to zoom in to somewhere near the resolution shown in the screen shot, and click the Loop button to turn on the loop and show its markers (Figure 7.9).

4. Drag the loop markers to :03.42 and :07.31. Figure 7.10 is a nice long loop, and these look like reasonable places to set our loop points relative to where the vibrato swells line up.

Figure 7.8 Drag in the F3 long vib file to create a Patch.

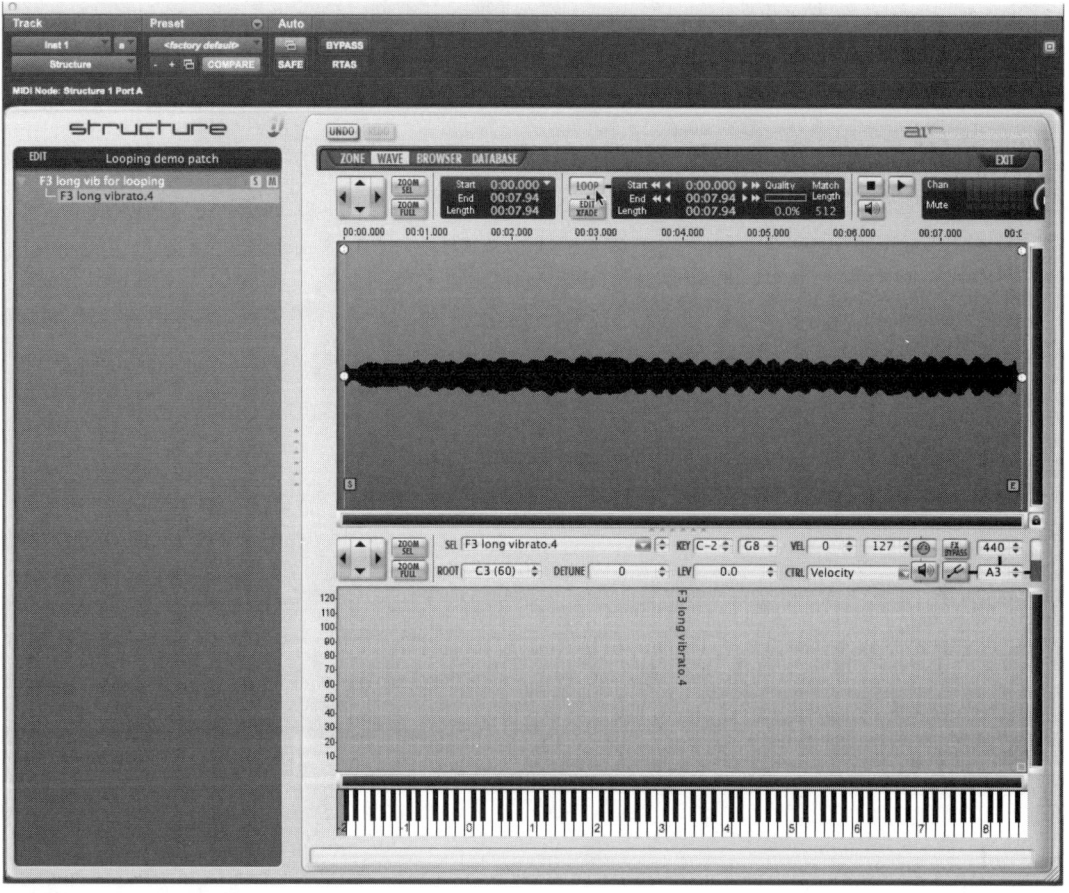

Figure 7.9 Click the Loop button.

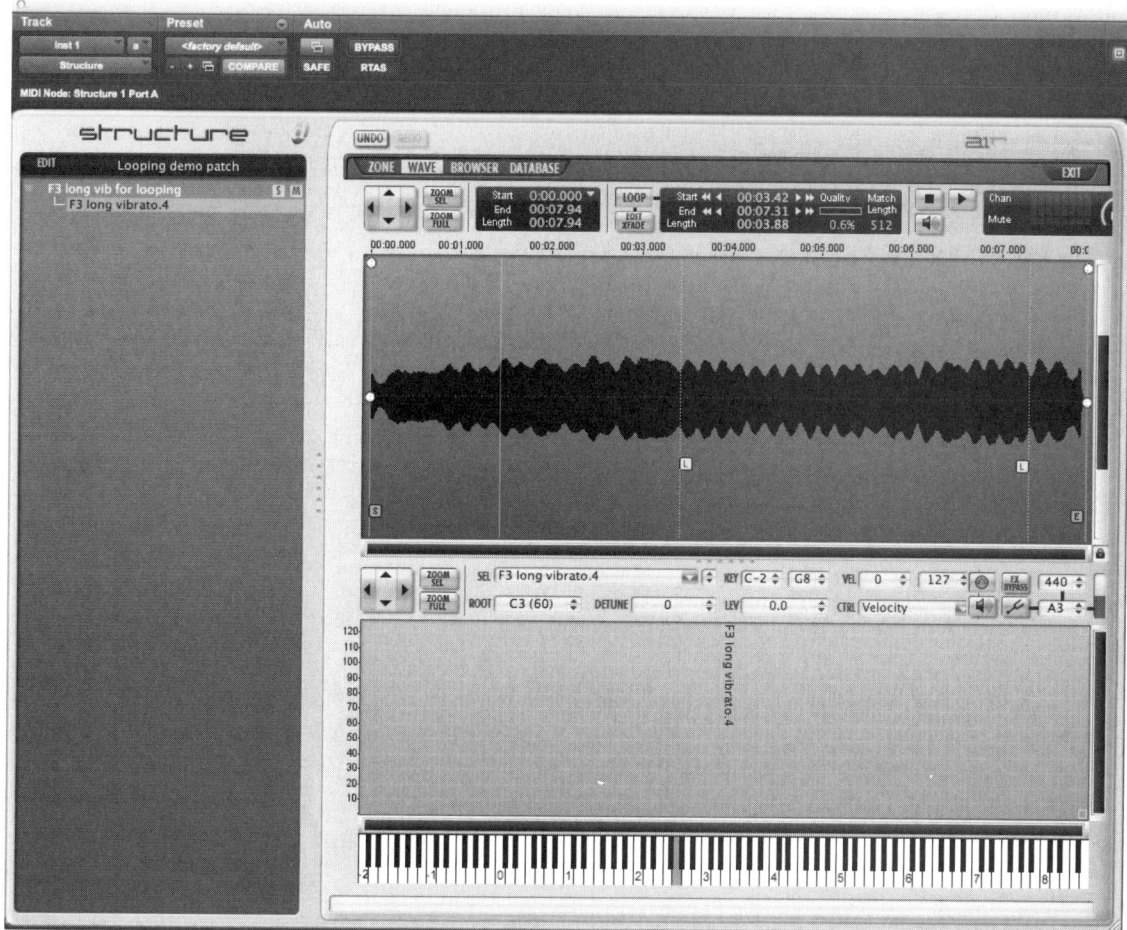

Figure 7.10   Drag the loop markers as shown.

5. Play. Overall, that's about as good as it's going to get with a vibrato sample, but there's a click. We'll get rid of that with a crossfade.

6. Click on the Edit Xfade button as shown in Figure 7.11.

7. Set a crossfade about as long as the one shown in Figure 7.12.

    If you play now, you'll hear that the click is gone. But you don't have to listen very intently to hear two notes layered during the crossfade. It's too long.

8. Try setting the crossfade to roughly the length shown in Figure 7.13.

    That's a pretty good loop. Now we'll see how much easier it is to loop the non-vibrato sample, since it doesn't have those tell-tale vibrato swells.

9. Drag in the F3 long no vib sample, stretch it across the keyboard, and mute the vibrato sample in the Parts list on the left so it's not heard while we loop the other sample.

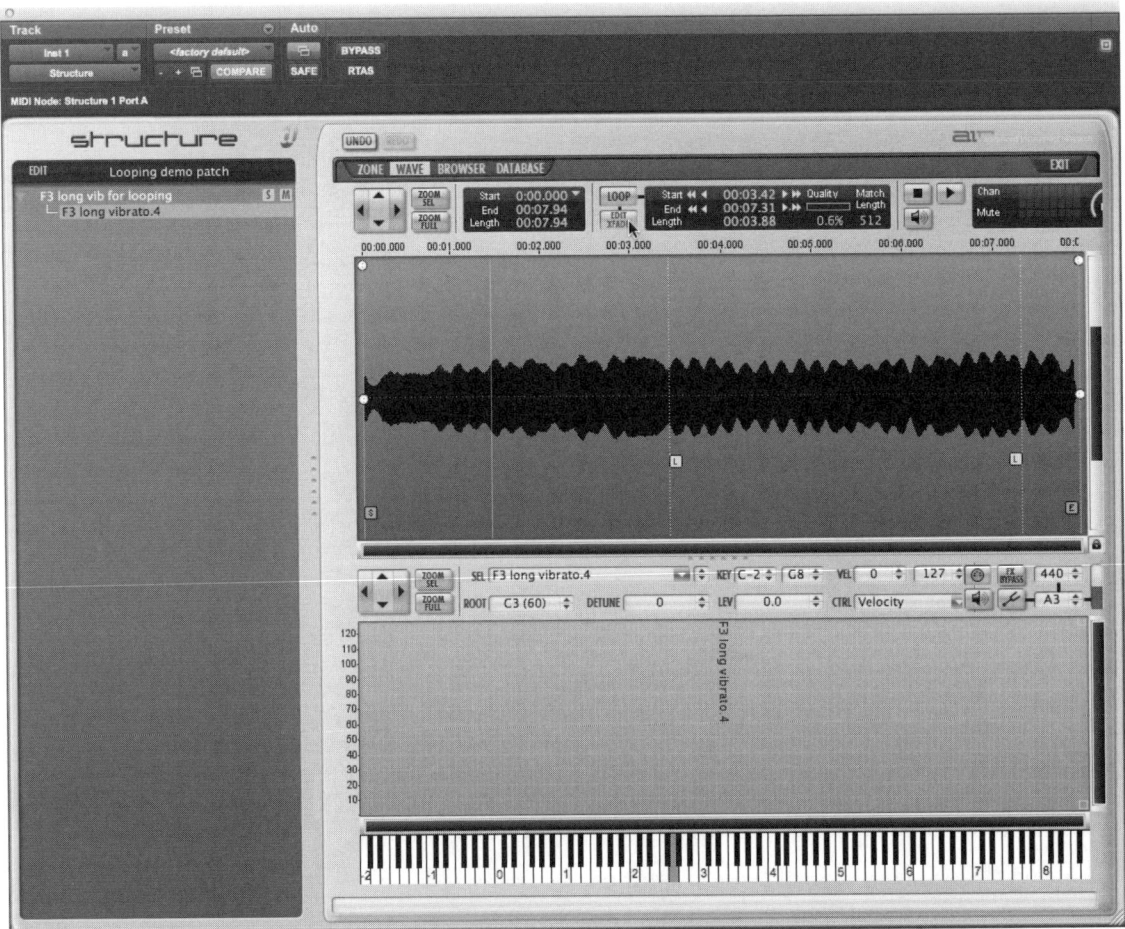

Figure 7.11 Click on Edit Xfade.

Set the loop points to a nice long loop (:01.22 :07.19), and set the crossfade to a moderate length as shown in Figure 7.14.

10. Play.

Nice, right? You can probably shorten the crossfade a little more. The idea is to make it as short as possible without being audible. But it's fine as shown.

Loop Points in NN-XT

1. Insert an NN-XT sampler from Reason's Create menu or by right-clicking in the rack. Remember to right-click on the sampler and initialize the patch to get rid of the piano program Propellerhead loads by default. Open the remote editor by clicking on the triangle at the lower left (Figure 7.15).

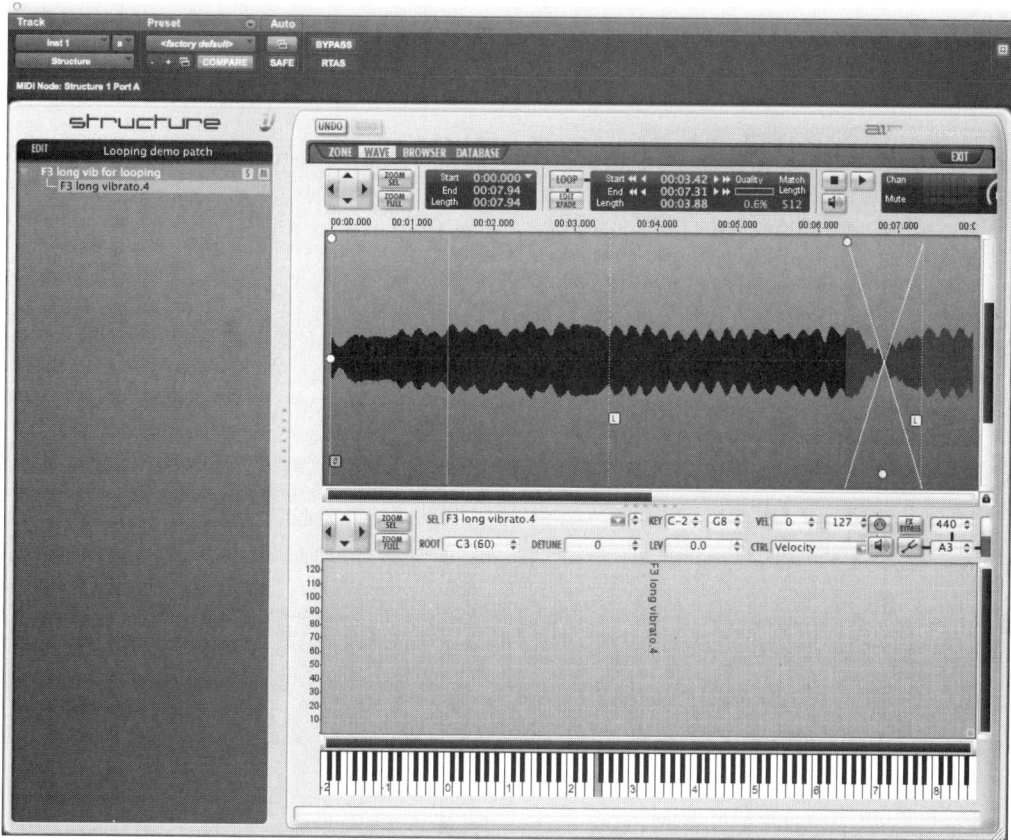

Figure 7.12   This crossfade is too long.

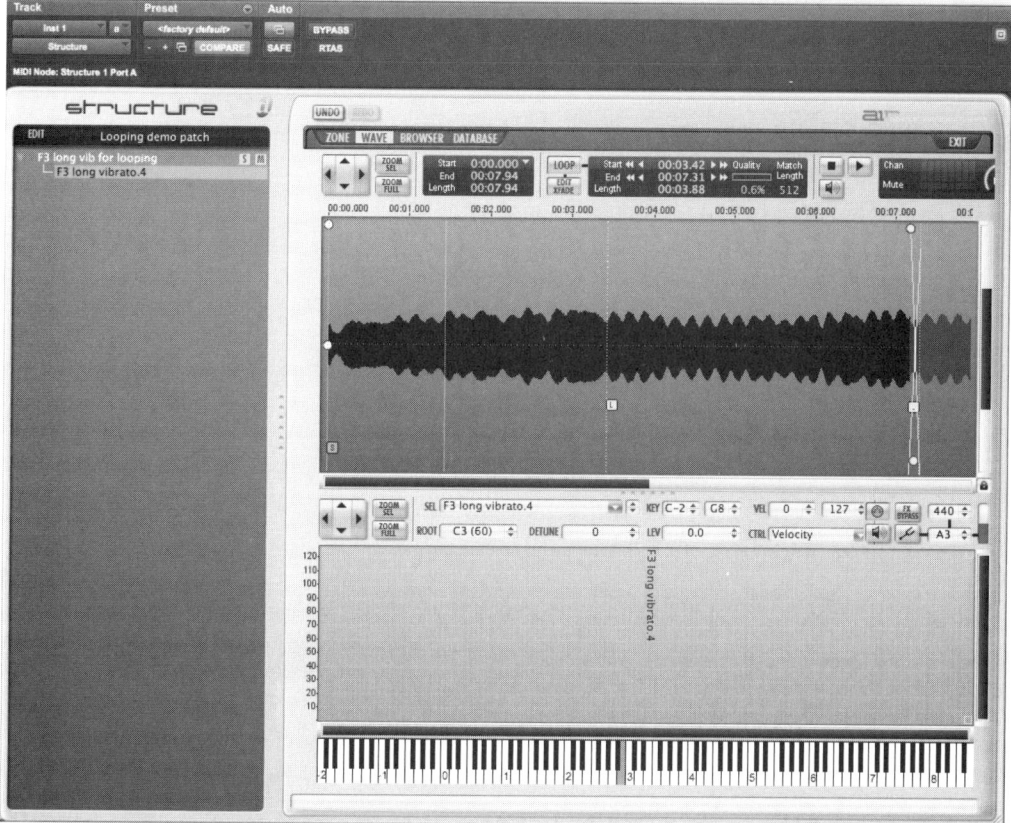

Figure 7.13   Looped okay, but the vibrato isn't perfect.

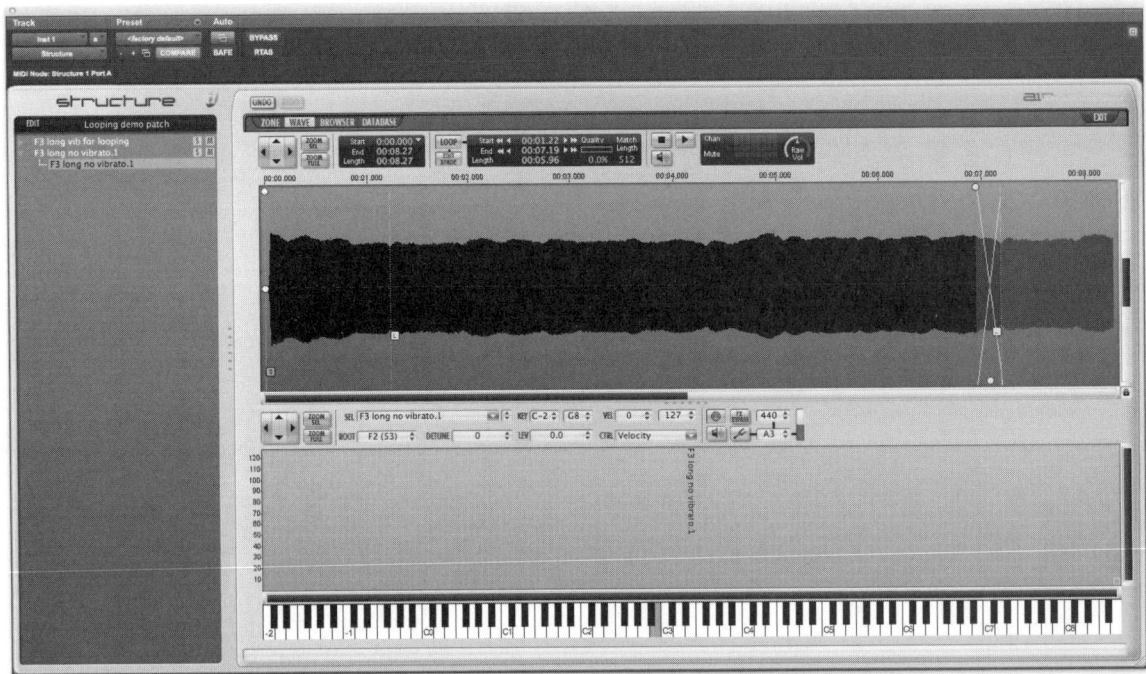

Figure 7.14 Try the settings shown.

Figure 7.15 Create and initialize an NN-XT.

2. Load the B♭2 long vibrato sample from the disk icon in the editor. You can't drag samples directly into the NN-XT, but you can audition them from the dialog box that pops up here (Figure 7.16).

Figure 7.16 Load the sample.

The sample is stretched across the keyboard.

3. Set the loop start and end to 25% and 90% as shown in Figure 7.17.

4. Play. This sounds like the rear end of a horse, right? It clicks and doesn't match up.

5. Move the sample start and end points around at random to see if you can find a good loop point. Stop before you get frustrated and start cursing me for sending you on a fool's errand.

As you can see, looping samples is very difficult if you can't crossfade into the loop.

Let's cheat and put in some loop points that will work:

1. Set the sample start to 37.9% and the sample end to 56.2%.

2. That loop is a little short; it doesn't sound 100% natural, but it doesn't click or pop. We'll live with it.

Figure 7.17 This loop is hopeless.

3. Set the Play mode to FW-SUS (forward-sustain) as shown in Figure 7.18.

    This tells NN-XT to play from the beginning and then repeat over the loop until you release the key, at which point it plays to the end of the recording.

4. Since the tail of the recording is a little short, let's add a little release time in the envelope.

5. 0.23 s is a good setting for the release, but you can experiment to get a feel (Figure 7.19).

The NN-XT doesn't have a visual sample editor, but more importantly it doesn't allow you to add crossfades to smooth out loops that click. However, you can use an external application like Redmatica Keymap to build NN-XT programs.

Let's put that more strongly: if you're going to use the NN-XT to build sampled instruments, use an external sample editor. Your sequencer probably has one built in.

Figure 7.18   Play mode FW-SUS.

Figure 7.19   Experiment with the release.

Loop Points in EXS24

Looping is very easy in the EXS24.

1. Insert an EXS24 on an instrument track and click on Edit to open the EXS24 Instrument Editor (Figure 7.20).

Figure 7.20   Insert an EXS24 and go in to Edit mode.

2. Create a new Instrument (Figure 7.21).

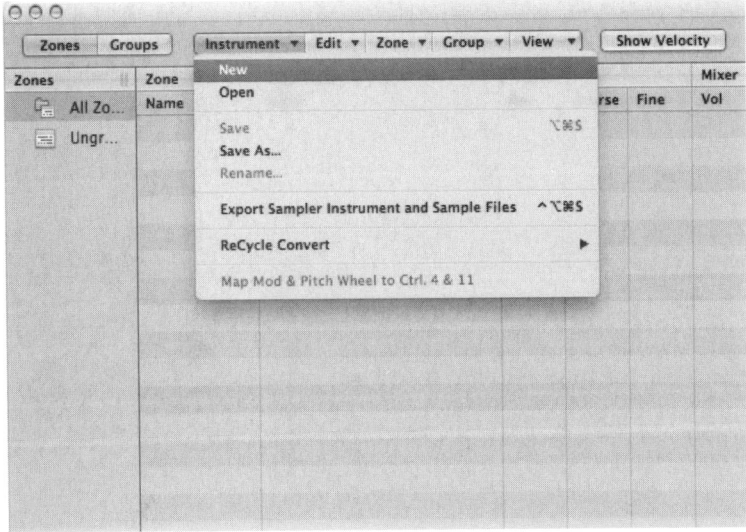

Figure 7.21   Create a new Instrument.

3. Drag the sample into the Zones list; it stretches across the keyboard automatically. Show Zone: Loop from the local View menu (Figure 7.22).

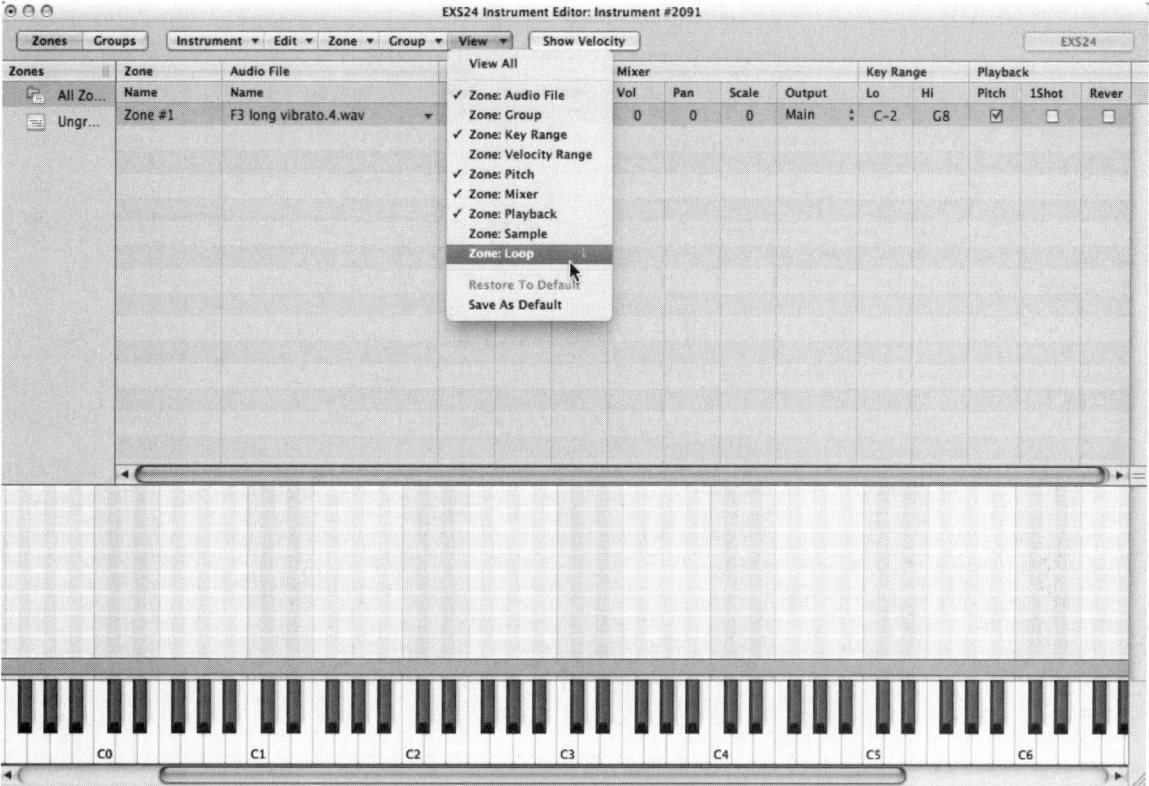

Figure 7.22 Drag in the F3 long vib sample into a Zone.

4. Double-click the F3 sample (you can see the mouse pointer where you click). This opens the sample in a Sample Editor window (Figure 7.23).

Figure 7.23 Double-click to open a Sample Editor window.

If you have an Arrange window open, it will open in a split window at the bottom; if not, it will open in a standalone Sample Editor window as shown.

5. Adjust the zoom level and window size so your display appears similar to the one that follows. Highlight the same section of the waveform (Figure 7.24).

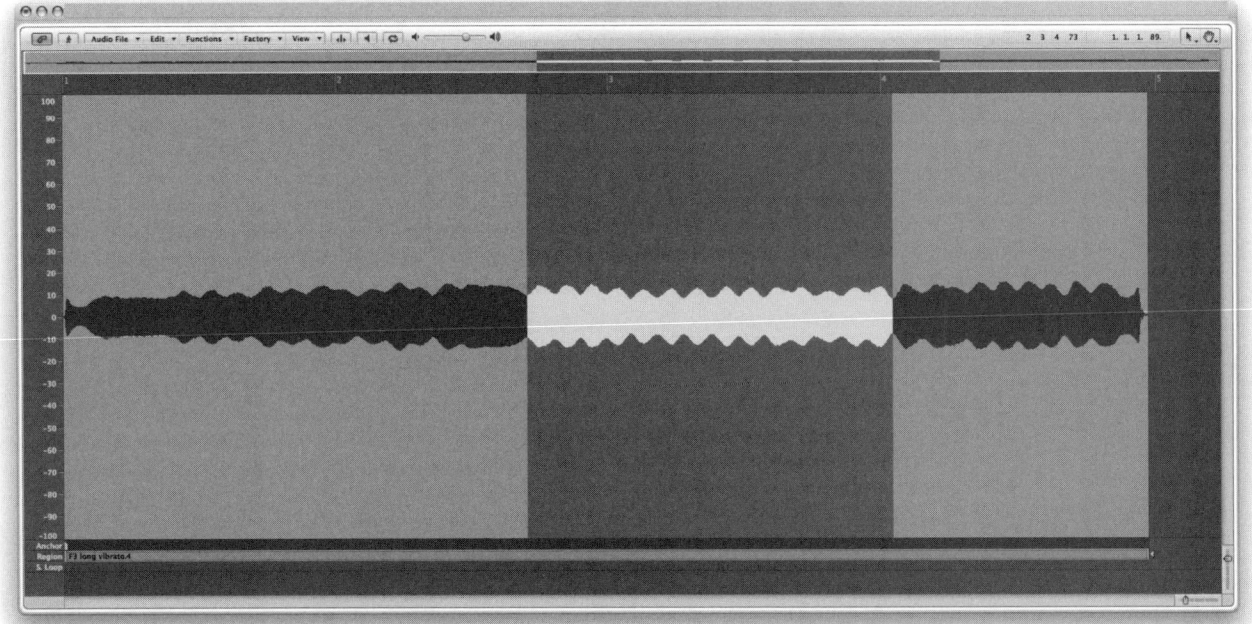

Figure 7.24 These loop settings may work.

This looks like a good candidate for our loop, since the vibrato has settled at a consistent speed over this section. If you zoom in on both sides, you'll see that the selection boundary has been placed on zero crossing boundaries. You can use the overview waveform display on top of the main one to navigate (Figures 7.25 and 7.26).

6. Select the Selection > Sample Loop command from under the local Edit window (Figure 7.27).

    If you look at the Instrument Editor, you'll see that the sample numbers of the loop boundaries set in the sample editor have been transferred automatically (Figure 7.28).

7. The boundaries are grayed out because the loop hasn't been turned on. So turn them on (Figure 7.29).

8. Play. That's a good loop, right?

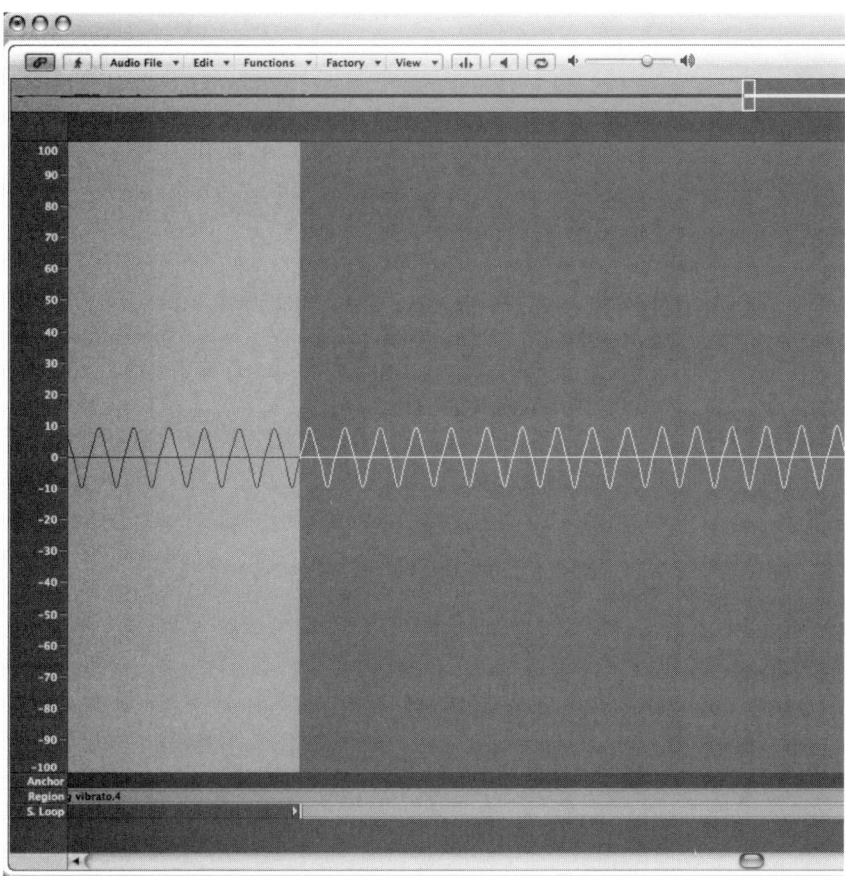

Figure 7.25 The loop starting on a zero crossing.

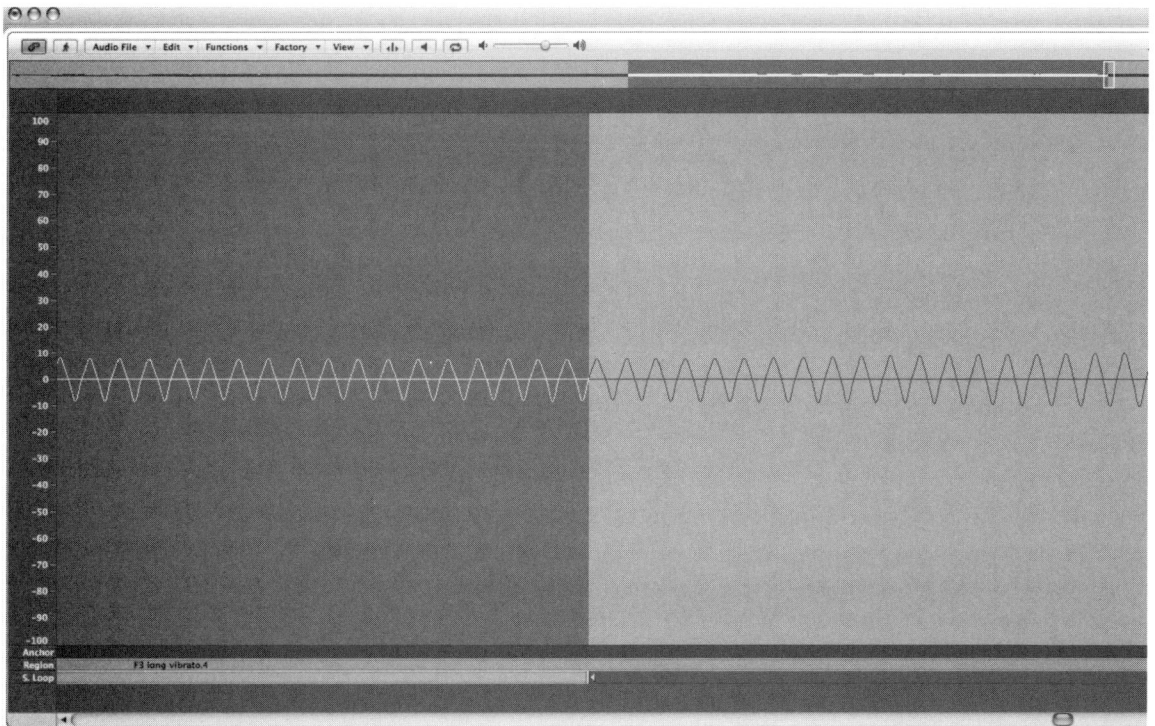

Figure 7.26 The loop ending on a zero crossing.

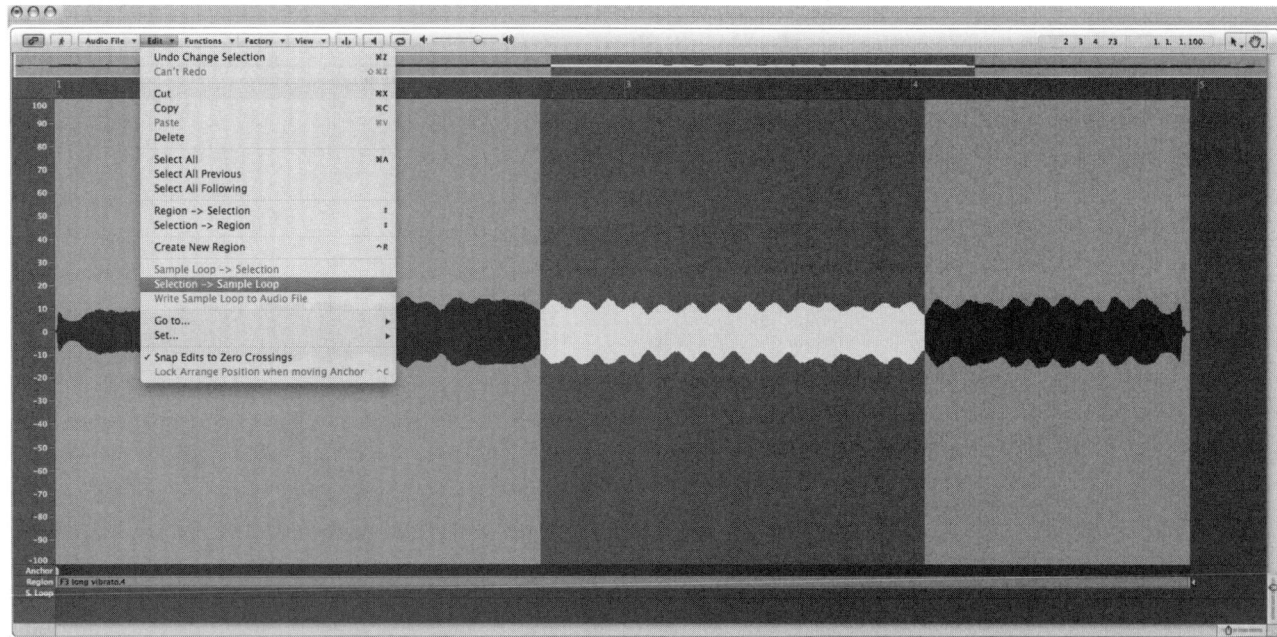

Figure 7.27   Selection > Sample Loop.

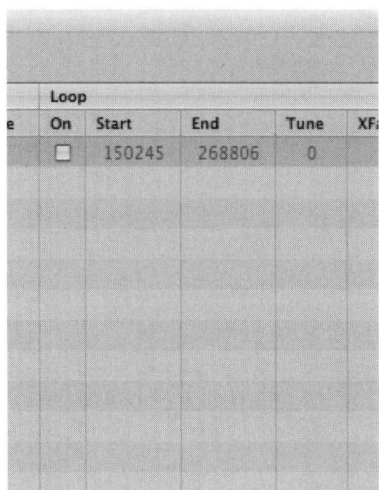

Figure 7.28   Changes reflected in the Instrument Editor.

9.   If not, enter the values 150245 and 268806 for the start and end. They'll work.

10.   Try moving the loop boundaries in the Sample Editor. Play. It's hard to go wrong with this sample.

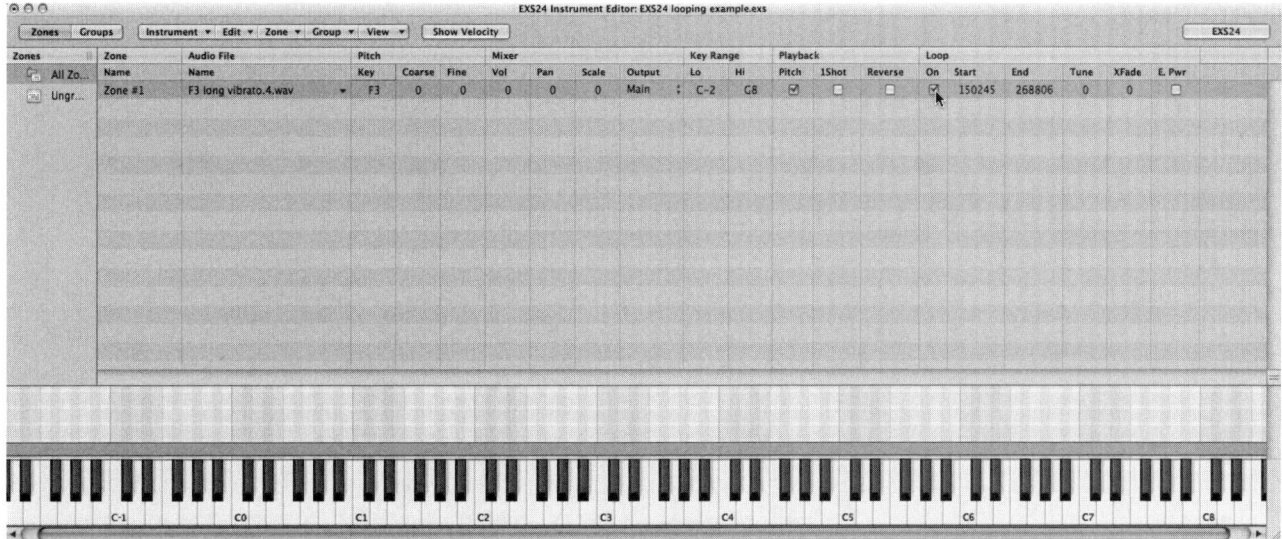

Figure 7.29 Turn on the loop. It works.

11.   Set the start and end points to a pretty bad loop: 57834 and 66069 (Figure 7.30).

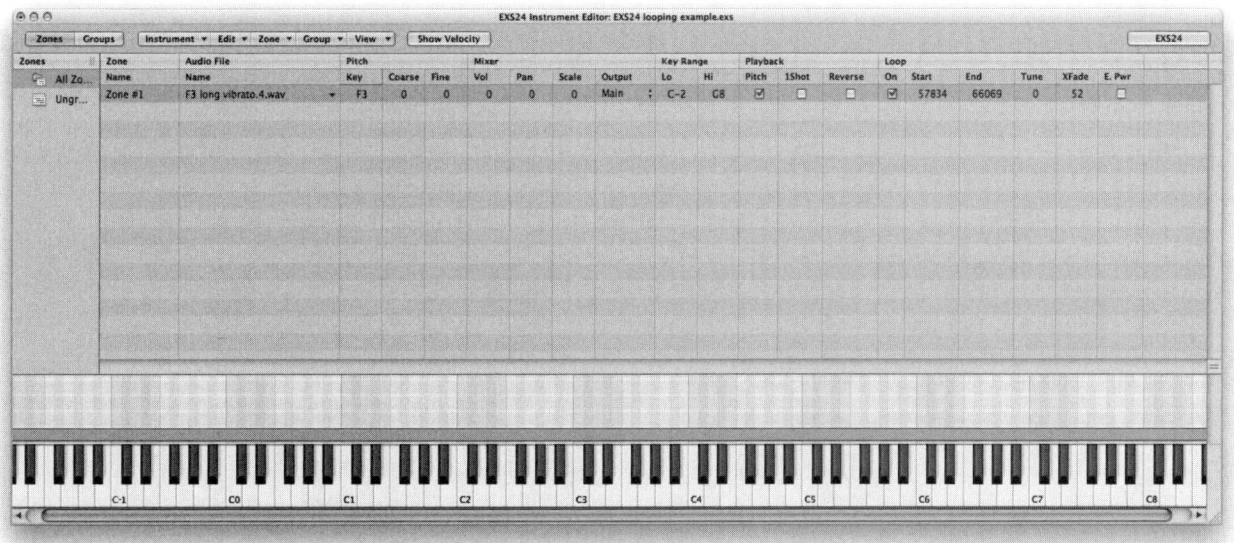

Figure 7.30 These settings produce a pretty bad loop.

The reason for these bad settings is to show the crossfade function, which makes a lot of otherwise unloopable samples loopable. What this does is replace the abrupt transition with a fade across the loop boundary, of course.

1.   Play.
2.   Try a setting of 52 (Figure 7.31).
3.   Play again. The click is gone, right? You might actually like a longer crossfade, say around 80.

Loop					
On	Start	End	Tune	XFade	E. Pwr
☑	57834	66069	0	52	☐

Figure 7.31 Try the settings shown.

Obviously, there's more to a good loop than hiding its edit points. This one is so short that the vibrato sounds horribly artificial. Longer loops put more time between repetitions of identifiable features in the recording, and that makes them less obvious.

One feature worthy of note is the E. Power checkbox at the right of the previous screenshot. Equal power crossfades are good for matching audio edits when the in and out points are at different levels. We don't need that in this case, but it can be a useful feature.

A final topic: the EXS24 doesn't let you play a loop and then continue to the end of sample when you release the key; you have to program a release sample if you want to do that. The next chapter is about exactly that—programming release samples—but while we're here we'll create a release sample that consists of everything following the end of the loop point.

But first: The easy alternative is just to add a little bit of release time to Envelope 2—the amplitude envelope—on the instrument front panel. After experimenting with longer and shorter settings, try a setting of somewhere around 100 milliseconds, which is just enough release to smooth out the end of the note (Figure 7.32).

Figure 7.32 Adjust the Envelope 2 release.

Creating the release sample is very simple, but it requires a few screenshots to detail.

1. In the Sample Edit window, select Sample Loop > Selection to highlight the loop (Figure 7.33).

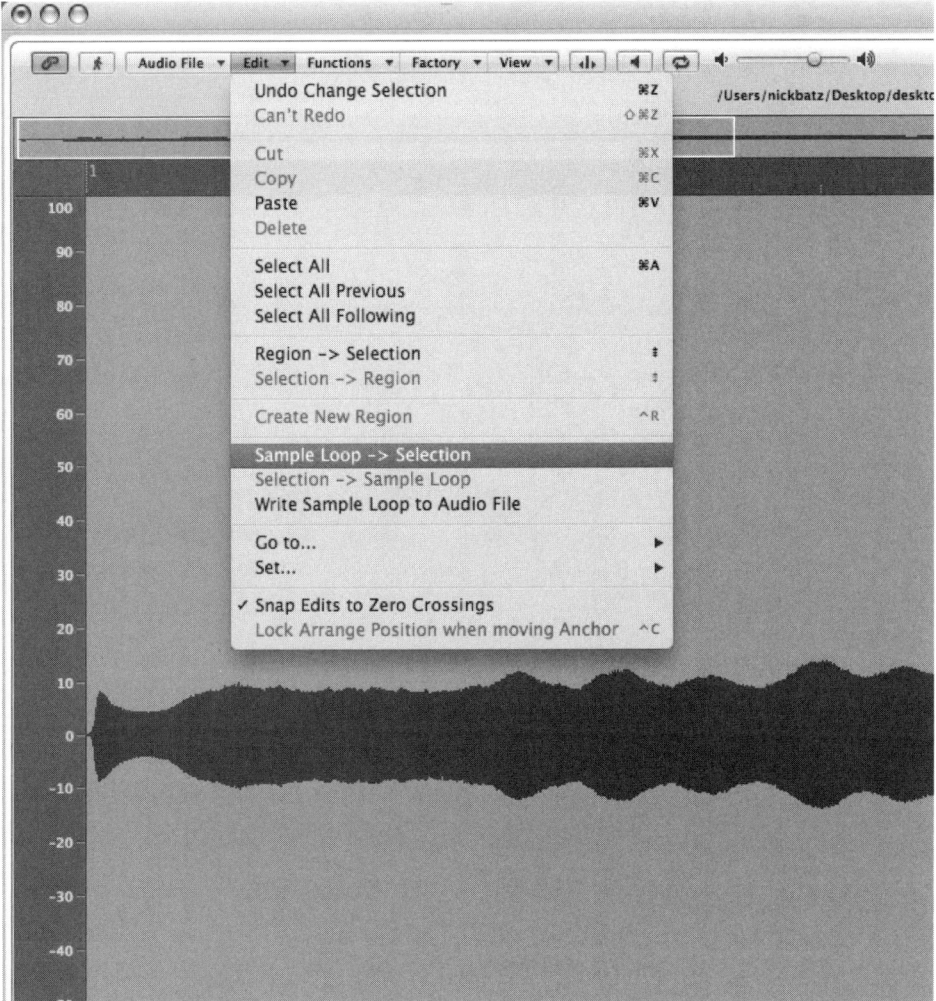

Figure 7.33 Sample Loop > Selection highlights the loop.

2. As shown in Figure 7.34, select the Zoom tool (the default command in Logic to bring up the tools is the Escape key).

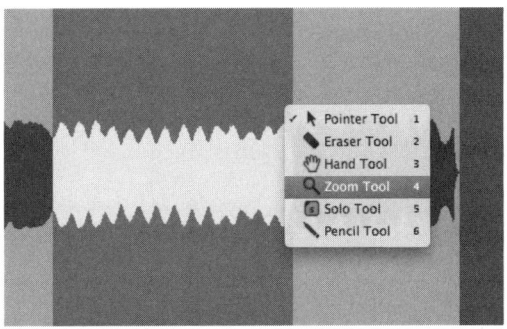

Figure 7.34 The Zoom tool.

3. Zoom way in to the loop end marker so you can see the waveform's zero crossing (Figure 7.35).

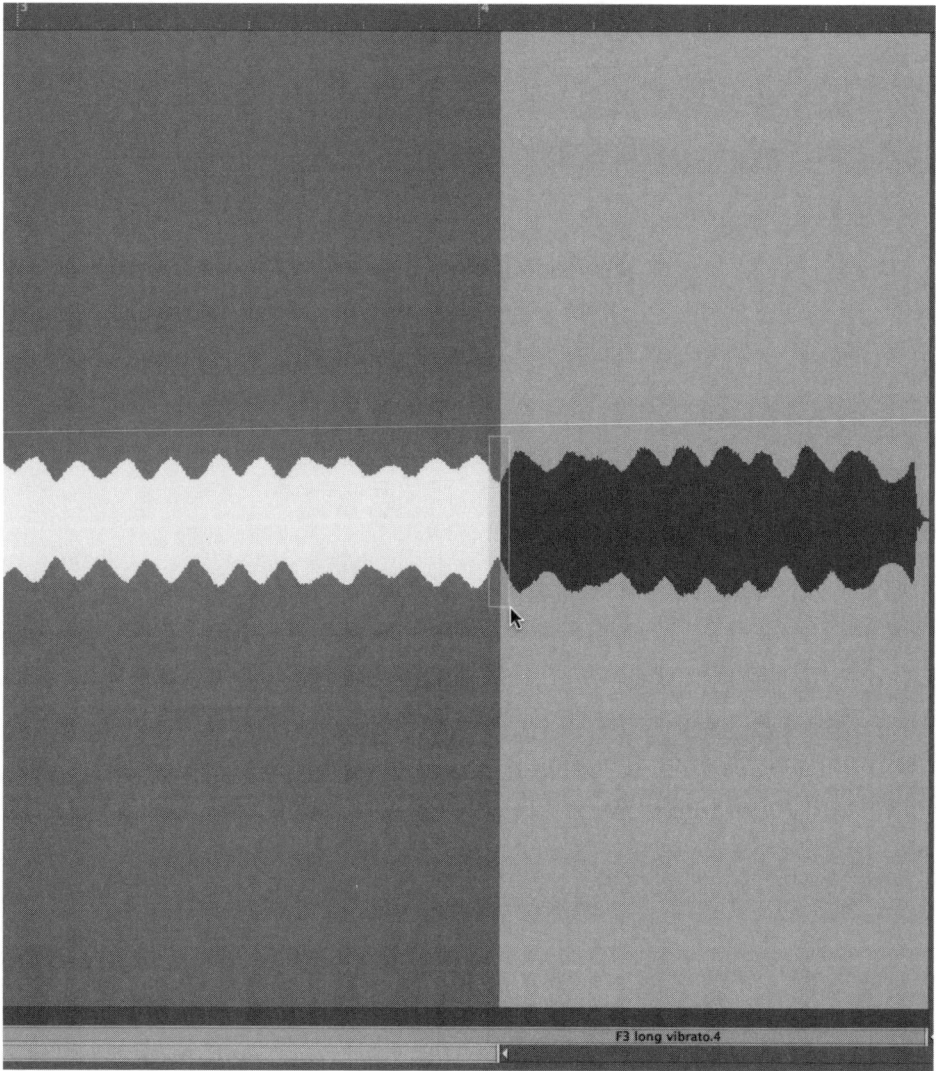

F3 long vibrato.4

Figure 7.35 Zoom way in.

4. Go back to the default Pointer tool and click exactly on the zero crossing to position the cursor at the end of the loop. This will deselect the loop (Figure 7.36).

5. Use the Select All Following command from the local Edit submenu to select from the loop end point to the end of the recording (Figure 7.37).

6. Issue the Save Selection As command from the local Audio submenu (Figure 7.38).

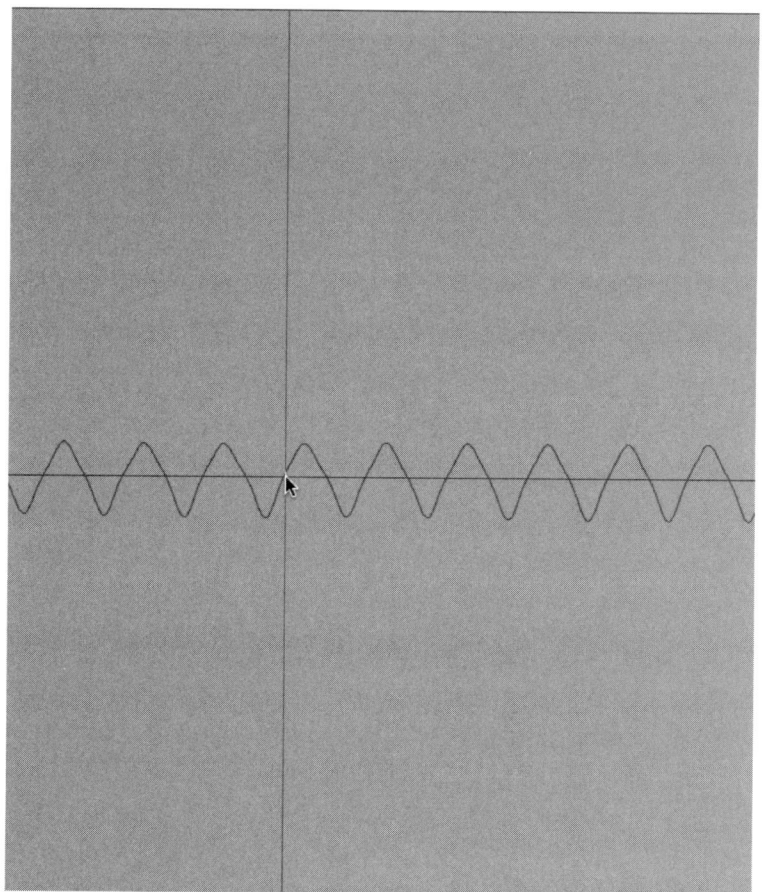

Figure 7.36 Click with the Pointer tool at the end of the selection.

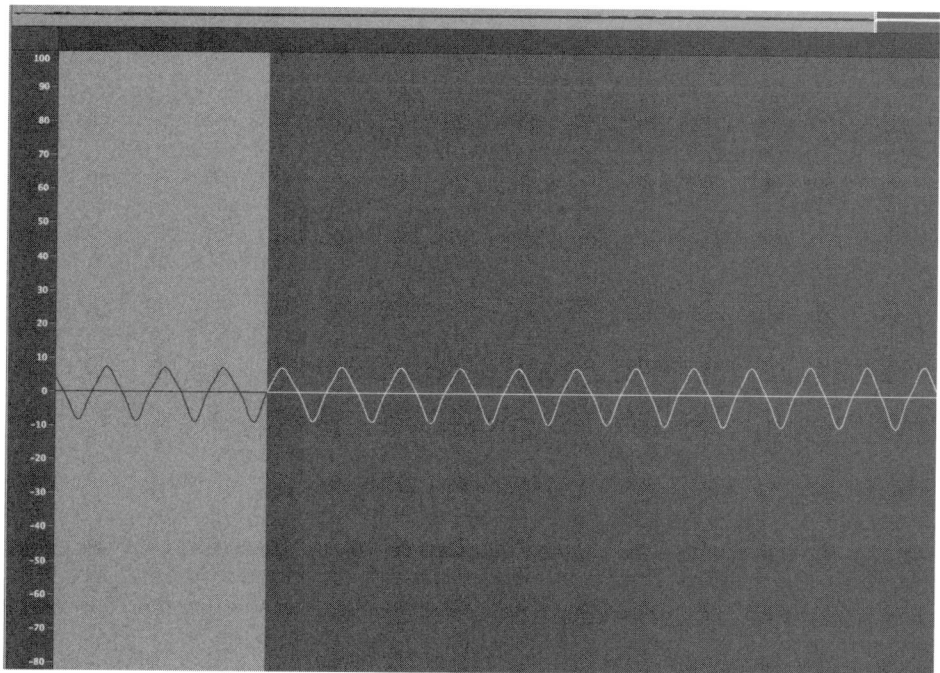

Figure 7.37 The selection is reversed.

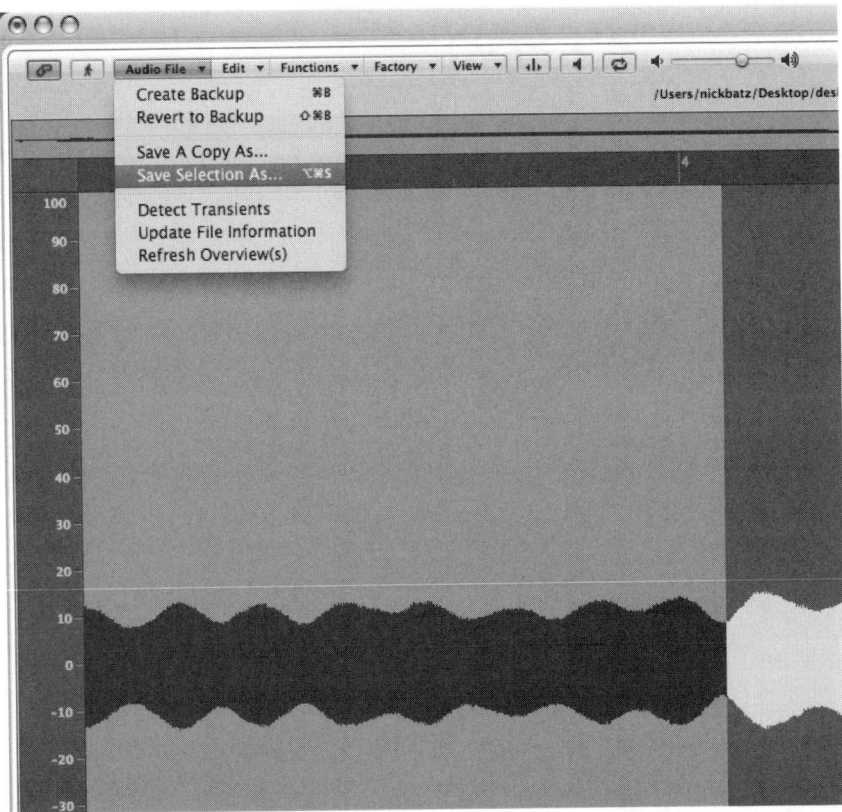

Figure 7.38   Save Selection As.

7.   Name the release sample. You'll want to use the default settings in this window so that all the formats remain the same (Figure 7.39).

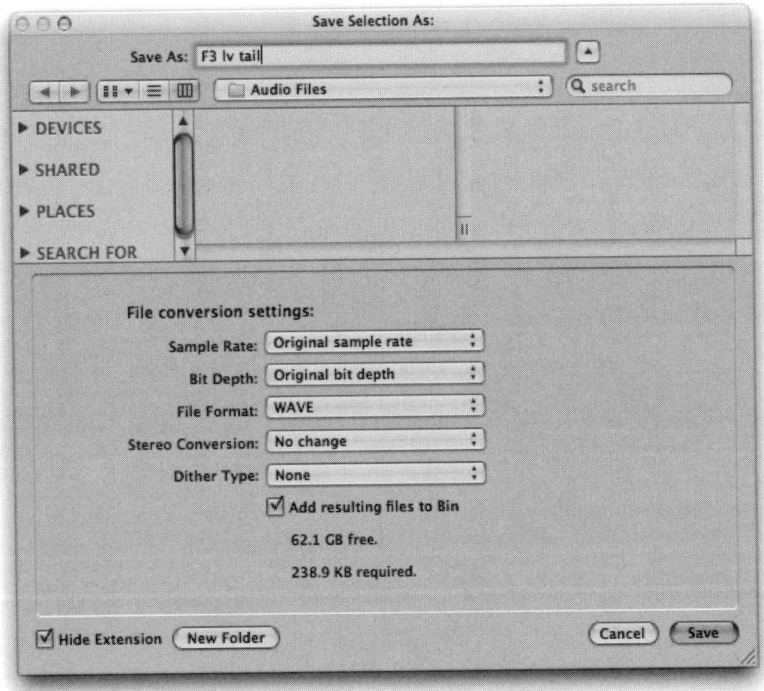

Figure 7.39   Use the default settings as shown.

8 Release Samples

Release samples, sometimes called release trails when they consist of room or hall ring-off, are recordings of notes when you stop playing them. On a piano that would be the sound of the damper(s) falling and the note ringing out inside the instrument; on a guitar it could be (among other techniques) the sound of fingers muffling the note. Release samples are triggered by the MIDI Note-Off command corresponding to the Note-On that triggers the regular recording.

Sometimes—as with our dry alto recorder—release samples are pretty subtle and may not be necessary. While some of the samples in the alto recorder do have a slight pitch dip at their tail ends, instead we're going to use a different set of long non-vibrato samples that we'll pretend were recorded from a distance in a studio with natural room ring-off. (These are actually the same samples run through a reverb, created to make the following tutorials more illustrative of the effect.)

The nice thing about release samples is that by definition you've already recorded them, so you can decide to program them by cutting them from your samples at any time. Sometimes it can take a little tweaking to get them to sound natural, but they're generally not very difficult to program.

Release samples aren't available in the Reason NN-XT.

Tutorial: Release Samples

The first step is simply to cut the samples where you want the release samples to start. This is mostly trial and error, but some pointers follow. We've already discussed cutting up samples in various programs, so we'll just show Pro Tools for this part; it will be very obvious how to do the same thing in your sequencer.

Here are the eight long no-vibrato reverb samples cut up in Pro Tools (Figure 8.1).

Be sure to zoom way in when you trim the recordings. This looks like the exact beginning (Figure 8.2).

In this case (Figures 8.3 and 8.4) we're being ridiculously picky, but if you zoom in...

Figure 8.1 The samples before separating their releases.

Figure 8.2 Is this the beginning?

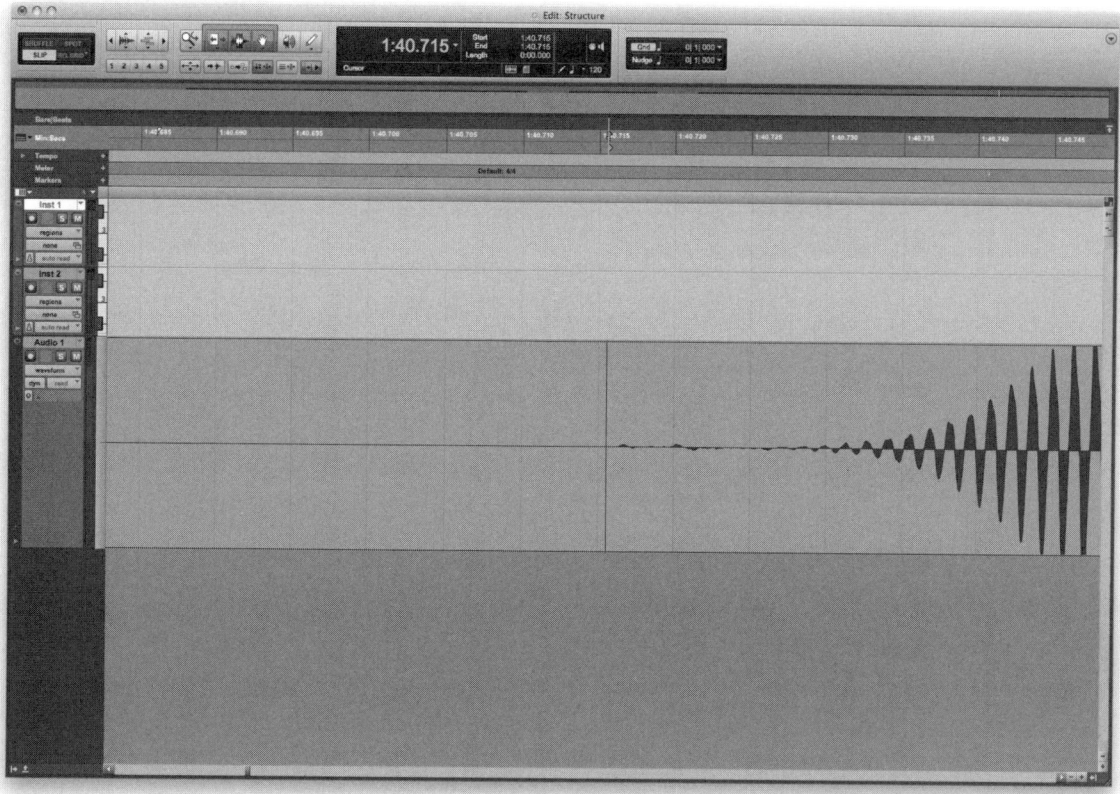

Figure 8.3 Zoomed in, it's not accurate.

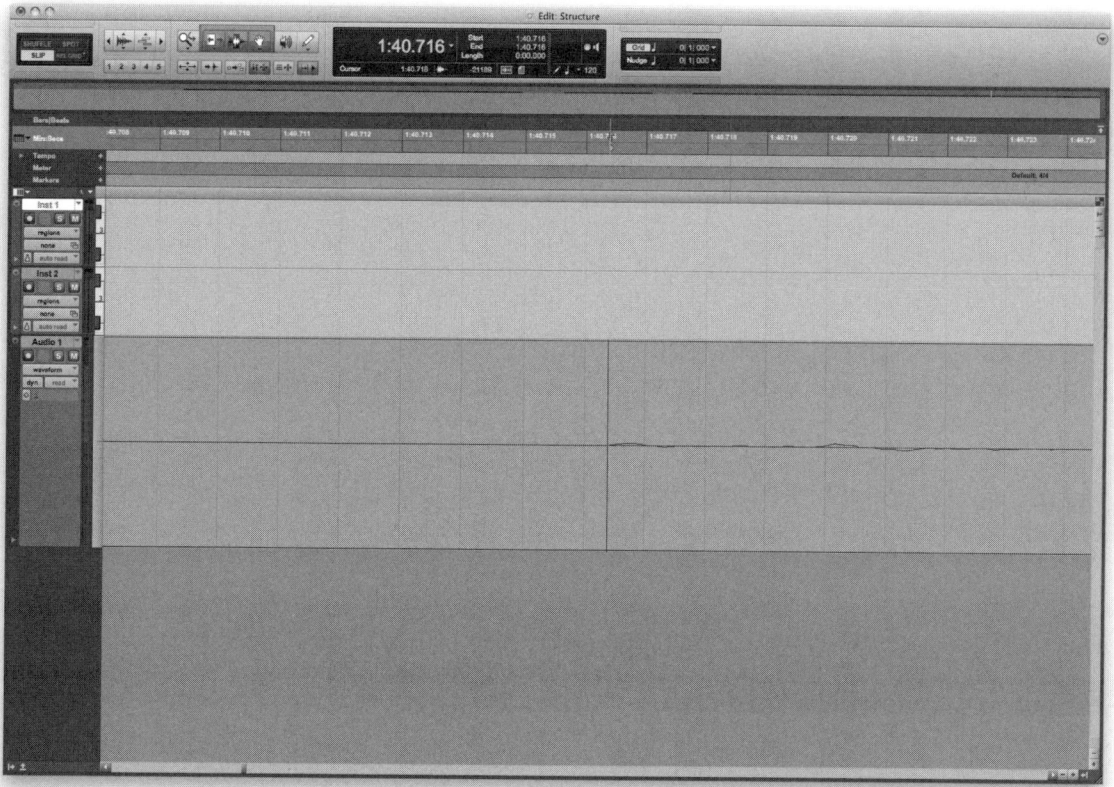

Figure 8.4 The real beginning.

When you trim the tail of the recording, you want to make sure not to cut off quiet room ring-off (Figure 8.5).

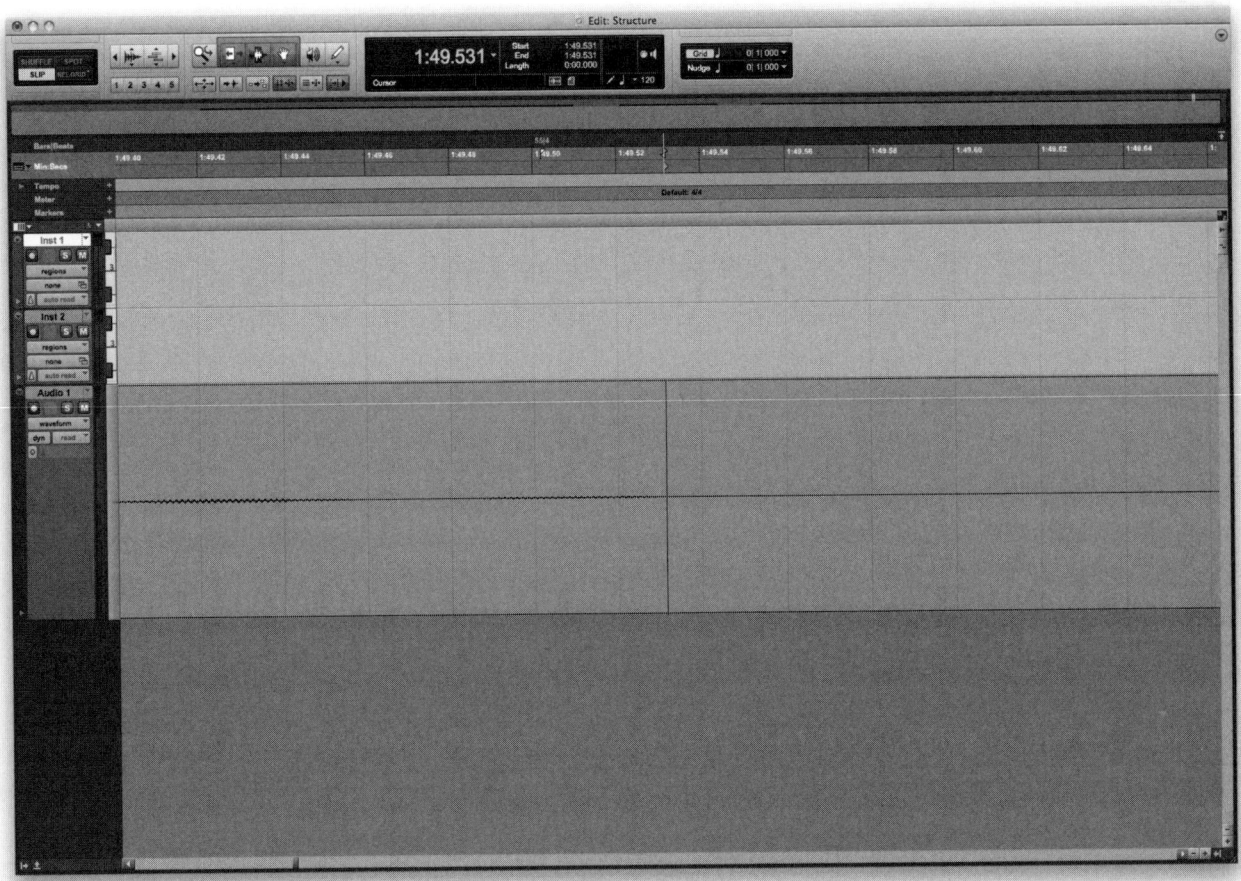

Figure 8.5 Leave the room ring-off.

Here you see the same note in its reverbed version with ring-off on top and the original dry sample shown below. The difference is very easy to see (Figure 8.6).

You want to cut the release sample just before the release, leaving a little room to fade it in (or crossfade). This is a good place to cut; each vertical line in the grid is .1 seconds, so we're leaving about .05 seconds before the reverb ring-off. That's enough for the alto recorder, which has a sound very close to a pure sine wave, but it won't be long enough for an instrument that has a lot going on at the ends of its notes (Figure 8.7).

With any audio edit, it's good practice to cut on a zero crossing, which is the point at which the waveform is between positive and negative excursions (or v.v.). There's nothing magical about zero crossings, however—you can still make horrible edits on them (Figure 8.8).

Figure 8.6   With and without reverb.

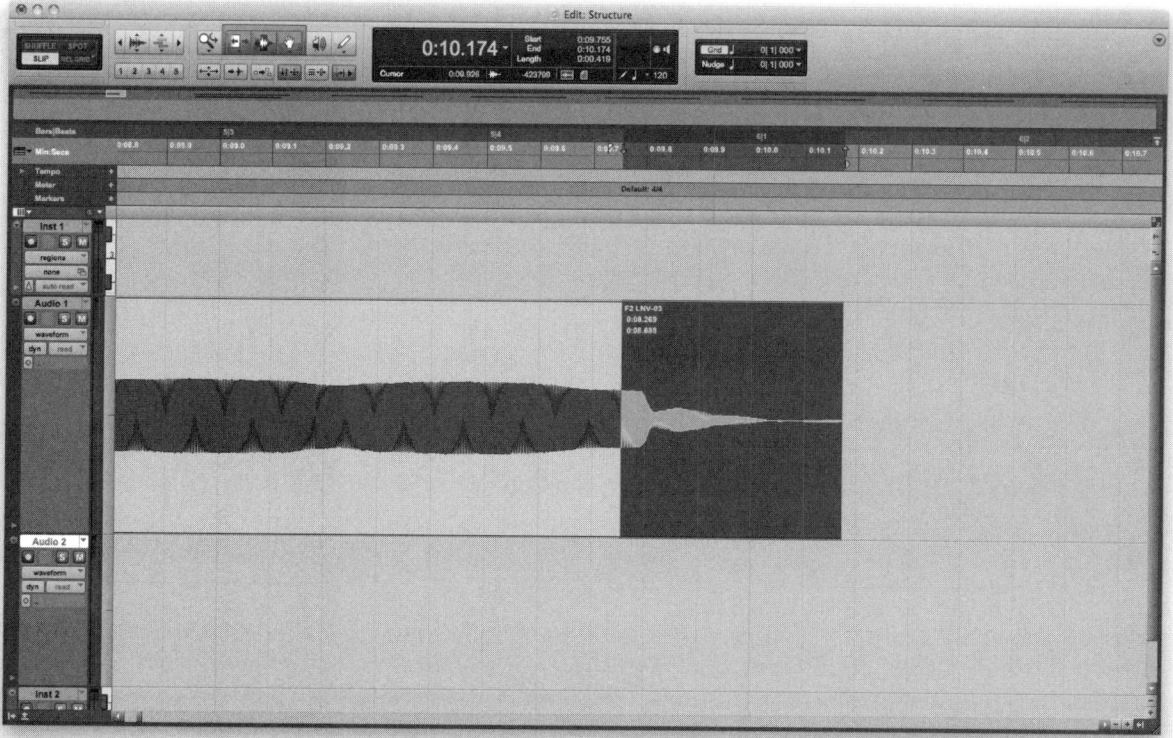

Figure 8.7   This leaves room for a crossfade.

Figure 8.8 A zero crossing.

In order to avoid getting bogged down with lots of editing, let's just take this single sample into the different samplers to show how to program release samples.

Tutorial: Release Samples in Structure

Just to show how this works, we're going to take a single F2 sample with its release. Programming hundreds of other samples is just more of the same process.

1. Create a new Patch and import the F2 sample (Figure 8.9). We'll stretch it across three octaves just to hear sound when those notes are played, and of course the process would be the same if we were using velocity layers (here we're not—the sample plays across the entire range).

2. Import the release sample corresponding to the F2 on another layer, and again for the purposes of the exercise stretch it across three octaves (Figure 8.10).

   Now we need to create a Sub-Patch to program the release layer sample as a release (Figure 8.11).

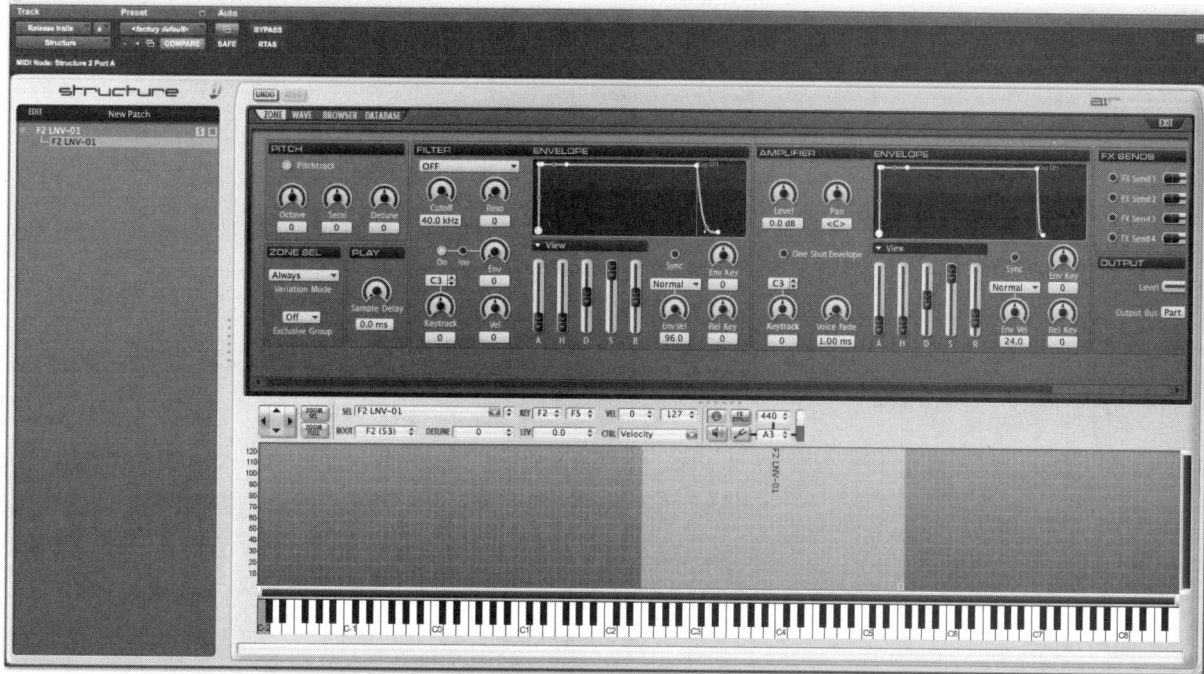

Figure 8.9   New Patch with the F2 sample stretched across the keyboard.

Figure 8.10   The release sample imported and stretched.

Figure 8.11 Add a Sub-Patch.

3. Attach the release layer to the Sub-Patch and set the Trigger On parameter to Note Off. This does just what it says: tells Structure to play the layer when you release the key (or sustain pedal), i.e., when it sees a MIDI Note-Off command (Figure 8.12).

Figure 8.12 The Sub-Patch triggers when you release the key.

4. Play. You'll hear the room tail when you release the key, but it glitches a little on the transition.

5. To get rid of this glitch, we'll fade in the release sample. The easiest way to do this is to slow down its attack in the amplitude envelope at the Part level, but we could also do it in the Zone screen if we needed more control over individual notes.

6. Click on the Amp tab and slow down the attack just a little (Figure 8.13).

Figure 8.13 Go to the Amp tab and slow down the attack.

Structure lets you view envelope parameters by text if you want to be very precise, but we're just going to use the faders and adjust the envelope using our ears and eyes.

Now play. The glitch is gone.

However, sometimes release samples are a little less forgiving. You may need to do a crossfade rather than just the fade-in we did here, in which case you'd slow down the release of the outgoing standard sample. Figure 8.14 is what it might look like.

Structure also lets you lower the level of the release samples using three parameters: Level Decay, Velocity Decay, and Decay Keytrack. We're not using these parameters, but they're present to prevent the release sample's level from jumping up unnaturally; for example, imagine how it

Figure 8.14 If you'd needed to crossfade.

would sound if you were to release a piano note that's been sustaining for ten seconds and then hear its damper at the same level as the initial attack.

Level Decay reduces the level of the release sample progressively as the note is held. Please see Figure 8.15. Velocity Decay does the same thing using velocity instead of amplitude, which means you can trigger different release layers, and Decay Keytrack halves the decay each time you go up an octave (which is what a plucked or hammered string instrument would do, for example).

Tutorial: Release Samples in Kontakt

As with the other samplers, we're going to take a single F2 sample with its release trail. Programming any number of other samples is just more of the same process (Figure 8.16).

1. Create a new Instrument.

2. Save As [we're calling it "Alto recorder w/release samples"] (Figure 8.17).

Figure 8.15   Choose your decay.

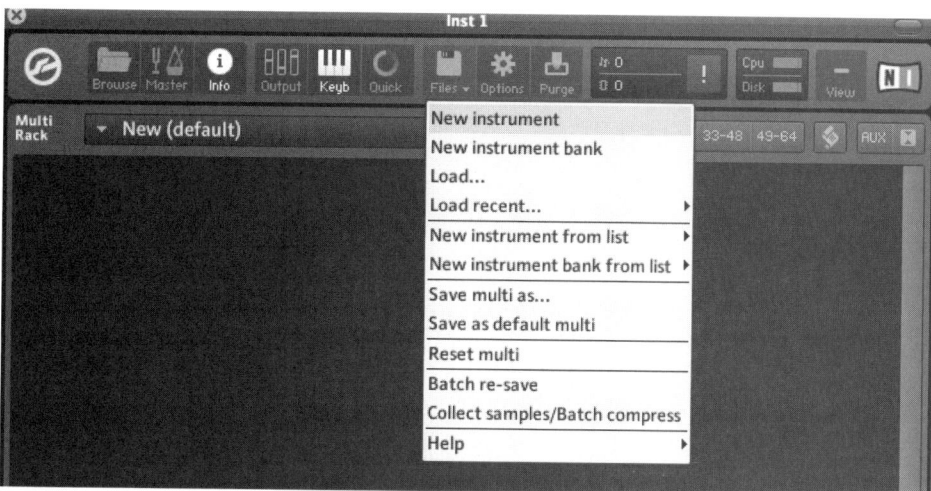

Figure 8.16   Create a new Instrument.

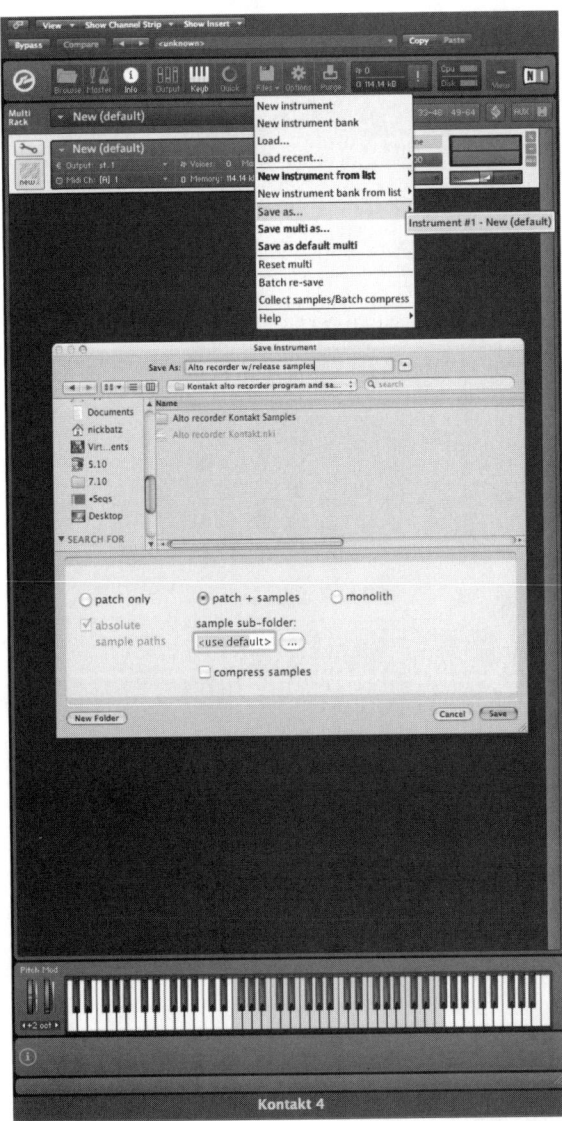

Figure 8.17 Save As.

3. Click on the wrench to enter Edit mode, then on the Mapping Editor tab (Figure 8.18).

The next three simple steps are all shown in the single screenshot that follows them.

4. Click on the Mapping and Group editors to unfold them and highlight Selected Groups Only to avoid confusion when editing.

5. Drag in the main F2 sample (as opposed to the release sample). This creates a new Group, and if we were mapping the rest of the alto samples instead of just this single one for demonstration, they would go in the same Group.

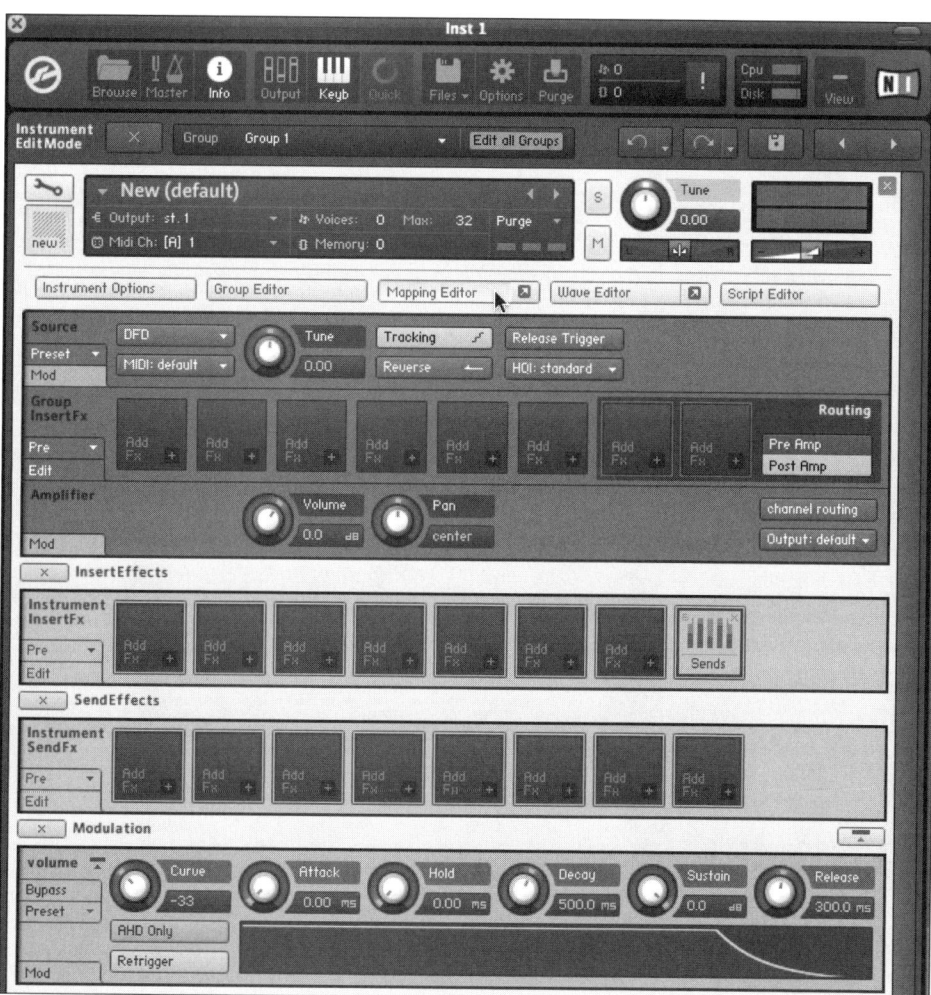

Figure 8.18 Go to the Mapping Editor.

6. Just for this exercise, stretch the single F2 sample to cover three octaves. This is an optional step to make the sample play across a range of keys (Figure 8.19).

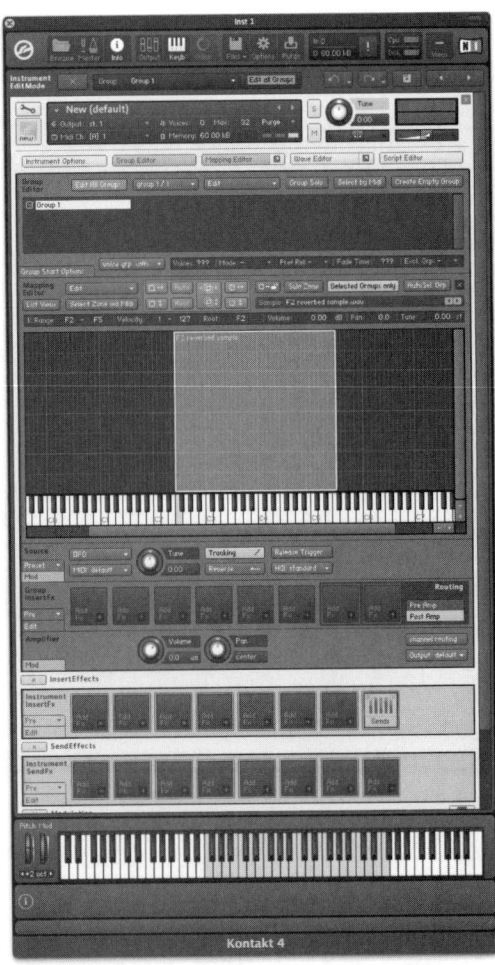

Figure 8.19 Three steps in one picture.

7. Now create a new empty Group for the release sample (the mouse pointer shows where you click), drag in the release sample, and stretch it across three octaves as with the regular sample (Figure 8.20).

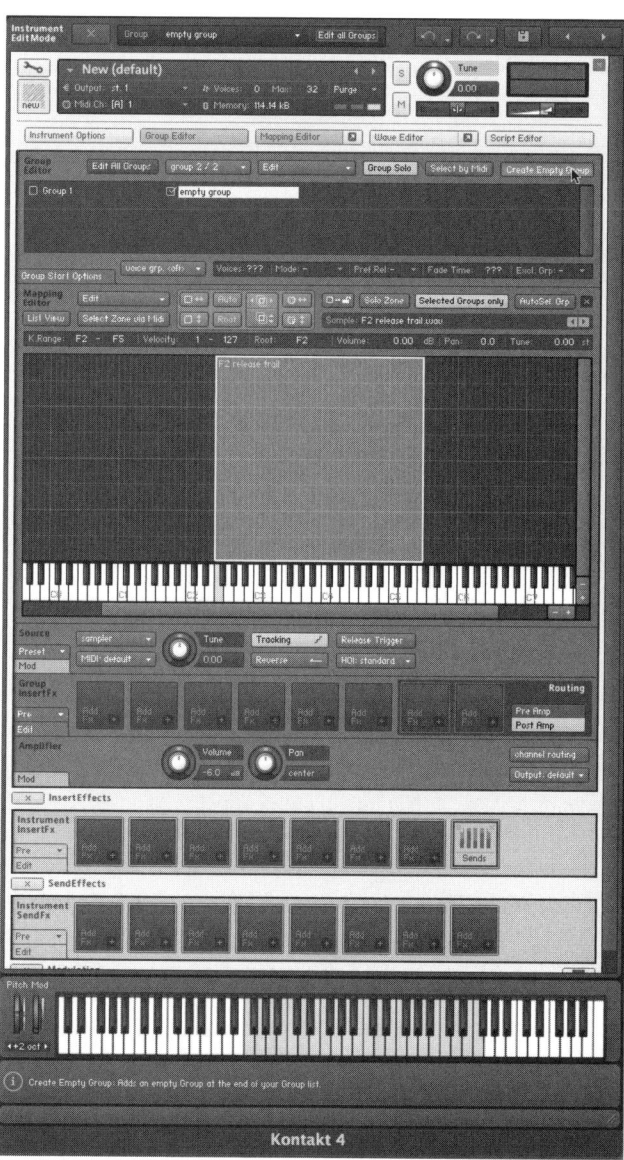

Figure 8.20   The release sample stretched in a new Group.

At some point in the process, it's a good idea to name the Groups. "F2" and "release sample" seem like reasonable choices (Figure 8.21).

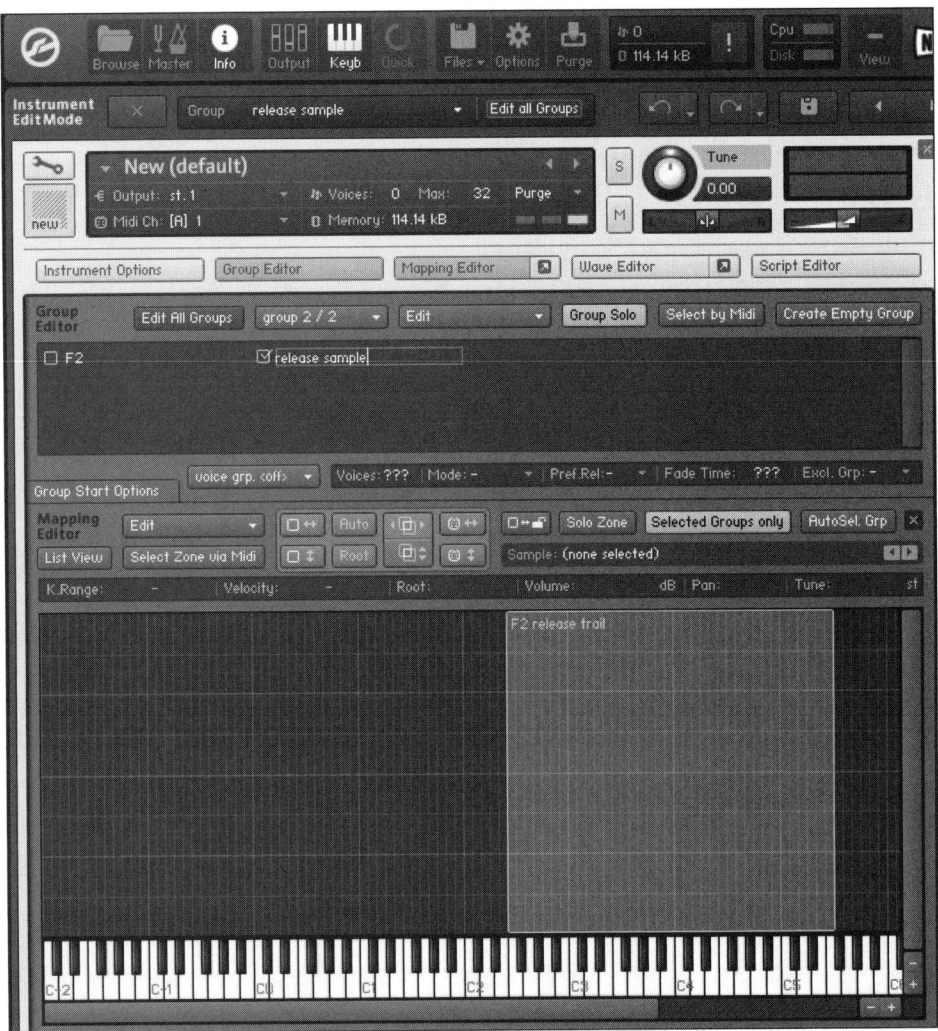

Figure 8.21 Name your Groups.

8. Select the release sample Group and click on Release Sample (in the Group editor area—again, look for the mouse pointer). This is shown in Figure 8.22.

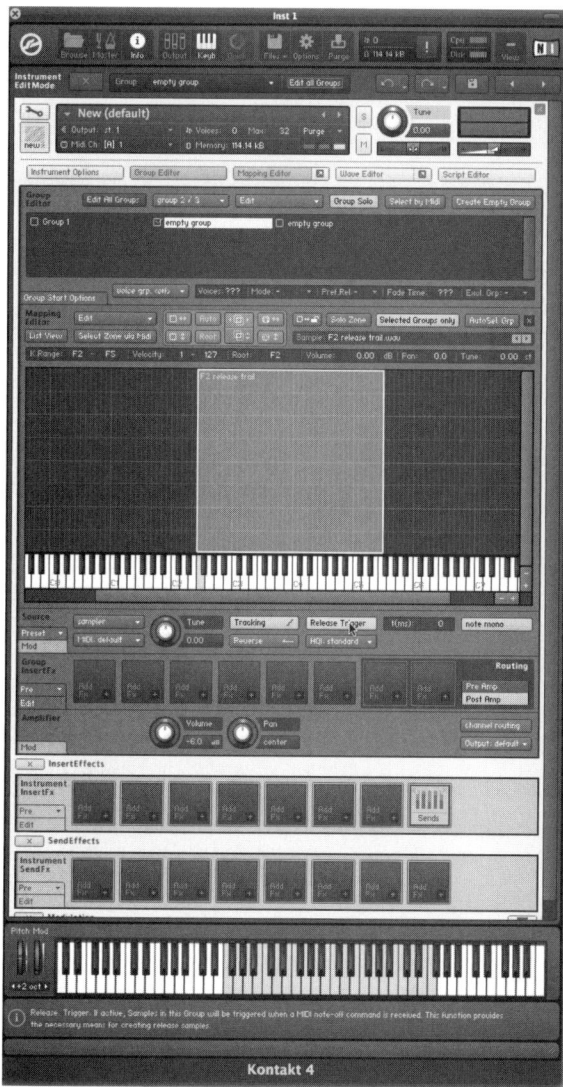

Figure 8.22 It's a release sample.

9. Play. The release sample sounds as soon as you release the key, more specifically when it sees the corresponding MIDI Note Off command. But it's glitching because it's jumping to the release from an arbitrary point in the sample rather than where it was recorded.

    The solution is to make the release sample fade in quickly. This requires an envelope.

10. Add an AHDSR envelope under the Add Modulator drop-down (Figure 8.23).

Figure 8.23   Add an AHDSR envelope.

11. Click on the little icon shown under the mouse pointer to display the envelope we've just created (Figure 8.24).

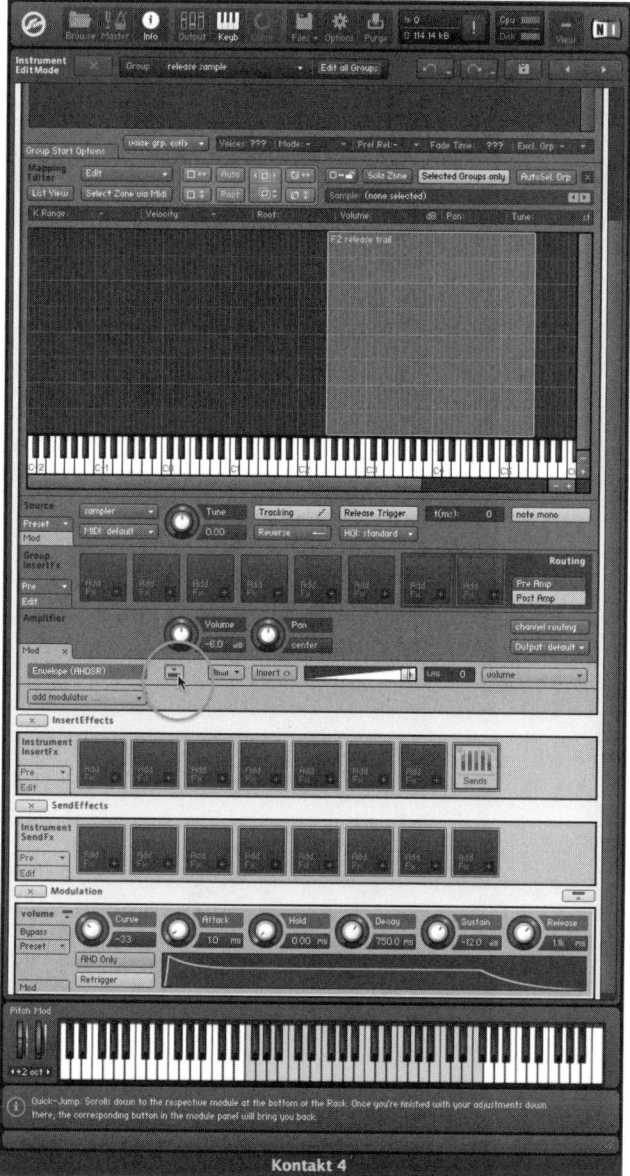

Figure 8.24 Show the envelope.

12. We're only concerned with the attack stage of the envelope, and 250ms (a quarter of a second) works well to my ears (Figure 8.25).

Figure 8.25 Attack.

If for some reason your other envelope stages defaulted to different settings, the ones shown above are neutral: Hold 0ms, Decay 500ms, Sustain 0dB, and Release 300ms.

We're done with this demonstration, but sometimes it's necessary to program a crossfade between the outgoing regular sample and the release sample. The way to do that is to add a volume envelope to the Group with the regular sample(s) just as we've done here and then slow down the release stage.

Tutorial: Release Samples in EXS24

Again, we're just going to program the single F2 note with its release sample for this tutorial. The process is the same no matter how many samples you have, and this will allow us to get to the point without getting mired in lots of editing.

Note   Programming release samples in the EXS24 looks very simple, but in practice we'll see that some aspects of it are counterintuitive.

---

1. Insert an EXS24 sampler on a Logic Instrument track and open the EXS editor (Figure 8.26).

Figure 8.26   Insert an EXS and click on Edit.

2.   Do a Save As and name your program (Figure 8.27).

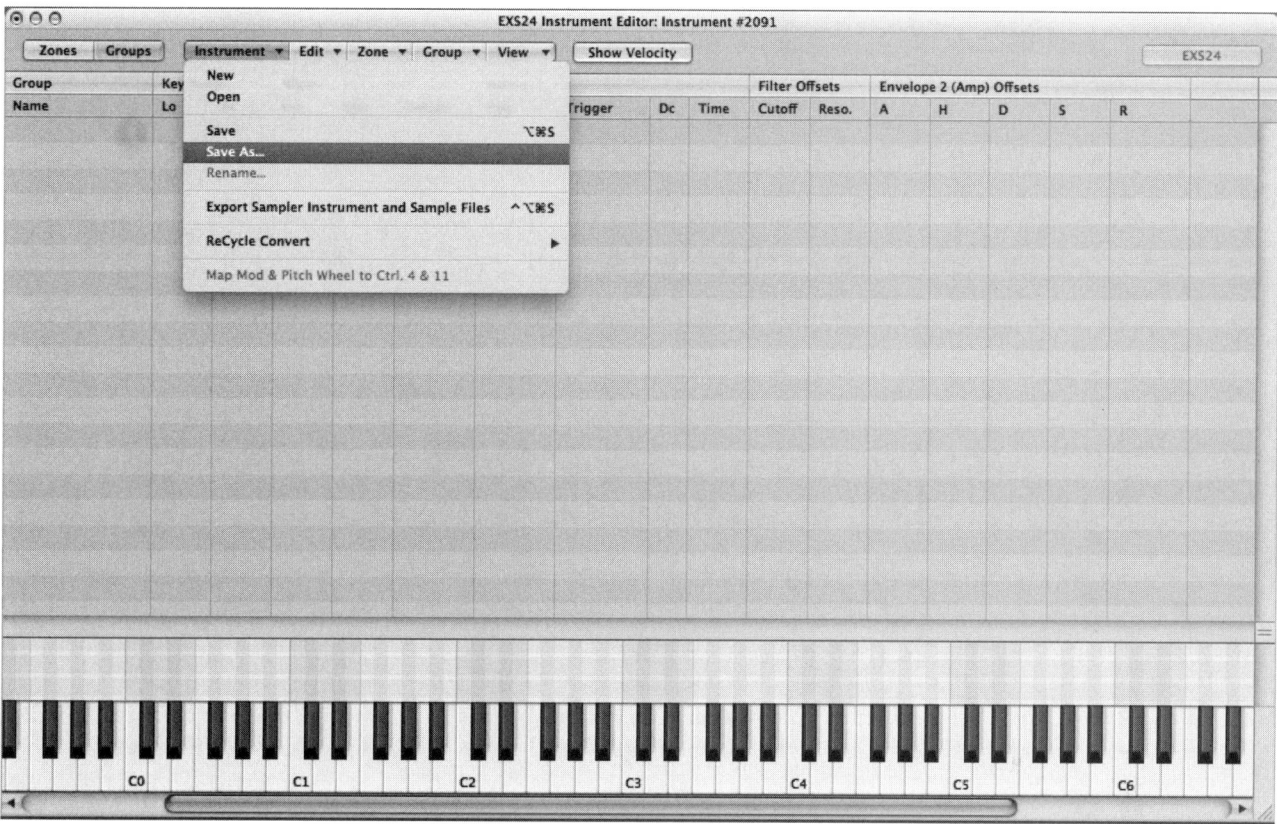

Figure 8.27 Save As.

3.   In Figure 8.28, we create a new Group for the main sample (we'll create another one for the release sample later).

4.   Give the Group a name (Figure 8.29), such as "Sample."

Figure 8.28 New Group.

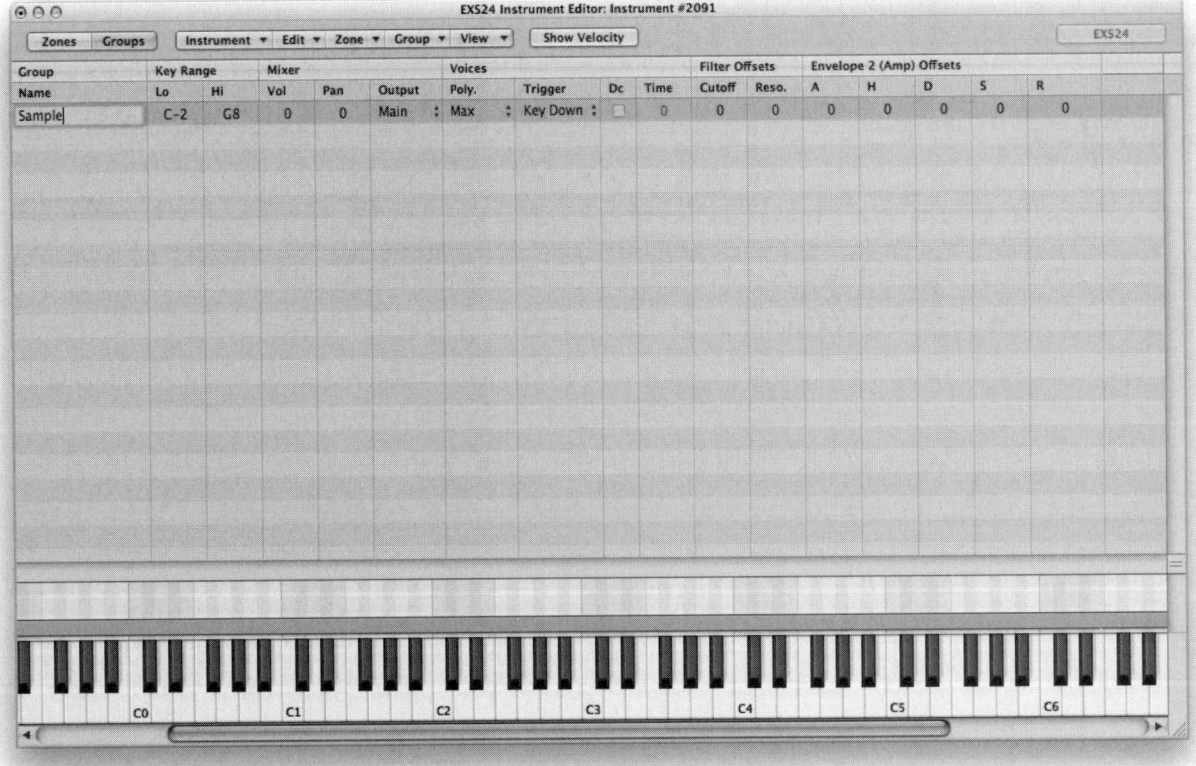

Figure 8.29 Name that Group.

5. Click on the Zones tab as shown and then drag in the main sample (Figure 8.30).

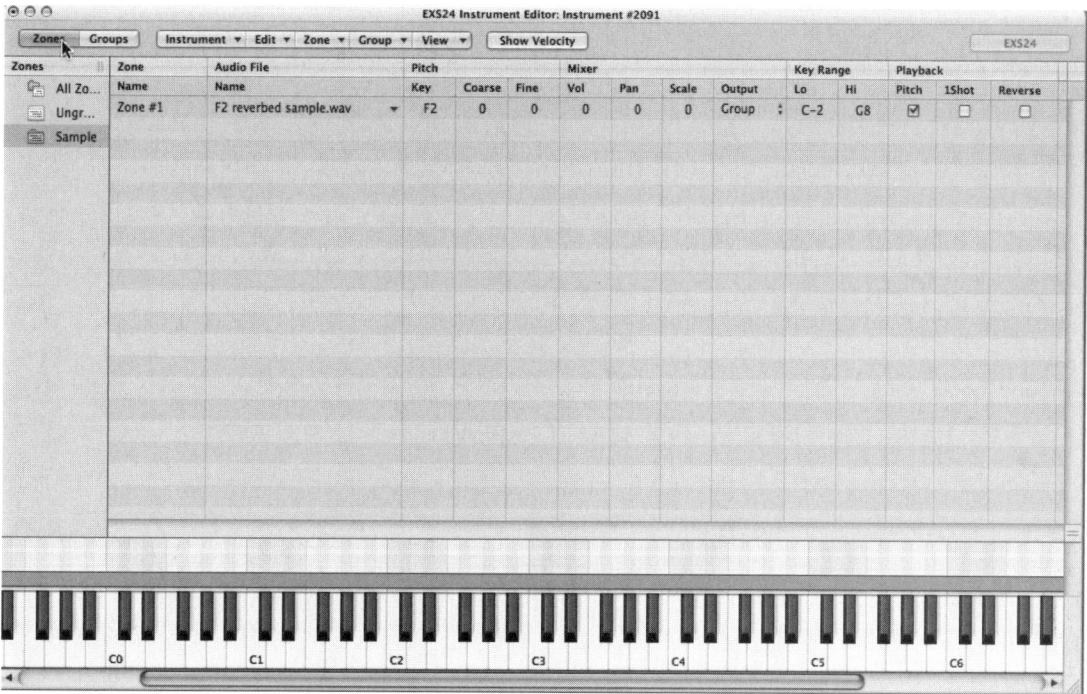

Figure 8.30 Drag in the sample.

6. Go back to Group view and set the range to the three octaves from F2 to F5. This stretching step is just so we can hear the sample over a range on the keyboard (Figure 8.31).

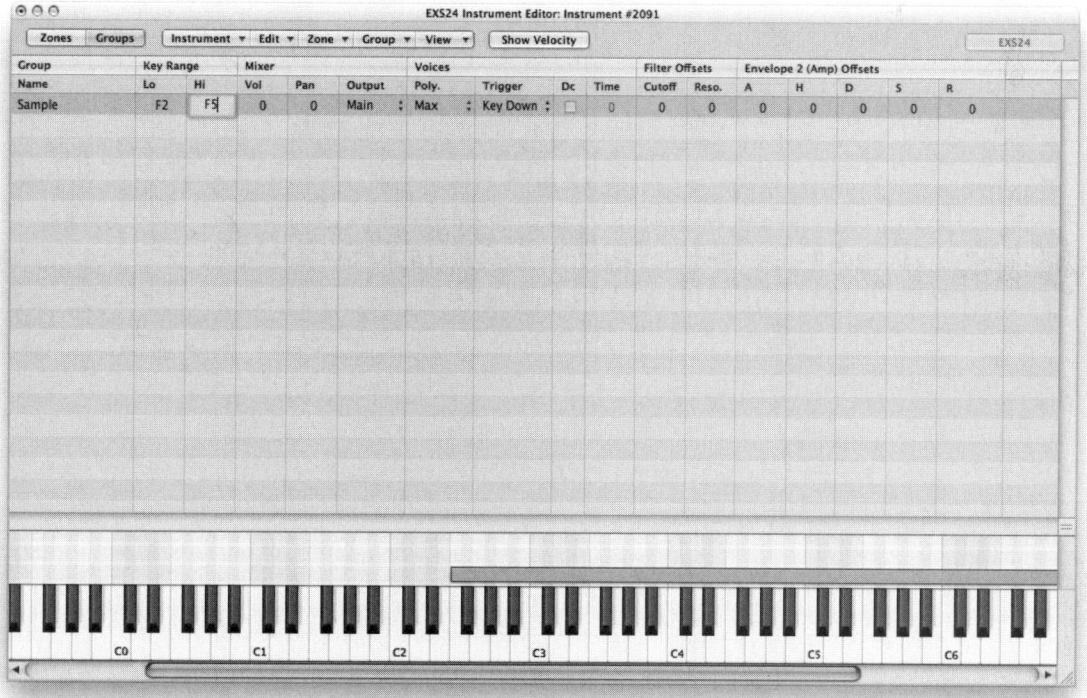

Figure 8.31 Stretch it across the keyboard.

7.   We've arrived at the moment we promised above—creating a new Group for the release sample. Give it a name like "Release sample" (Figure 8.32).

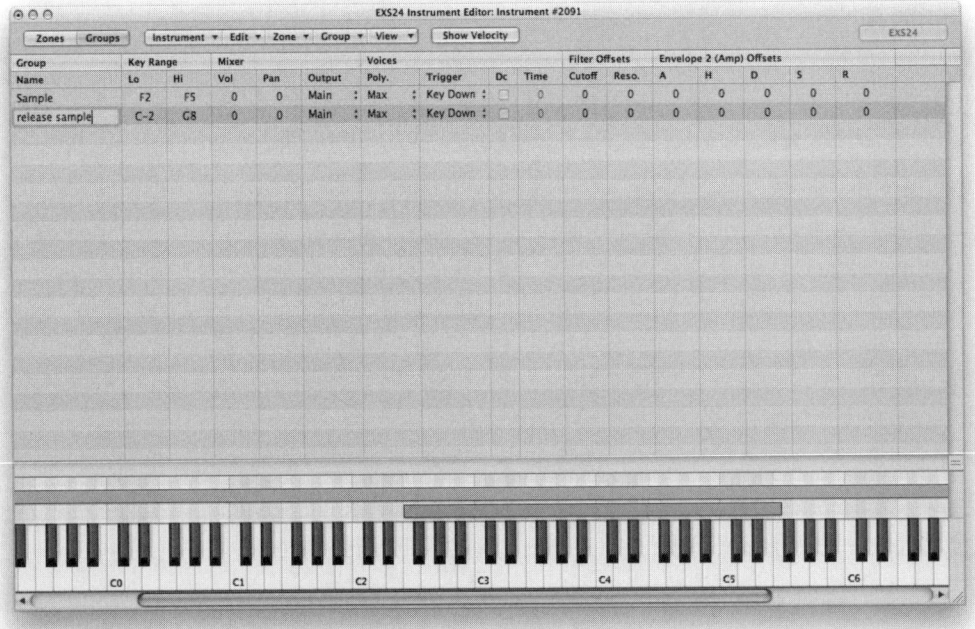

Figure 8.32   A Group for the release sample.

8.   Go back to the Zones tab and drag in the release sample (Figure 8.33).

Figure 8.33   Drag in the release sample.

9. As before, go back to Group view and set the same F2–F5 range for the release sample (Figure 8.34).

Figure 8.34 Stretch that release sample.

10. Set the trigger of the release sample Group (only) to Key Release so that they'll play when they see the MIDI Note-Off command following the Note-On that triggered the regular sample (Figure 8.35).

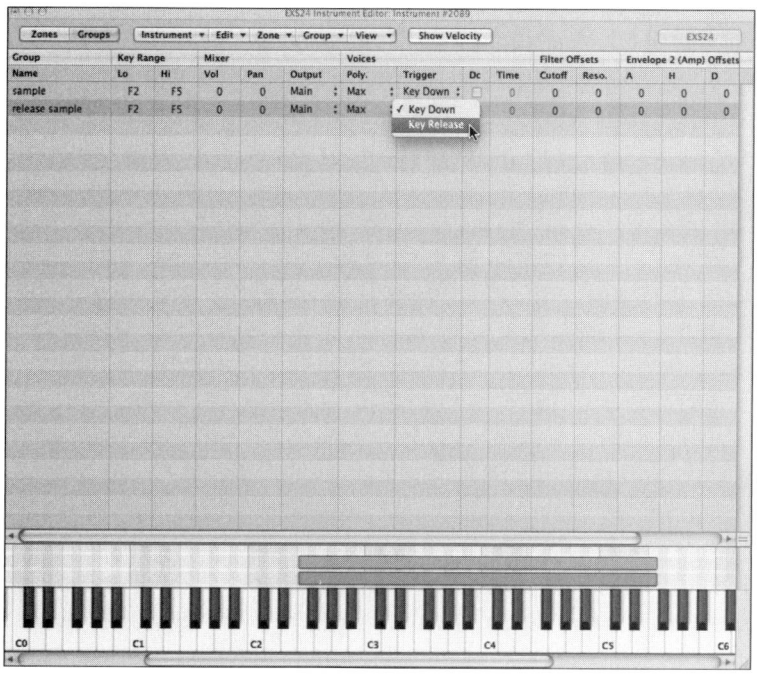

Figure 8.35 Trigger set to Key Release.

If you play the keyboard, you will hear a stupid noise instead of our beautiful release sample. Why? Because the EXS24's release sample implementation is counterintuitive and undocumented.

The EXS now has a convoluted feature that attempts to set the release sample's level relative to the outgoing sample (see sidebar: "The EXS 24 Note Counter"). That's part of what the Dc (Disable Counter) button in Figure 8.36 is supposed to do; when it's on it enables the Time parameter next to it, which is a note counter that measures the time between the MIDI Note-On and Note-Off. If Time is 2000, that's two seconds (2 × 1000 milliseconds); release the key after one second, and the level of the release sample should be half the original volume. You might also expect it to take the setting of ENV 2 on the front panel—the one that's hardwired to amplitude—into account, but you'll notice that ENV 2 has no effect on release samples.

Again, that's how it's supposed to work. In practice you'll find yourself poking around in the dark, and nothing will change. I suggest turning on Dc (which actually turns it off) and setting the Time parameter to 5000 (Figure 8.36).

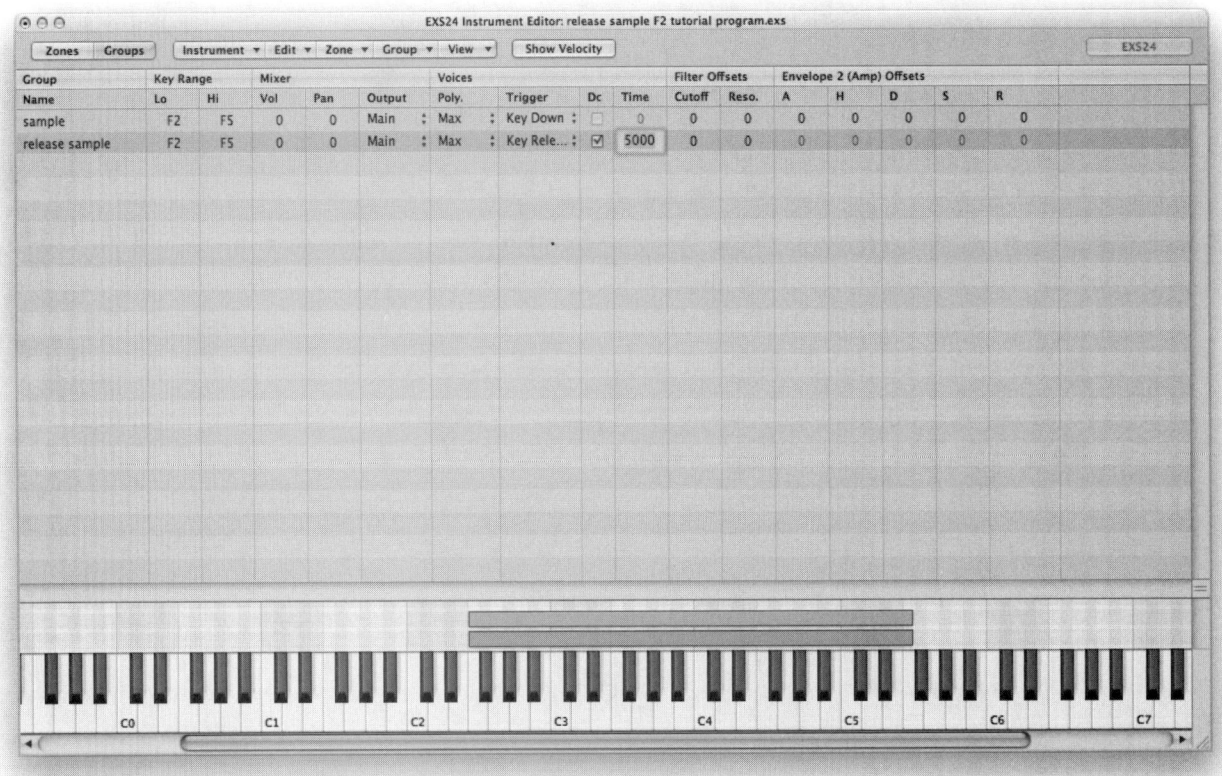

Figure 8.36 Settings so you can hear the release sample.

The EXS24 Note Counter   It's quite difficult to make heads or tails of the EXS24's release sample feature, if for no other reason than that it's undocumented. However, the feature actually works the way you'd normally want it to. With special thanks to Garth Hjelte of Chicken Systems, whose company publishes Translator (a program that translates programs between sampler formats), here's how it works.

In Groups, the check box marked Dc should probably be called Disable Note Counter. Right away, the first funny thing is that checked means the note counter is off, and unchecked means it's on.

An internal amplitude envelope (the NoteCtr Envelope) is calculated, lasting the duration of the source sample (the regular sample, not the release). For example, if you release a note three quarters into the length of the sample, the amplitude will be attenuated 75 percent.

There is a bug in this feature, though: if the sounds aren't looped, the NoteCtr works as long as you release the key before the NoteCtr expires. If you release it after it expires, the release sample plays at full volume. However, if the sound is looped, then the NoteCtr Envelope never expires. A workaround for unlooped sounds is to turn on the loop and set both the loop start and end to the end sample; the loop won't sound, and the EXS24 will behave properly.

While Envelope 2 on the EX24's front panel is assigned to amplitude, its attack and release stages have no effect upon release samples. However, its decay and sustain settings affect the note counter's timing!

If the sustain has a positive value, the decay has no effect. But if the sustain is set to 0, the decay can shorten the note counter envelope. The formula is simple: four times the decay time = the length of the NoteCtr Envelope (with the restriction that it can't be longer than the source sample).

9 Using Kontakt Scripts

Scripts in this context are plug-in programs that interpret incoming MIDI data and use it to control internal Kontakt parameters. They are the main feature that distinguishes Kontakt from any other sampler currently available. (EastWest has announced a pro version of their Play sampler with user scripting, but it isn't out as of this writing; however, their libraries in the playback-only Play all use scripting.)

Most commercial sample developers who release libraries in Kontakt format use pretty advanced scripting these days. In fact, there are programmers who hire themselves out just for writing scripts. But there's also a surprisingly large group of serious users writing them. Kontakt comes with a sizable assortment of useful preset scripts, and there are lots of very sophisticated ones available for download on the Web.

Sidebar: Writing (or Editing) Your Own Scripts It's a good idea to get a general feel for Kontakt scripting just to be able to edit parameters in preset scripts. But if you're interested in learning the KSP scripting language yourself, there's a great resource at http://nilsliberg.se/ksp. I'd suggest starting with Nils Liberg's excellent introductory tutorial found at http://nilsliberg.se/ksp/scripts/tutorial/. It's a quick read. While you're there, download his free script editor; creating your scripts in it is much more convenient than using the small script-editing window in Kontakt (scripts are just text—you can copy and paste them in).

Unlike the very clear manual that came with Kontakt 2, the Script Reference manual installed in the Kontakt 4 Documentation folder is just a code reference; it's not very useful for people like this author who had previously never programmed anything more complicated than a word processor mail merge. But if you have an idea for something you'd like a script to do, there's an excellent chance that just a quick read-through of Liberg's tutorial will show you the path. Then if you have questions, pose them in the Kontakt forum on the Native Instruments Web site—where you'll also find the links to Nils Liberg's site. The www.VI-control.net discussion group also has an excellent Kontakt scripting subforum.

Tutorial: Adding a Preset Script

Please load the completed alto recorder Kontakt program we worked on in Chapter 3.

You can browse the factory preset scripts in two places, as shown: the browser and the Script Editor, which is the tab that's highlighted (Figure 9.1). (Remember, you access the Instrument Editor by clicking on the wrench at the upper left.)

Figure 9.1 Where to find the factory preset scripts.

Load the Randomize Pitch script (Figure 9.2).

Note the parameters displayed in the gray area, specifically the Tune dialog box. Play the program, and you'll hear successive notes being randomized by up to ±.05 cents; considering that 1.00 cents is a half step, this is audible but pretty subtle (the decimal point is shifted two places to the left in this box; a half step is actually 100 cents).

Figure 9.2   The Randomize Pitch script.

Try setting the Tune parameter to 1.00, a half step (Figure 9.3).

That's a useful effect for some applications, but it's obviously way too much here. A more likely setting is .09, but of course this is subjective.

You might want to play with different scripts, and if you like one, save the program with it loaded. If you don't, just reload the program to revert to the previous state.

Let's take a quick tour.

Figure 9.3 Tune set to a half step.

Click on the Edit button (circled) to access the Script Editor (Figure 9.4).

This is where the KSP language resides. The first command is "on init," which sets the starting point for the script. A little farther down it says "declare ui_label $label1," and so on. This is creating the text label that says Randomize Notes. Any parameter can appear in the user interface, where it can be adjusted; in this case the script has numeric entry fields, but they can also be buttons, knobs, or even custom graphics.

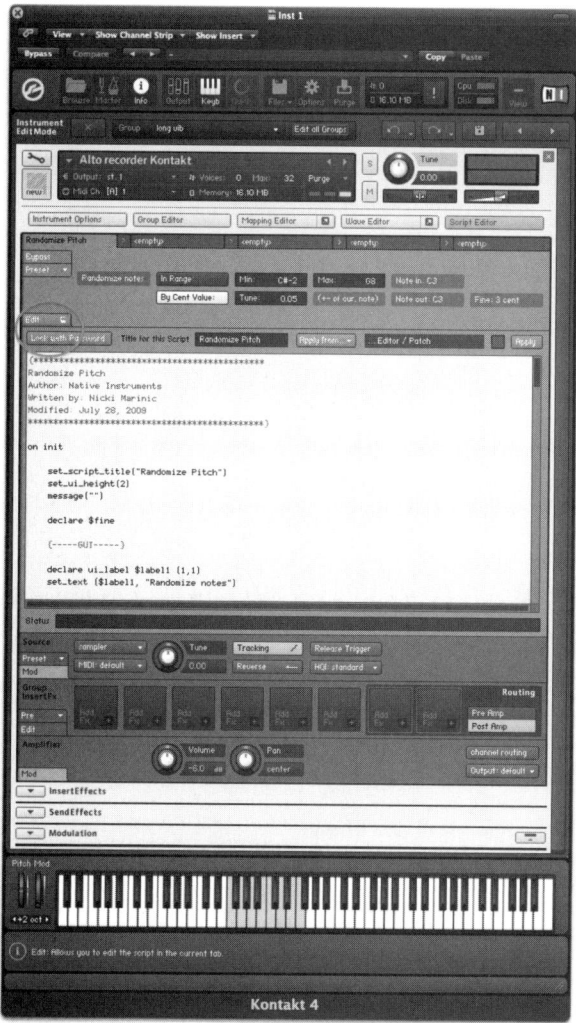

Figure 9.4   The Script Editor.

Click on the second tab, labeled Empty for obvious reasons (it's circled in Figure 9.5).

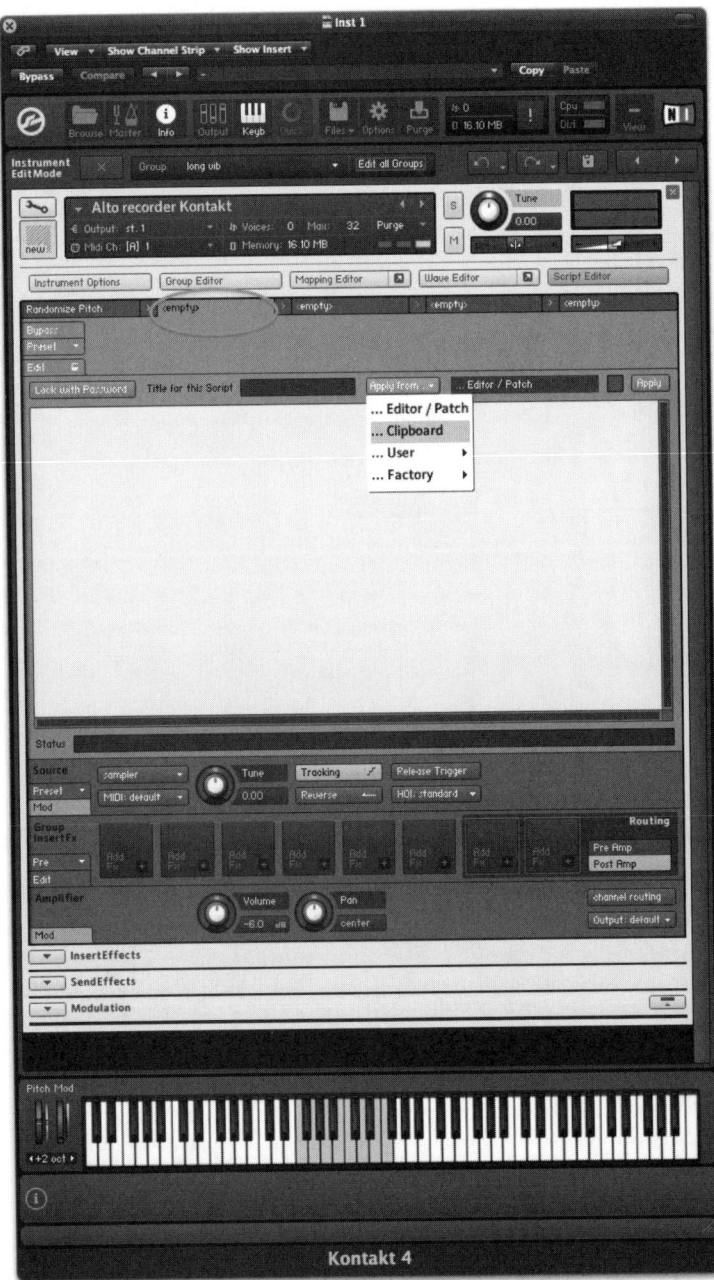

Figure 9.5 Paste your scripts here.

This is where you write scripts or paste them in (as shown in the Apply From drop-down). You can also lock scripts with a password here, if you want to keep them private.

Index